Creating Music and Sound for Games

❋ ❋ ❋

G.W. Childs IV

COURSE TECHNOLOGY
CENGAGE Learning™

Australia • Brazil • Japan • Korea • Mexico • Singapore • Spain • United Kingdom • United States

COURSE TECHNOLOGY
CENGAGE Learning™

Creating Music and Sound for Games
G.W. Childs IV

Publisher and General Manager, Cengage
   Learning Course Technology PTR:
   Stacy L. Hiquet

Associate Director of Marketing:
   Sarah O'Donnell

Manager of Editorial Services:
   Heather Talbot

Marketing Manager: Heather Hurley

Acquisitions Editor: Orren Merton

Senior Editor: Mark Garvey

Marketing Coordinator: Adena Flitt

Project Editor: Tonya Cupp

Technical Reviewer: Casey Kim

PTR Editorial Services Coordinator:
   Erin Johnson

Copy Editor: Kim Benbow

Interior Layout Tech: Digital Publishing
   Solutions

Cover Designer and Illustrator:
   Mike Tanamachi

Indexer: Sharon Hilgenberg

Cover images from the RTS game *Trash* by
   Inhuman Games

Library of Congress Control Number: 2006927156

ISBN-13: 978-1-59863-301-6

ISBN-10: 1-59863-301-5

Course Technology
20 Channel Center Street
Boston, MA 02210
USA

Cengage Learning is a leading provider of customized learning solutions with office locations around the globe, including Singapore, the United Kingdom, Australia, Mexico, Brazil, and Japan. Locate your local office at:
international.cengage.com/region

Cengage Learning products are represented in Canada by Nelson Education, Ltd.

For your lifelong learning solutions, visit **course.cengage.com**

Purchase any of our products at your local college store or at our preferred online store **www.cengagebrain.com**

Printed in the United States of America
   2 3 4 5 6   15 14 13 12 11

FD292

I'd like to dedicate this book to my mom, Suzanne. Thanks for your support and for staying on top of me to get it done!

} Acknowledgments

So many people assisted me in making this book that it's difficult to know where to begin thanking everyone. God is definitely first on my list, but a close second is Orren Merton for being the "whip the shoulder" and the encouragement. You knew what hat to wear in every situation and I really thank you for it.

Next up is Mike Prager. Without you this would have never been possible. Thank you for thinking that I was up to the challenge.

This book also would have been completely impossible without the people I interviewed:

The very first interviewee I'd sincerely like to thank is J. White. You were always so helpful and full of useful information. The book wouldn't have been the same without you.

Next, I'd really like to thank Ben Burtt. Your enthusiasm and artistry are legendary and I was so blessed to have some of that light spill over into the book. Thanks for lunch, too!

Peter McConnell, your expertise and incredible insight really helped make the composer section of this book.

Julian Kwasneski, I've never met someone who works as hard as you. I know you had unbelievable obstacles when you answered my questions. Thanks so much for taking the time.

Thanks to Mark Griskey. Mark, you are a composing machine and I'm so thankful for your time and information.

Nick Peck, I don't know how it's humanly possible to stay on top of everything you do. Thanks for all of your help and encouragement.

Jory Prum, we've been friends for so long, but we've never actually worked on a project together. It was great to finally hear how you do things. Thank you for sharing!

Thanks to my friend Jim Diaz. We've been friends since the beginnings of our careers and the friendship is always a treasure.

Doug Beck, thank you so much for your time. It was a pleasure to get to hear how you work.

Steve Tushar, you're another one who amazes me with how you tackle all of the different jobs that you do. Thank you for your time and information.

Last but not least, the technical end:

Thanks to Mark Garvey and Tonya Cupp. Mark, thanks for giving me the opportunity, and Tonya, thanks for your hard work and patience with me!

I'd also like to take a moment to thank some of the people who helped me get together photos and (when I needed it) first-hand, up-close-and-personal use of the software.

Thanks to:

Mike Prager (Cakewalk), Erin Hutton (Native Instruments), Angus Baigent (Steinberg), Stefan Leiste (EastWest), Paul De Benedictis (Spectrasonics), Jon Gillham (Apple), and Bela Canhoto (Liga).

Thank you as well to all the people who were there for me, keeping me going, putting up with me, and giving me unbelievable support. Thanks to Kurt Kurasaki: I've really treasured our talks and your wisdom. Also, Andrew Mamaliga, Eddie and Judy Briscoe, Ruby Briscoe, Joe Gonzales, Ashley Horstman, Ed Love, Kristen Simpkins, Rover, Jay Tye, Kait Lewis, Ozzie Ozkay, John Buzolich, Phillip Berry, Alex Von Bromssen, James Perry, Angela Goodman, Kate Luce, Mike, John, Beckey and Mona Riley, Jerusha Hoffman, Amber Rose, Peggy Burtt, Bonnie, Frank and Anita, and everyone at the Open Door.

A very special thanks to my friend and mentor, Christian Petke. Thanks for continually showing me the ropes and believing in me when I didn't believe in myself. Isn't it funny that I finished this book before we finished the album?

Thanks go to my mom, Suzanne, and my dad, Bill. I wouldn't have made it without you. Also, I've greatly appreciated all of the cooking tips while writing this book, Dad! And last but not least, to my daughter Taylor. I miss you.

} About the Author

G.W. Childs IV has worked on over 25 video games in his long career in the video-game industry. Some of the titles he has worked on include *Star Wars: Knights of the Old Republic II: The Sith Lords*, *Star Wars: Battlefront II*, and *Mercenaries: Playground of Destruction*. Additionally, he's been a sound designer on Reason 3.0 and Cakewalk's Rapture.

G.W. lives up in San Rafael amidst several deer and many coffee shops where he is a regular. He plays in two bands: Soil & Eclipse (www.soilandeclipse.com) and Deathline International (www.copint.com /deathline and www.myspace.com/deathlineinternational) that often play in various clubs and can be heard at clubs in your area or on iTunes. You can learn more about G.W. and his bands at www.myspace.com /gwchilds4.

TABLE OF } Contents

❋ ❋ ❋

} Introduction

Hello and thank you for picking up this book. Hopefully, you noticed the title and found it completely intriguing. If so, I commend you on your fine taste. This book is about a couple of wonderful jobs within the video-game industry. Sound designer and composer are highly creative positions and generally filled by people who can think fast and create fast.

Have you ever played a video game for hours, into the morning, and thought to yourself, "Man, that sounded great! I wonder how they made so many cool sounds for that game?" If so, then you've wondered how a sound designer does his or her job.

Have you ever played a video game on your home-entertainment system and wondered how such beautiful music made it into the game? Maybe you wondered how you could get your music into a game. If this is the case, you've wondered about the job of a composer.

These are two of the most mysterious jobs that I know of within the video-game industry and I've got good news for you: This book tells you all about how each job works.

What You'll Find in This Book

This book is filled with information that has, for the most part, been available only to people within the video-game industry. Why is it such a secret? Most of the people in this business are so busy they don't have time to write a definitive book.

Here's what you'll find in the book:

- ❄ Tips for breaking into the business.
- ❄ An inside look at the various roles within the video-game industry and how the composer and sound designer interact with each.
- ❄ How to organize your sound-design project into a database and how to organize your own personal database.
- ❄ A walk-through of the tools of the trade, including careful explanations of the various types of software.
- ❄ Sound design and compositional ideas that save you time and make you more efficient.

Who This Book Is For

This book is for the guy or gal who loves video games and has always wanted to hear his sounds or her music in a video game. As I said earlier: It's true that these are two very mysterious professions. I used to be like you—standing on the outside wondering what I had to do to break in. I've laid out everything I've learned with help of others from within the video game industry.

How This Book Is Organized

This book is organized into two parts. Part I is directed at mainly the sound designer. However, I recommend reading this part even if you're a composer, as it offers information that you will find helpful.

Part II is for the composer. However, a sound designer can benefit from what's here as well. It's good to know everything you can about every job within this industry.

Part I: The Sound Designer

- ❄ Chapter 1 describes the video game team players. It also talks about your role within that team and what to expect at team meetings.
- ❄ Chapter 2 tells you how a sound-design project database and a sound designer's personal sound database are organized. These tools help you get the job done!
- ❄ Chapter 3 tells you how to record your sounds for use in your game. You learn the tools used in field recording and practices.

* Chapter 4 reveals the sound designer's necessary tools. It tells you what software is used, as well as how and why it's used.

* Chapter 5 talks about the basic tools found within wave editing programs and how they benefit audio editing.

* Chapter 6 goes into advanced techniques and some simple exercises that let you get your hands on creating your own sounds.

* Chapter 7 is an exercise in using software samplers (in this case, Reason) to make new sounds from existing sounds.

* Chapter 8 describes why and how you use batch converters to save yourself time and energy.

* Chapter 9 walks you through mixing the cut scenes, or short movies, that are found in every video game. Learn how to mix all of the elements: ambiences, sound FX, voice, and music—and all in surround!

Part II: The Composer

* Chapter 10 walks a composer through the first moments on a project and explains what questions he or she should be asking.

* Chapter 11 describes the composer's tools of the trade. It lays out programming, recording, and editing software, along with virtual instruments.

* Chapter 12 is all about software samplers, arguably one of the most vital instruments within the modern composer's arsenal.

* Chapter 13 guides you through editing licensed or pre-existing music into a cut scene and making it fit seamlessly within the length of the video.

* Chapter 14 shows the tricks for scoring cut scenes.

* Chapter 15 tells you what to do to break into the industry. Who do you talk to? Where do you go? What Web sites can you visit? It's all here.

* Chapter 16 ties together all the information you've learned.

1 } Meetings

In the beginning, the video games industry started off as a couple of guys working out of a garage. Games were a labor of love, not the money-making industry that we all know and love today. Back in those days, things were simpler. Artistic decisions, programming decisions, even sound and music choices were all based off a Yay or Nay from the programming guy. As garage companies evolved, one man's job was split.

These days each major game company has these main departments:

* Production
* Level Design (or just Design)
* Art
* Quality Assurance
* Marketing

Some companies have sound departments, others don't. The companies that don't tend to contract out to individuals or small companies specializing in sound for video games. Incidentally, agents (or agencies) represent artists for the express purpose of landing their talent video-game sound gigs. With that knowledge in your head, you should know one thing: Sound for video games is very competitive.

One of the first things you notice about the game industry is the enormous number of meetings taking place during game title development. Granted, the number of meetings may vary depending on the company you are working for, but make no mistake—there will be meetings.

Remember that one guy in his garage who used to do everything? Remember how his position got broken up? The meetings are there for him, you, and people in other departments to explain what they're doing, so everyone knows what's going on.

Who's Who in Game Design Meetings

With all of the different departments, you can see the need for an open forum; people need to discuss their workflow, problems, and ideas. Team meetings facilitate this kind of open endeavor and through them, many ideas flourish and grow. Consequently, many ideas get knocked out as well. Remember: It's a team endeavor, but not a democracy. The title producer has the final decision on pretty much everything. Figure 1.1 shows you a diagram of what a hierarchy of game designers will look like.

Figure 1.1

The chain of command as it exists on a modern game project. Keep in mind, this can vary from company to company.

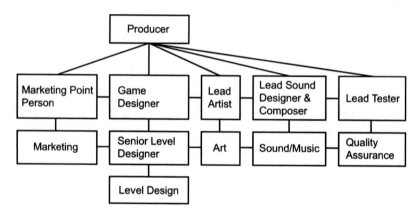

Producers

Producers all come from different backgrounds. At some companies, producers can fill many different roles, like in the old days. They can be the designer, producer, and writer all in one. These days, they are usually from production backgrounds and have had a serious amount of time in the trenches. They understand the companies' inner workings, what management wants, what constitutes a good game, and what to delegate. And here's one thing that they know all too well: how to stay within budget. Ultimately, the producer is the big boss for the game and only answers to the company executives. They know budgets well because producers tend to have been in the game industry for several years.

Producers always have assistant producers as well. The assistants work hard to pick up all the extra work. After all, there's only so much that one producer can do! Assistant producers do everything from keeping an eye on the bug count to making sure that everyone working overtime has food to eat at night. A **bug** is something that is not right within a game. It could be a clerical error in the text, a problem with the art, or, in its worst form, a chain of events that crashes the game. It's important to find every bug within a video game because one bug can completely ruin the game.

Level Designers

Level designers create the levels and overall game play. One level designer usually is assigned to a couple of levels in the game, essentially creating a series of puzzles and events that form an overall experience within one level. A **level** is basically one chapter of the story within a game. For example, when you beat one maze in Pac-Man, the next maze is restocked with more dots and the ghosts are there again. This is the next level. When you beat the level, you move further into the story and up to the next level. Level designers, at times, also work with the sound designer on sound placement, or wiring. (See the explanation of wiring later in this chapter.)

Level designers individually answer to a senior level designer, who answers to the main game designer. This is the person who converts the writer's story in to a full-fledged game. He's also the guy working with the producer to ensure that this game comes out the way it's planned. Basically, he's ultimately designing how the game will play. Incidentally, he's usually the guy creating the design document.

Art Team

A project's **art team** may seem like a pretty straightforward group but it's technically pretty complicated. Art department jobs include

- ❋ **Lead artists** supervise all the artists.
- ❋ **Concept artists** create paintings and sketches of the main characters, the game world, and the individual levels within the game.
- ❋ **Technical artists** are highly creative engineers who understand how to make software fulfill many different visual effects within a game. If a modeler is having a tough time getting a flag to wave within a game, he consults with a technical artist in achieving this end.
- ❋ **Modelers** use 3D design programs to create individual items, people, buildings, and streets within the game. They create all the 3D art within the game.
- ❋ **Texture artists** make 2D graphics to fill in the 3D objects within a game. When a modeler creates an item, it's a shape with no color, or **texture**. Modelers rely on texture artists for that.

Everything starts with the lead artist who, at the beginning, works with the concept artists. Later on, these paintings (which are usually quite beautiful) act as visual inspirations for all the other departments, like sound. Later in this book I talk about how sound designers and composers alike can use these paintings to fuel their creativity.

The art team definitely has more positions than this, but this gives you a good idea of what it's all about.

Quality Assurance Team

The **quality assurance (QA) department** is comprised of testers. Testers are invaluable to every department because they see what the end user will see—the actual game. These people do whatever they can to **break the game**, playing in every way possible hoping to crash the game. The QA team includes

- ❋ A **department manager** is usually a former tester who has shown enough responsibility to run the test department. This person oversees each project, oversees the department's administrative functions, and makes sure all the testers get paid.

- ❋ **The lead tester** is someone a sound designer should definitely buddy up with. These people have worked on several titles and know what's going on. Most project teams have one lead tester and one assistant lead. They maintain the test databases and ensure that all testers are doing their job.

- ❋ **Testers** sometimes spend night and day trying to find bugs within a game.

What usually happens in a sound designer/tester relationship? A tester is assigned to mainly document sound problems that occur in the game. She usually lands this position due to some background in sound, or may just be the tester who happens to write up a ton of sound bugs. Either way, this particular tester is invaluable to a sound designer because she helps you keep track of how your work is being implemented, how it sounds, and how it fits into the overall game.

❋ **Bugging Me**

A bug is an isolated occurrence in the game—something that isn't supposed to happen. For example, if your game crashes every time your character jumps the barrel, that's a bug. You're probably asking yourself why a sound designer would care about bugs. Sound bugs do happen quite frequently. You'd be surprised how often a particular sound will play too softly or just doesn't work in the game. It's okay: Bugs are there to ensure that you're putting out a quality game. They help you check your work and make improvements.

Marketing

There's always going to be a head marketing person, and he will have a small staff. A company always assigns a marketing person to a project at the beginning so that person knows what the game is about from the beginning. The assigned marketing staff decide when the game can be announced, how it should be marketed, and to some degree, how it should play in order for it to be marketable.

At some point in the project, don't be surprised if a marketing person approaches you to supply some audio for a promotional trailer or a promotional Web site. In a meeting, marketing's role is usually to listen to what's going on with the game and to let the team know where they are in their marketing campaign.

Questions to Ask the Design Team

While they may be long and boring, a good sound designer knows to take full advantage of these first meetings. You need to ask several questions at the project's start, and the first meeting is as good a time as any.

What's the Timeline?

One of the first and foremost things you need to know are the dates of each phase's production cycle:

- ❄ Alpha
- ❄ Beta
- ❄ QA
- ❄ Gold

Each milestone dictates where you should be at any point of the project, all the way up to completion. Not every project is the same in this regard. Be clear on what they consider Alpha. For more on that, see the following explanations.

With the game industry getting more and more competitive, publishers are forcing developers to complete games more expediently and efficiently. To say that this is what actually happens is somewhat laughable. Sometime you may get recruited for a title whose deadlines are too ambitious. The seasoned veteran can easily tell if the schedule is reasonable. For the new sound designer, it can be a little more difficult. You don't exactly know what your workflow is and how quickly you can work. Chapter 16 discusses creating a demo reel. If you are new to game sound design, I recommend keeping track of how long it takes you to put the reel together and use that as an average later on when dealing with your first projects.

Alpha Phase

Like the name suggests, **Alpha phase** is the very beginning of a game production cycle. At this point in the game's lifespan, it should be relatively playable, most of the art should be in, and the story should be present within the game. Generally, you are only delivering placeholder sounds at this point. Most of your production (like field recording) takes place during the Alpha phase. To explain this stage in more detail, Alpha titles still have Temp textures in some parts. The menus have temporary artwork. Some characters run around completely disproportioned and hideous.

I recommend you play the game you are working on, but this phase will make you cringe at times. There is simply no immersion at this point. Oh, and I haven't even mentioned the amount of bugs that you will encounter. Nothing like getting close to the end of a level with your disfigured main character (who is supposed to be a beautiful heroin) only to fall out of world and get some crazy error message. Occasionally, you get a title in great shape by the time it reaches Alpha. Treasure the moment; it won't happen often.

Beta Phase

At the **Beta phase** you see what the game is really going to look, play, and sound like. All the art is in, all the game-play elements are in, and the bugs are in, in spades. In the Beta phase you make regular deliveries to the team where the deliveries, or sounds, are **wired** (programmed) into the game. Production is still in progress, but your field recordings should be done at this point. Additionally, you check bugs on a regular basis. It's during Beta that you get the bulk of your feedback from the team on how the delivered sound is working in the game. In other words, Beta and Alpha are your busiest points in the entire schedule.

❄ **Wiring What?**

You can't simply drop a folder full of sounds into a game and expect them to start working. Someone has to go through and tell the game engine where to pull the sound, where to play the sound, and how to play the sound. This is wiring. On certain projects you will wire in the sounds that you create. This can be a very, very tedious endeavor, and it definitely doubles your work. The good thing about doing your own wiring is, you get more control of how the game treats your sounds. Occasionally, the programmers will have implemented a light GUI (graphical user interface) that lets you not only tell the sound where to go, but in some cases lets you tell the game from what direction the sound should play or how much real-time reverb should be triggered when the sound plays.

QA Phase

When the **Quality Assurance (QA) phase** has started, all the sound must be in the game. At this point you are only doing bug fixes and tweaking the mix of the game. That's when all of the bug fixes are taking place between the test team and the programming and design teams. To put it in basic terms, you are at the easy point while the rest of the team is going crazy.

Don't get me wrong, you'll still be attending many meetings and there will be plenty of bugs that come your way, but it won't be nearly as busy as Alpha or Beta. As a rule of thumb, I'd suggest spending a good amount of time playing the game. This is a wonderful opportunity for you to write your own sound bugs and fix things that have been bugging you, if the schedule permits the changes.

Gold Phase

Your involvement has ended at the **Gold phase** ... most of the time. At times, QA can spill over into this phase for the sound designer, especially if upper management has gotten involved and are not happy with how things are sounding. This phase is called Gold because the **gold masters**, or final, CD/DVD copies of the game are distributed to the team to double-check their work. These masters are also known as **release candidates**.

Unless a major sound bug is causing a problem (and that does happen from time to time), you can't change anything. Everything is locked in and the whole team is praying that the testers will quit finding major crash bugs that keep the game from shipping. If it is a console game that you are working on, you are also praying that other parties (which I won't mention the names of) will not find additional bugs as well.

Do You Have a Design Document?

A **design document**, or design doc, describes the game and how it will play. Additionally, the design doc contains artwork, the main story, each level description, and so on. Not all design docs are created equally; some are more informative than others.

If there is a design document, you can base most of your sound-design decisions on what is in this document. If the answer is No, you need to view the game in the condition it's in and make some creative judgments of your own.

When a team fails to supply this vital piece of information it creates a lot of extra work for everyone on the team. Why? Because it's the game's blueprint. Without it, the team can rely only on the vision of the design team and the producer. I've seen some design docs that have had just a quick paragraph what the game was about and how it's going to play. I also saw how that project went after the fact. Basically, everyone on the team—art, design, test, production, programming—had a different idea of what type of game they were making. As a result, the game was pushed back a year and heads rolled. If you're a contractor (who isn't too hungry for work) and encounter a title like this, it might be best to move along.

On the swing side of things, I've seen very detailed, very well-planned design docs that let the team and the product flourish. It's the same as yours truly writing this book. I did an outline that spelled out what the book was going to be about in great detail. As a result, I'm having a pretty easy time writing because I know how it starts, how it ends, and what it's about!

What Are the Sound Engine's Capabilities?

A lot of the time, this information can be found in the design doc. If it's not there (or there is no design doc), it should be on the tip of your tongue. Knowing the sound engine's capabilities lets the sound designer know what kind of additional tricks he may have at his disposal. With every new sound engine getting more sophisticated, it behooves you to know what's going on under the hood—especially if you consider how increasingly powerful some of the new game consoles are. With this in mind, the savvy sound designer might think about becoming best friends with the sound programmer because the programmer can tell you everything the sound engine can do. Keep in mind that as I write this, new and bolder engines are coming out.

At any rate, here are some things to look for in a sound engine:

* The number of audio channels that can be streamed during game play.
* To what extent sound is positional within the game.
* Any real-time Digital Signal Processing (DSP) effects: chorus, reverbs, delays.

Miles Sound System

Miles Sound System has been around for years and lovingly upgraded over a vast period of time. I've worked with it on many titles. Like other sound engines for actual video game engines, it has a slew of plug-ins that grant cool sound features to your game. Some examples of plug-ins for the Miles Sound System include EAX 4.0, EAX 3.0, Dolby Surround, SRS Circle Surround.

However, just because you add a plug-in doesn't mean that the game is actually going to play in surround optimally. For example, some developers just slap in the plug-in and assume that real-time reverbs work in every cave area. When this attitude abounds, sound sources reverberate that shouldn't, stereo support is poor, and filtering events are strange.

Here is a list of some Miles Sound System features:

* On-the-fly resampling and format conversion
* Dozens of independently stackable DSP audio filters
* Software reverb with high-quality EAX emulation
* 3D digital audio positioning up to 8.1 channels
* MP3 support

2 } Sound Database

Shepherds have a difficult job if you think about it. Not only are sheep their only company, but they are also the shepherd's bread and butter. A shepherd is toast if something happens to the sheep, so he must track all the sheep—no small task. Wouldn't it be great if the shepherd had a database to help out? He could name each sheep and create a status field: Is Rusty alive, sick, or dead? Check the database! He could make a description field in case he forgets their names. (Granted, all sheep look very similar, but they all have certain features that set them apart … maybe.) With a database, the shepherd could be more on top of things.

As a sound designer, you're not too different from the shepherd. You have to know these things about each sound:

* Location
* Status
* Type
* Where the sound plays

A sound designer's other key responsibilities follow:

* Determining what sounds the game needs
* Supplying the game with quality sounds
* Creating audio for cut scenes within the game; see Chapter 9
* Working with the programmers to ensure that the game engine makes optimal use of the audio
* Determining the overall sound mix, ensuring that all sound volumes and music are optimum

That sounds like a pretty daunting task for one person. With the help of an organized database, it can be a lot simpler than it sounds. A database is one of the first things to work on in preparation for your sound-design gig. I don't list the actual steps for creating the database because there are several software packages to choose from.

You go through a design document to make an elaborate list of what sounds you need for every level:

* Weapons—What do they sound like when they are fired, reloaded, and so on?

* Environment—These sounds would occur due to certain environments. If a desert is the game's backdrop, what does a desert footstep sound like?

* Environmental ambiences—The natural sound of a level all by itself. If you're in a forest in the day, that might include birds chirping and wind blowing through trees.

* Characters—These sounds, specific to the main character, may occur during all portions of the game and include talking, sneezing, and opening things such as knapsacks, yelling, or injury sounds.

* Enemies—These guys and gals make sounds, too.

A working knowledge of spreadsheets comes in very handy when you're making these lists. You can break down lists by sound source, levels, type, and so on.

As a sound designer you're responsible for two databases:

* Project

* Personal

Granted, you don't have to database everything, but the seasoned pros do. The philosophy is that the more you document, the less time you spend looking for sounds later.

Database References
Frankly, entire books could be written on creating a sound database. I encourage you to pick up a how-to book on creating a general-purpose database in conjunction with this book. This chapter lists the fields and options you want in your sound design database and recommends proven software; it doesn't take you through each step involved in creating a database.

Project Database

The **project database** is devoted directly to the project. It explains where the sound appears in the game, what character a sound may be associated with, the description of the sound, and so on. Every game you work on will need its own sound project database. You'll use this information from the moment you start the title to the moment you finish it. Even after the title has shipped, the information in a project database is helpful.

For example, assume this ugly scenario: You are starting a new title and need a sound that exists in the previous game you worked on. You open up the directory that holds all of the files, each of which is labeled in the naming convention of the last title. Unfortunately, the filenames don't help with this project. You play each file individually, for hours, until you finally find the sound you were looking for. You play the sound a couple of times and realize it's not quite what you currently need. You just wasted hours finding a file that you aren't going to use!

Now, envision this lovely scene: You have a database for the last title that you worked on. You know that you are looking for a particular sound. You search the database, which brings up 30 sounds. It takes you 5 minutes to find the perfect file. That's the beauty of the project database.

Keep in mind that there are several game engines, and filenames are handled differently from one project to another. Many times a team programmer instructs you to name your files within certain parameters.

> ❈ **Project Sound Databases and Filemaker Pro**
> What kind of software should you use to create a project database? Every sound designer I talked to for this book uses Filemaker Pro. This chapter shows examples in Filemaker Pro. There are definitely other worthwhile databases for this kind of work, but none is used more often in this industry.

Project databases vary depending on the needs of the project team. Make a master template of your project database and change it as necessary. For example, the terminology for certain sound attributes may change from title to title. In one title, Type may be the field name describing a kind of character. In another title, Class is the field name describing characters. (You may have to meet with a team to make sure everyone uses the same terminology.)

To get a really good idea of what a database is like, take a look at Figure 2.1. It shows a picture of a database supplied by Bay Area Sound, who has done titles like *God of War* and *James Bond 007: Everything Or Nothing*. The database is one of their keys to success, so let me start breaking the database down.

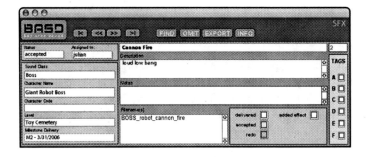

Figure 2.1
Notice the different fields and their contents in this Bay Area Sound database.

Status

The Status field appears in the top left in Figure 2.1. Usually this field has three options: Accepted, In Progress, and Delivered. Accepted is currently chosen, which means the sound designer has declared the sound as a file that he's going to work on. Indicators vary, but here are common ones you'll see:

* Not Begun
* In Progress
* Ready
* Delivered
* Redo
* Cut

Assigned To

On the majority of the projects you won't be the only sound designer. In that case you want to keep track of who is doing what. From the lead sound designer to the assistant sound designer, there has to be accountability. After all, you don't want three people working on the same sound!

Sound Class

Most video games have several character classes. **Classes** are essentially categories of creatures and characters and how the game organizes them. There are creatures that exist only in the background, generic enemies that exist in abundance on different levels, friendly character classes that aid the player throughout the game. The character in Figure 2.1 is obviously a boss-class character. Generic characters appear more than once in a game level. You know, like thug A and thug B? These kinds of characters would be known as Enemy. Some sounds are emitted from natural sources, like the environment, and are referred to as Ambience.

Character Name

Some fields may seem so simple that they are redundant, but you'd be surprised how frequently someone forgets to include them. Character Name fields let you enter the name of the character making the sound effect. If it's not a character making the sound, then the name of what's making the sound is entered in.

Character Code

This field holds the character's name as it appears in computer code. Examples include CC_01 or BG_03. When coding the game, programmers don't—and much of the time can't—code a character's appearance. You're more likely to see $(%& than Big, Bad Robot. Programmers shorten the filename so the name works in the syntax in which they are coding.

Level

This field points out the sound's level and its character. In this particular case, Toy Cemetary is the level; it's where all the action will take place!

Milestone Delivery

This field's important because meeting milestone is crucial in game development. Failure to meet a milestone can ruin marketing strategies or cancel a project. A **milestone** is a deadline, the point that a certain amount of progress has to be made. In Figure 2.1, for example, you can see this sound is due on Milestone 2 (M2), which occurred March 31, 2006 (3/31/2006).

Filename

At the top of the middle column, the filename appears in an unlabeled field. This is the short, descriptive filename of the sound as it appears to the sound designer and the team. Don't mistake this for the *game's* filename, which is usually coded (and appears in the Filename(s) field in Figure 2.1 as BOSS_robot_cannon_fire). As explained before, different game engines handle filenames differently. This is how the naming convention worked for this particular title.

Description

The Description field lets you insert a brief description of how the sound should, you know, sound. This lets you know what you're building. For example, someone might describe a certain sound as "a distant explosion produced by a cannon." This description is the first bit of information you can work with. From here you can make plans to hang out at a fireworks extravaganza with a mic!

Notes

In this section, you can leave any kind of helpful information:

❈   Describe how you created the sound. For example, say you use a compressor setting for a compressor plug-in. In your notes, you mention the setting filename and what plug-in you used.

❈   Explain to your assistant how you'd like the sound to be created. For instance, the lead sound designer may have specific ideas of what source material to use, so he will leave a note explaining where to get the material.

❈   Note what you used for source material in creating this sound. Maybe you used a rhino from a commercial library?

❈   Note a specific combination of sounds used to create the final sound.

Filename(s)

I warned you about the Filename(s) field earlier. Here it is: where you type the name of the sound as it's assigned within the game. When the game engine calls up this sound, it's going to pull BOSS_robot_cannon_fire, not Cannon Fire. Let me break down the name:

- ❋ **BOSS:** The first part of the filename reveals the sound class to the person wiring the file. In this example the sound class is Boss.

- ❋ **robot:** The second part of the filename lets the person wiring know that this sound is coming from the robot boss.

- ❋ **cannon_fire:** Here's the sound's basic reference, based on the filename. The underscores are necessary because spaces can cause a problem for programming and wiring. The Boss is capitalized to help confirm the character classification.

This particular database lets you enter more than one filename in this field. Yep, certain sounds can be used all over a game. This way you know what other names this sound is going by. For example, BOSS_robot_cannon_fire is the boss robot in a particular level. BOSS_robot_cannon_Fire (notice the capitalization of Fire) indicates the pirate ship in another level.

Status Checkboxes

In this area you'll notice several checkboxes:

- ❋ **Delivered** is selected when the sound has been delivered to the team to be placed in the game. This is the box that's checked to let you know that the sound has been completed and no longer needs any attention.

- ❋ **Accepted** is selected when the request to make the sound has been accepted and is in the work cue. The Status field is capable of giving more answers as well, besides simply Accepted. It can say things like Cut and Not Begun.

- ❋ **Redo** is selected if the sound was not accepted by the team (or the lead sound designer) and was marked as a sound that needed to be done again to really fit the game, or for whatever reason it wasn't accepted.

- ❋ **Added Effect** is selected if additional processing was used on the sound. Maybe a reverb was added or a chorus. Sometimes the initial sound doesn't seem 'big' enough, so effects are used to make them larger than life, etc.

Status checkboxes are quick, easy ways to tell what the situation is with a sound. At a glance you can tell if it's been delivered, if it's a redo, and so on.

Tags

Tags are specific to the person who put together the database. Tag checkboxes are generic and can take different meanings from project to project. For example, the lead sound designer on this project may decide that his assistant will assign all his sounds as B sounds. This is helpful because when the sound designer or his assistant want to search for and differentiate between sounds the lead has worked on and the sounds the assistant has worked on, they can search by tags. Another example: Say the sound designer is applying a process on certain files. In this case, he marks these files as C files. If he wants to search for all the files that have run through this process, he can search for C files.

Find

The Find button, at the top of the screen in Figure 2.1, provides one of the most important database functions. Find initiates a Search function, much like a search on the Internet. When you click Find, every field goes blank. At this point, you type in a description, select a certain field, or both.

Once you press the Find button again, the database displays information based on your searching. For example, say you are looking for all delivered loud bang sounds. You type Loud Bang in the Description field and select the Delivered checkbox. Once you press Find again, the database displays all the loud bang sounds that have been delivered.

Omit

Use the Omit button with the Find function. After initiating a Find and you enter search criteria, press Omit if there's certain criteria that you don't want brought up in a search. For example, say you are searching again for delivered loud bang sounds, but you don't want any of the loud bang sounds that Julian created. First, you press the Find button to start your search. Then you enter Loud Bang in to the Description field and check the Delivered box. Now press Omit. The fields go blank; select Julian in the pop-up menu so it isn't brought up under the Assigned To field. Now when you press Find, all the records that come up are loud bang sounds that were delivered but not assigned to Julian.

Export

Occasionally, you'll want to export your database records and all of the information to either an Excel document or to another program, such as Word, that handles text. Once you click the Export button, Filemaker Pro asks you where to send the information and what type of file it should be. For example, ASCII is basic text that can be used in any program like Word.

Certain pieces of information in your database may come in handy for meetings or with documents. Use the Export function to get that data out to those other programs. You can send files to programs like Word, PowerPoint, and even Wordpad.

Info

In this database, extra information has been neatly tucked away to avoid clutter. When the Info button is pushed, more information is displayed revealing things like the Sample Rate, Number Of Channels, and so on.

It's not required to set your database up this way, but you may find it handy to. With an Info button you can look at all the options when you need to but avoid it when you just want quick reference on a file.

Other Handy Fields

No two project databases are the same. As I said before, every team has certain needs. The way your database is set up directly affects the way you deliver a sound to the team, the way you organize, and the way you name sounds.

You can add plenty of other fields to help organize your work. Here are some common fields you might find helpful:

* **Loop:** This standard checkbox can indicate if the sound is a loop. Every game has ambiences that flesh out each level's sound, and ambiences always loop.

* **Shared File:** It's not uncommon for one sound to be used in different parts of a game. You may want a checkbox to indicate that a sound is used on many levels. After all, there are going to be lot of characters with lots of footsteps. It would make sense that you wouldn't have different footsteps for every character in the game, right? Especially if they are of similar build.

* **File Specifications:** Use such a text box to list technical elements such as sample rate, bit resolution, and number of channels.

Personal Database

The **personal database** is a catalog of sounds you've supplied for every title you've ever worked on. As technology changes, you'll want to adapt your database; as your workflow changes, you'll want to adapt your database. So many things can cause a database to change—new programs, for instance. Keep the database as meticulously as possible, making sure you include data like this about each sound:

* **How it's been used:** You may want to add a field like Type and then list it as some of the things it could be used as. Examples include Impact, Explosion, Menu Sound, and the like.

* **Where it's been used:** A field like Titles would list what games this sound has appeared in.

- ❄ **Where it was recorded:** You may have an Origin field that lists the specifics of where this sound originated. It could even have the time, date, and location.
- ❄ **What microphone recorded it:** Include a field like Microphone or Field Recorder. Each of these pieces of gear would let you know what you used to record the sound.

Your personal database is just as important as the project database, though the former can end up being a little empty if the sounds you develop are claimed as a company's intellectual property after a title ships—and they almost always are claimed. Does this mean you're keeping an empty database? Absolutely not!

What if the sound is claimed as the company's property? All sound designers keep copies of their work. It is perfectly acceptable to back up your work during the project. What if the company loses the library and needs a backup? The most important point is that you do not use the exact sounds again with another title.

Modifying Source Material

Modifying source material falls into a grey area of the sound-design business and is something you cannot ignore. You should always archive your work. Sure, you may not be able to use an existing sound in the future, but it doesn't mean you can't have it as reference for later work. For example, say you need a sneezing sound. You root through your existing library and find a sneezing sound you used on a title two years ago. You read the description of how this sound was made and get an idea how to make a new, better one.

Another thing to keep in mind about personal databases: You may not have the right to use an individual sound anymore, but you can still use the **source material** (original recorded material before post production) to make a sound for a current title. Perhaps you have the fabled sneezing sound source material. It's really a recording of your cat hocking up a hairball. When you got the sound-design gig two years ago, you used that recording. You modified it, however, pitching it down and adding some effects. After you were done, it sounded like a sneeze, and that's exactly what you needed two years ago.

Two years later, you are trying to come up with a sound simulating a robotic leg joint that has a slight squeak and, for whatever reason, you decide to use the sneeze as source material. Maybe it has a slight squeak? You pull the original recording from your personal database, pitch it all the way down, add a little compression, and boom—you have a robotic leg joint! With current audio software, you can modify any sound to resemble almost anything. That's one reason it's great to have a personal library.

Personal Database Software

What kind of database software should you use for a personal database? Whatever you decide to use, it should include the following:

* Detailed: It should be capable of listing everything possible about each sound. You never know what information you'll need later.

* Audio specific: Much of the time project databases are accessed by more than just the sound designer, but you are the only person who'll access this database.

* Easy and fast: As a sound designer (especially if you're a freelancer), you have to be organized and fast. Many sound databases allow you to drop files, on the fly, into programs like Pro Tools and Nuendo. The database can tag the files with descriptions, allow quick access, and track thousands of files.

You can use Filemaker Pro, as suggested for project databases, but the following sections (whose headings tell you acceptable platforms) describe software perfect for personal databases.

BaseHead for PC

BaseHead, pictured in Figure 2.2, is a competitively priced sound-database program for the PC that makes it easy to add and scan through thousands of WAV files on your hard drive. It then allows you to filter the results, audition the sound to preview, and transfer directly to your target application or copy to a specified directory. It even lets you open sounds in a wave editor such as Wavelab for destructive editing.

BaseHead is available online at www.baseheadinc.com. BaseHead supports Avid, Avid Express, Cool Edit, Cubase SX, Nuendo, Pro Tools, Samplitude, SAWstudio, SONAR, Vegas Video, and any other program that supports drag-and-drop support from the desktop.

Figure 2.2

BaseHead is in development at the time of this writing, but looks like it will be an excellent choice for a personal sound database.

Soundminer for PC or Mac

Soundminer is another very adept sound-database program, and it appears in Figure 2.3. The program's features are numerous, even allowing batch conversion and editing processing. It has ReWire support, so it works with any ReWire-compatible program, but its main support is for Nuendo and Pro Tools. The program also features brilliant things like Sound Digger, which searches your database on the spectral properties of one sound in order to find other sounds with similar spectral properties. A VST rack can have up to nine VST effects in a chain for real-time and applied transfers. There is a multi-channel mixer for listening to up to six multi-channel files. For more information on VST effects, see Chapter 4.

The two platform versions vary but the main features are all there in each. For more information, visit www.soundminer.com.

Figure 2.3
Soundminer has been a favorite for organizing sound effects for some time now. It offers loads of features that go above and beyond.

NetMix for PC and Mac

NetMix is a very versatile program that allows multi-track editing, project management, and digital video, as well as acting as a database for your sound files. Many companies currently employ the program, and that's not a bad thing since the companies are paying sound designers.

Besides the previously listed features, it allows mixing before audio even makes it into your host DAW and the ability to build complex sounds. It syncs to picture, which is great when you're auditioning for cut scenes and the like. The program even has multiple output capabilities for surround support. NetMix, pictured in Figure 2.4 works with Pro Tools, Sound Designer, Nuendo, Logic, and Peak. For more information, visit: www.creativenetworkdesign.com.

> **DAW**
>
> DAW stands for digital audio workstation. It's another name for a multi-track audio program like Nuendo or Pro Tools. See Chapter 4 for more details.

Figure 2.4

NetMix has a very straight-forward interface that allows a thoroughly customizable database.

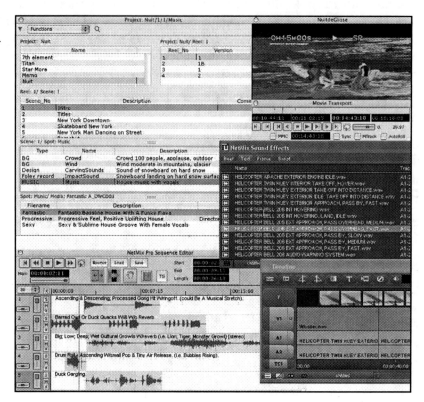

Making Prototypes

Before beginning the Alpha phase (described in Chapter 1), it's crucial to get some placeholder sounds as quickly as possible. A placeholder sound is referred to as **prototype**.

Prototypes give you plenty of help:

* An early idea of how the sound engine will play back the audio you supply

* What the game play will be like with sound

* More direction regarding what kind of sounds to create

I've heard everything from car horns to cowbells acting as prototype sounds. It's not necessary to spend a lot of time on these sounds. In most cases you may use something from your pre-existing library. However, I suggest supplying prototype sounds close to what the actual sound should be. Table 2.1 gives some overall ideas by genre.

Table 2.1   Prototype Suggestions by Genre

Genre	Prototypical Sound
All	Footstep shared by all surfaces
All	Interface sounds (beeps in menus)
Action	Default for many kinds of attacks, vehicles, ambiences (jungles, city, and so on)
Sci-fi	Aliens, laser guns, explosions, impacts, alarms, space vehicles, ambiences (starship interiors, alien planets)
Fantasy	Sword clangs, damage, spell casts, armor clanks, ambiences (dungeons)
Kids' games	Cowbells, music boxes, kazoos, blocks, vehicles
Sports	Impacts, referee whistles, ambiences (stadiums, crowds)

One thing to consider though: In the beginning, there will be far more audio cues than sounds you can provide. The game engine can trigger an infinite number of audio sounds, but you will have delivered a limited number. With this being said, it's perfectly acceptable to have one sound filling several purposes. Later, you can go back and customize each sound to fit each cue. You can replace the sounds after designing all your sounds and creating a library for the game.

3 } Field Recording

Field recording is an adventure. When writing this chapter, I spoke with the infamous Ben Burtt, the sound designer behind movie series such as *Star Wars* and *Indiana Jones*, and who recently worked on *Munich*. He likened field recording to being on a safari where you aren't hunting animals, but sounds. If thinking about field recording in that sense doesn't get you excited, I don't know what will.

Imagine it for a second: You're traipsing through the jungle. It's hot and sticky and you're constantly pushing leaves out of the way. While wondering what in the world made you want to come out here in the first place, a shrill cry in the air makes you remember! You pull a microphone from your bag and power up your field recorder. With a sigh of relief, you notice that the battery is full. Unlike the conventional hunter, you don't see, but you hear. You don't want a pelt from your prey; you merely want to capture audio. It's too good to be true—you hear them shouting like inmates during a prison brawl. Monkeys—tons of monkeys—are yelling, and you're recording every bit of this. Just imagine how great this will be after you clean and process it in the studio! Can you see the similarities? The hunter journeys through dangerous jungles, going to great lengths to capture prey. The hunter has equipment that he must maintain. The hunter even has to clean his prize. But unlike the hunter, no life is taken. In fact, a part of the creature will be kept alive forever! Are you excited yet?

I think field recording is one of the best parts about being a sound designer, period. It's where you get to explore, experiment, and ultimately contribute to your ever-growing library. Every sound in your collection is a different story, a different adventure, a window to your past. This chapter covers some of the equipment pros use, explores ideas for locations, and reveals methods that make things easier as you take your first steps into field recording. By the end of this chapter, hopefully you'll run out and buy a new field recorder (or at least vow to start saving for one). Hopefully, instead of slamming the window because of those noisy birds, you'll stick a microphone outside to record them. This chapter seeks to inspire that much passion.

When to Go Out in the Field

Do you need a fresh set of sounds for every game you work on? Absolutely not! The first step in determining if field recording is necessary is to go through your sounds and see what you have already. Are you working on a World War II game? If you have machine gun sounds, that's half the work right there. Save yourself some trouble and go with what you have. Game schedules are always crunched and the more time you can save, the better. Keep in mind, I'm not telling you *not* to field record. You need to! You need to keep expanding your library. I just want to stress knowing when to record and when to use your library.

Be Prepared

The night before you have a field-recording assignment, make sure you have these things done:

* Batteries charged, verified, and double-checked
* Microphones packed
* Accessories packed: shock mounts, wind socks, and any other items that you use on a regular basis

Plan based on what type of field recording you're doing. Will you be outside? Will you need a microphone stand? Will you need earplugs? All these things can come up.

Keep It Simple

One of my biggest all-around recommendations for field recording is to keep it simple. When it comes down to it, how many microphones you use or how nice your field recorder is means nothing if you aren't ready to grab a sound.

Remain mobile so you can go toward a sound at any second. You can easily duplicate many ambiences, effects, and so on in post-production. Sometimes trying to record a sound in stereo may not be necessary. For instance, say you're trying to record a car driving by. It's fairly easy to get a stereo recording of just such a sound. But perhaps you have ready the monaural microphone when the car has almost reached you. Are you going to stop, change microphones, and risk missing the sound? No! Get the drive-by in mono! Later on you can go back and pan the sound left to right in the studio. If you lose part of the sound, however, it's gone forever.

Slate

When possible, always **slate** your field recordings by saying, into the mic, a small description of what you're going to record. This saves time later on when you're going through your recorded files and are trying to remember what a certain sound is. With a slate, you can know with absolute certainty what your subject was. For example, say you're getting ready to record the whooping of an exotic crane at the zoo. Say, into the microphone, "Exotic crane at the public zoo, take 1." You can even get more specific than that: "Exotic crane using a Shure SM58 at the public zoo in a tiled room on October 5, 2006."

Recorders

Now that you know to be prepared and to slate, what exactly will you slate into? This following sections cover some of the available digital field recorders. The prices vary from expensive to astronomical; somewhere in there you should find something that works for you.

This section does not seek to tell you that you have to use a digital recorder, however. It's been said that some great recordings were achieved from the portable tape decks used for office dictation. In the end, it's all about how you use your gear!

❊ Nagra

From the early 60s up until the early 90s, the Nagra was the ultimate field recorder for movies and later for games. The recorder, which is shown in Figure 3.1, was rugged and captured the sound the way that it was supposed to be heard. However, in the last several years, digital recorders have taken over as the new force in field recording. They sound great, they can record at high sample rates, you can transfer the sound digitally to your computer (if you have the hard drive space to burn), and they are light and compact.

Figure 3.1

The Nagra III, a classic field recorder responsible for many of the sounds you've heard in many of your favorite movies.

Sound Devices

This is the one all the big boys are using, and for good reason. The Sound Devices 7-Series field recorders are designed to be highly rugged and very simple. Simple's good, right? You bet! When you're in the field, the last thing that you want to be bogged down by are clumsy controls and intense digital menus. You need to be sharp and ready to go, and so does your equipment. The Sound Devices guys kept this in mind when designing these recorders. Notice in Figure 3.2 that the sound device has big, clearly explained buttons, much like an old tape deck. The buttons may not seem like such a big deal until you're taking a smoke break and some amazing sound starts up, catching you off guard. You're going to want reliability and simplicity.

Figure 3.2

The Sound Devices 702 field recorder has standard rewind, fast forward, play, and record buttons.

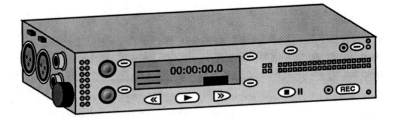

Beyond the obvious, the Sound Devices field recorders are known for their extremely good recording quality. They can record at 24 bit and 16 bit with sample rates from 32 kHz to 192 kHz.

24 and 16 to What?

Recording at 24 bit or 16 bit with sample rates up to 32 kHz to 192 kHz means the recording quality available to the recorder. When referring to sample rates such as 32 kHz, I'm referring to the number of samples per second that can be taken from a contiguous signal (in this case 32). If I were to increase the sample rate, the recorder would take up to 44.1, 48, 96, and so on. The higher the sample rate, the better the recording.

Bit rate refers to the amount of detail stored per unit of time. The higher the bit rate, the more perceived clarity in a recording. Essentially, recording at a higher bit rate brings forward nuances or frequencies that may not have been perceived otherwise.

It is common practice to record at the highest possible sample rate and bit rate. Later on, when you're delivering your sounds to your team, you'll convert your sounds to a lower sample rate and bit rate. Why? The higher the sample rate and bit rate, the more room the files take.

They store their recording on either internal hard disks (only on the high-end 722 and 744T recorders) or on CompactFlash cards (type I or II). They write WAV files (with Broadcast WAV metadata). All data can be transferred via FireWire directly to a Windows PC or Macintosh for post-production or archiving. The 7-Series recorders use two channels of a high-resolution analog microphone pre-amp on the input section. The pre-amp is designed for high-bandwidth, high bit-rate digital recording. Also, they have two XLR inputs and can be adjusted for 48V phantom power.

You're probably thinking that they sound pretty cool, but wondering how big they are. You'll be happy to know that size and portability were kept in mind when constructing these little devils. They were built from the ground up with regard to documentary and recording engineers. As a matter of fact, they weigh fewer than 3 pounds and can fit into a standard accessory case.

The Sound Devices field recorders are on the pricey side. Check them out at www.sounddevices.com.

Edirol

Edirol, who are known for a variety of different audio/video products, feature a small digital recorder. The R-4 is a portable four-channel digital recorder and a wave editor. It's designed as a cost-effective alternative to some of the higher-end digital recorders, but it still has many of the same bells and whistles.

One of the first things I should mention is that it ships with a 40 GB internal hard drive. That's great because with the R-4's ability to record up to 96 kHz, you're going to need it. To put it in clearer terms, the higher the sample rate, the more hard drive space you'll use. For example, if you were recording at 44.1 kHz 16 bit, you wouldn't take up nearly as much space recording at 96 kHz 16 bit.

Another cool R-4 ability is recording up to four channels simultaneously. That's great if you want to set up multiple microphones to get different angles. The recorder even has four XLR inputs to help you achieve this. When recording sounds that you're only going to get one chance at, it's really important to have microphones set up at different distances. After you've recorded the sound, you get an idea what distance works best. The closest mic might sound best, the farthest mic, picking up the sound reflection, may be better.

Here's another thing that you might find handy: When you're in the field, the last thing that you want to worry about is the sound that you're recording peaking out the input of your recorder. The Edirol R-4, seen in Figure 3.3, eliminates this worry with its on-board limiter. A **limiter** keeps a sound's volume from going past a certain level. Having an on-board limiter keeps you from

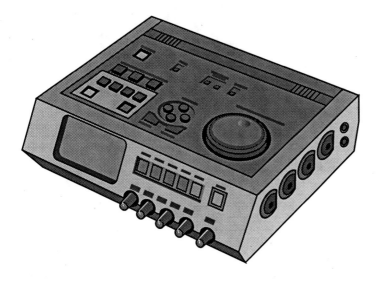

Figure 3.3
The Edirol R-4 packs a lot of pro features in a really good price.

having to constantly mind your meters. If you don't have a set of mics to work with at the start, you'll be happy to know that the R-4 has a set of built-in stereo mics. This is okay, but it's always better to have a set of external mics designed with a little more quality.

❄ **Those Funny Little Meters**

Perhaps on your home tape recorders or computer you've noticed the VU or PPM meters that show how much volume is coming in from your recorded source. It's extremely important that these meters are kept from going over the red, or **peaking**. If these meters do go into the red, your recording can be severely distorted.

For file transfers, you can connect the R-4 to a USB 2.0-compliant computer. Since USB 2.0 is on every current computer, you should have no problem with compatibility.

For such a cost-effective unit, the R-4 offers a ton of high-end features. Check out www.edirol.com.

M-Audio

On the very small and very affordable end, M-Audio has released the MicroTrack 24/96 shown in Figure 3.4. This little device is about the size of an iPod but boasts some features. Like its name implies, the MicroTrack 24/96 can record in either 16 bit or 24 bit, from 44.1 kHz to 96 kHz. It can even record MP3 files at 44.1 kHz or 48 kHz. Just imagine something that small recording with that kind of quality!

Figure 3.4

The M-Audio MicroTrack 24/96 is the smallest in this chapter's recorder round-up, but holds up in features and price.

It doesn't have XLR inputs but it does have 1/4″ inputs that supply phantom power. **Phantom power** is a method of supplying current over a cable to power a microphone. Additionally, it has a 1/8″ mic input and comes with a small 1/8″ stereo mic for when you're on the go. There's even a mic/line switch. This is handy for musicians as well as sound designers. For example, say you're playing a show and decide to record it with this device. There's no need to use a mic when you can get a direct line coming from the house board, right? The recorder even has SPDIF input in case you want to make a field recording directly from a digital device. SPDIF (Sony/Phillips Digital Interface) is a digital input type that allows a digital stream of audio instead of an analog stream. Digital transfer is preferred because it eliminates harsh hums and artifacts that can be present in an analog transfer.

Like the Sound Devices mobile recorder, this device has a very simple interface. There are basic volume, record, and level buttons. The MicroTrack records to microdrives for easy, portable storage and actually comes with a 64 Mb CompactFlash card which, of course, does not hold a whole lot of data. Like an iPod, you can charge it via USB from your laptop or use the handy wall adapter that comes with it. It has an internal lithium, rechargeable battery.

There's really not much more to say about this slick little device that's built sturdy and contains a lot of bang for the buck. Be sure and check it out at www.m-audio.com.

Inexpensive Recorders You May Already Own

You may not be in a position to spend money on one of these devices. That's okay. Of course, high-end recorders are preferred, but you may get some cool recordings with what you already own. Experiment! Personally, I've gotten some interesting recordings from a small digital recorder that I carry around for interviews, ideas, and sounds. The microphone that's built into this device doesn't give the best recording, but sometimes the sound's beauty is in the ear of the beholder. Keep in mind that many sounds can (and will be) spruced up in the studio.

Digital Video (DV) Camera

Some people have digital video cameras to record family outings, class trips, and first steps. If you have one, see if you have a mic input. If you do, you're in business. You can get a small condenser mic and be ready to go. Even if you don't own an external microphone, you can still use the built-in mic.

Portable Tape Deck

A small, portable tape deck, like those used for lectures or interviews, is another option. Ben Burtt mentioned to me getting an extremely good recording of the space shuttle on one such device, when all his other high-end recorders failed.

Microphones

Keep several things in mind regarding microphones when you're field recording:

* Start with a small diaphragm condenser microphone. They're very sensitive. If you do go with one, make sure your field recorder can supply phantom power. Not all mics need phantom power, but condenser microphones need it to power the circuitry contained inside of them and to supply voltage for the transducer element.

* Even better, go with a matched *pair* of small diaphragm condenser microphones. You want a matched pair to achieve a stereo recording. If you're using two different microphones, one channel of your stereo recording will sound different than the other. Most field-recording people have a monaural microphone and a stereo microphone at the ready. Still, having a matched pair allows you to set up your microphones to capture a specific scene. For example, there is a lot going on within a certain area of a forest clearing and you decide to spread the matched set of microphones farther apart.

* Use a **zeppelin**, or **windscreen**, (also called a wind sock) as pictured in Figure 3.5, to keep wind from interfering with your microphone during recording. Of course, if you are recording in doors, a wind sock isn't necessarily needed. But for outdoor recordings with sensitive microphones, a wind sock definitely saves you from *whooosh* sounds in the background.

Figure 3.5

A windscreen prevents wind from ruining your recordings.

* Use a **shock mount**, as pictured in Figure 3.6. It prevents vibration and impact noises that occur when the microphone is moving around. The last things that you want are the shuffling sounds of your microphone as you're walking along trying to keep a sound in range of your microphone.

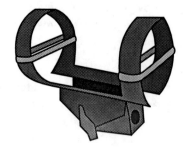

Figure 3.6

A shock mount keeps vibrations from being picked up in the recording.

❄ Consider using a shotgun microphone. They allow you to track a sound from a distance and keep it coming into your recorder as long as you're following it.

Here are some field-recording microphones that won't break the bank.

Audio-Technica AT897

The Audio-Technica AT897, pictured in Figure 3.7, is designed for field recording in film. The short shotgun works equally well for wildlife and broadcast. It also mounts on the side of a DV recorder without adding much weight.

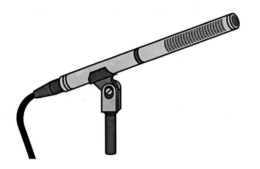

Figure 3.7
The AT897 is a worthy short shotgun.

This mic is priced right and should do the job well for you. Check it out at www.audio-technica.com.

Shure VP88

The Shure VP88 is a single-point, stereo condenser microphone for use in professional studio recording and field production. It combines two condenser cartridges in a single housing to create a stereo audio image of the sound source. **Stereo audio image**, or audio image, is the audio as it sounds when recording in stereo.

The great thing about having a stereo microphone is quick, simplistic reliability when you need to get a stereo recording quickly and efficiently (see Figure 3.8). It's recommended that every field recording engineer have one in their possession at all times, and this one is great for the money. Check it out at www.shure.com.

Sennheiser MKH 418S

The Sennheiser MKH 418S, pictured in Figure 3.9, is another short shotgun microphone with one startling difference: It can record in stereo and in mono! As I said earlier, having a stereo and a mono microphone on your person at all times is ideal when doing field recording. This microphone is both and it's a shotgun to boot. Basically, you can record at a distance in mono or in stereo and can toggle back and forth with the flip of a switch.

Figure 3.8
The Shure VP88 is a sturdy
microphone with great
sound and a good price.

Figure 3.9
The MKH 418S may seem
a little pricey, but it's really
two rugged microphones
for the price of one.

Don't even sweat durability. The mic is built to withstand harsh outdoor conditions; the body is weather resistant. This microphone is a little pricey, but it's kind of like getting two microphones in one. For more information, check out www.sennheiserusa.com.

Rode NT5

This matched pair of small diaphragm condenser microphones are intended for musical instruments. As they are a matched pair, you may use one for mono recordings and then add the other when you need stereo. The frequency response on these microphones is quite nice: 20 Hz to 20 kHz, with a maximum dynamic range of up to 128 dB. Basically, not a lot gets by these little fellas. I think one of the best traits about these microphones is the price. Be sure to check them out at www.rode.com.au.

Figure 3.10
This Rode NT5 microphone
set is extremely good and
extremely cheap.

Locations

You've got your equipment charged and packed. Now where do get your field recordings? Anywhere! And when I say anywhere, I do mean anywhere:

❋ **Your friends.** Someone may have an intriguing job—a mechanic, maybe? You'll get access to hydraulic lifts, power tools, air compressors, and other lovely sounding devices. A pilot, maybe? Just imagine how much you could record if you could hang out at an airport for a few hours! Military reserve units, maybe? Ask if you can go on a field expedition.

❋ **Your neighborhood.** Where do you live? If it's near the woods, you could get some nighttime ambiences in the forest. If you live near a farm, you could get some cool animal sounds. Cities and even the suburbs are filled with useful sounds.

❋ **Your house.** You have easy access to a garage door, a car alarm, a dishwasher, a fireplace, a blender. If you think about it, you could spend days recording and manipulating sounds around your house!

Meanwhile, remember these things:

❋ **Keep your field recorder with you at all times.** I often think of a particular door at a previous job. When I pressed my access card over the card reader, a metal bolt unlatched. I always wish I had a stereo recording of that lock, and I truly meant to get it. Suddenly, my job moved from that building and I no longer had access to the sound. Don't let this happen to you!

❋ **Enlist help from friends and family.** Kids love looking for new sounds! You'd be surprised how many people will start getting into it.

Ultimately, field recording is a fun art. Even if you don't have access to audio that you need, start looking around for great substitutes. If you need a space ship, try using some of the engine noises from your car. It may only sound like a car at first, but after you tweak it in post-production, you may get some great results. If you need alien noises, try using animals. When you tweak animal audio, you can get some otherworldly sounds. The bottom line? Don't take No for an answer. There is a solution waiting to be found. You just need to start the scavenger hunt!

When Field Recording Isn't What You Expected

You'll get an opportunity to record something in particular and the actual sound may not be what you expected. For example, Mr. Burtt told me of a time when he went to record some missile launches in the desert. Everything went smoothly. The only problem was that the missiles didn't make interesting sounds! He described the rocket take-off as sounding like fingers running down a comb. Later on that night, he was lamenting the trip and noticed that the air-conditioning unit in his hotel made a great rumbling noise. He placed his microphone on top of the air conditioner and recorded it. He used its rumble for the rocket sound.

This is a great example of being aware of your environment and how it works to your advantage. Sure, the audio you want may not end up sounding the way that you want, but something else might be right under your nose and do the job just as well!

When Recording Is Done

It's most important that you import your recorded material into your current database as soon as you get back. You'd be surprised how many major companies forget to do this and, as a result, have a huge clerical mess. Having an organized library is essential to your success. It's really easy to relax after getting back from a long day of recording. That's fine! Kick back. But as soon as you get back to the studio, get those new files into your database and break them down into categories. And then, start your tweaking! You'll thank yourself for this later. If you have your files properly organized, you can find them based on descriptions and use them in more ways than you may have originally thought.

4 Sound Design: Tools of the Trade

When I think of the sound designer's list of tools, I think of certain action movies. The hero, at his base of operations at the beginning of the film, has just learned his mission. At this point he's dressed in his civilian clothes and looks like a normal guy. Slowly and confidently he walks over to a polished mahogany wardrobe, unlocks the padlock, and opens the doors. Inside of this thing is every weapon known to man, his uniform, his sunglasses, you name it. Methodically, he picks out certain pieces that are well worn and cared for. He lovingly inspects each piece as he moves it from the wall locker into a metal briefcase.

It may be overdramatizing what occurs for a sound designer, but is it really that different? We all have that one computer, those several pieces of software, and the specific database that we most like to use. The list can get quite extensive. Why do you cling to these particular items? They worked when you needed them most. Sure, they have their quirks, but you've learned through experience what they are and how to work around them.

I know I have my fair share of workarounds. I have one particular combination of software strung together to perform a specific task through macros. A macro program called Quick Keys pulls filenames from an Excel document, and then I rename the sample file in Reason. Essentially, I use Reason to process files and Quick Keys as the batch converter. Was it elegant? Not by a long shot. Was it stable? Yes, if I avoided doing certain things. Did it work? Yes. Would I use it again? Yes, because nothing out there can do what it does. I took the tools that were available at the time and made them do their jobs; at times, you will have to make them do things their designers never thought of.

I can tell you from experience that when you finish your first project, you will feel this way about more than one piece of gear, software, or computer. I can tell you also from experience that there will be other pieces of gear, software, or computers that you will never touch again. They may be good, and they may be highly praised, but they let you down.

If you are new to the sound-design game, this chapter is here to help you decide what tools are good for sound design. And when I say *tools*, I mean software. I'll touch on computer platforms and hardware. But these days, the software is where it really tends to be. If you are an old timer, I invite you to peruse my opinions. Some you'll agree with and some you won't. After all, you've had different experiences in the trenches. Some things worked for you that didn't work for me. If we ever run into one another, perhaps we can have a drink and talk about it. But I will say this: Please take a look. You might find out something about this software that you missed before. Maybe I'm talking about a newer version that you haven't checked out yet. The great thing about software is its continual development.

Computer Platforms

I'd like to first take a moment to talk about the computer platform that you use. Before you even start thinking it, I'm going to diffuse the fire. I'm not here to say that Macs are better than PCs. It's an ongoing debate that I'm going to steer this book away from.

Do I have a preference? You bet. I'll tell you right now that I do. So why am I not talking about my preference? Because that's exactly what it is, *my* preference. Everyone has his own way of working. What I always say is that if you've been using a Mac all along, you should use a Mac. Why? Because it means you already have a decent knowledge of the machine and its operating system. You know how to get around and get things done fast.

But what if one platform has software that looks attractive? When you switch from Mac to PC, you have to learn not only the attractive program, but the operating system. And it may be simple to open a folder and create a new document, but there's also the effort of learning how to tweak an unfamiliar operating system to run audio in a stable fashion.

It might actually be a better idea to try to run things on the machine that you've been using. If it's not fast enough, pick up a machine that uses either the same operating system or a newer version of it. Taking this precaution just means that you'll have one less thing to tweak. This goes for either Mac or PC users. In my humble opinion, it's just better to go with what you know. But what of that attractive software question? In my experience, one piece of software that doesn't run on your platform will have a comparable piece of software that does the same thing on the other platform.

Visit online forums. Later on in this chapter I suggest several different software packages. Each of these bundles has forums for people just like you. These people have all been through just what you're possibly going through right now, trying to figure out what software is right for them. Don't be afraid to ask questions. These sites have real people talking about their experiences in an unbiased and uncensored fashion. You can get the real scoop on the programs that you want before you buy them. You can even go as far as putting up your equipment specifications to find out if other users think that your computer is powerful enough to run the program.

Recommended Software

Now I get to play the part of the sidekick inventor in the action movies. I think you know the kind of guy I'm talking about. He's eccentric and clumsy; he dresses funny; and he spends all his time in the lab. His whole purpose in the movie is to outfit the hero with the tools you need during the mission.

What's the mission? Your first sound-design gig. It may not have happened yet, but if you're reading this book, you obviously have an interest. If you're interested, it probably means that you are trolling for gigs (if not now, soon). There's no point in looking for a mission without the proper weapons, right?

All right, let me put on my bifocals and lab coat. Check! Now, let me put on my pencil holder. Check! Where's my sexy lab assistant? Darn, I forgot this is a book. We don't usually get sexy assistants in those. Walk with me through the dusty lab door and try not to trip on all the strange little gadgets. Here, let me open the wall locker. First, you'll notice two big weapons inside the cabinet. The first one is labeled Wave Editor with Ol' Two Track in parentheses. The other weapon is a little bigger and has more switches and buttons. This one is labeled Multi-Track Editor. These are the two standard-issue software for sound designers. They come in several makes and models, but they are the two things that you must have.

Wave Editors

The first big gun in the sound designer's arsenal is his two-track editing program, or wave editor. I like to think of wave editors as an old two track reel-to-reel from studio days long past. Back then you could record a sound on one of these big lugs, and then trim the sound (very carefully) with a razor blade or run it through external effects. You could splice two sounds together and reverse the sound. There was just a slew of fun to be had with a two track.

Essentially, **wave editors** are the same thing: multi-function editing tools used to perform precise, microscopic sound edits. And when I say *sound*, I mean audio files. You can literally see an audio file's wave form in front of your eyes.

❋ **Surf's Up**

A **wave form** is a visual representation of a sound. Essentially, you are seeing the compressions and rarefactions that make up a sound. When it gets lower, the wave form gets thinner. When it gets louder, the wave form gets thicker. If there is an abrupt loudness, you see a spike in the wave form, and so on.

You can cut and fade the wave form. You can even change its volume. The list of the other things that they do is quite extensive, but let me tell you a few common uses.

- ✳ **Trim the heads and tails off of the beginning and end of a sound.** That may sound like a small, irrelevant feature but it's not easy to do in multi-track programs.

- ✳ **Fade.** You can put small fades on the beginnings and endings of sounds. I can't tell you how handy this is when you run into a sound that fits what you are looking for but is abruptly cut off.

- ✳ **Quickly render effects.** A good wave editor offers a two-click render—much faster than with a multi-track program. **Real-time effects** run directly off your computer's processing power. Every time you play a real-time sound, you may notice subtle variations; you can modify it on the fly. When an effect is rendered onto an audio track, it means the effect is no longer in real time; it's now a part of the audio file. To **render** an audio file means to have your currently open program create another version of the audio file with the processing that you were adding in real time before as part of the audio file.

- ✳ **Undo multiple tweaks.** If you think several of the adjustments you just made aren't helpful, go to the Edit menu and select Undo until you are back where you want to be. Once you select File, Save, the adjustments you made are permanently part of the file.

- ✳ **Stack effects.** To **stack** means you are running several effect plug-ins at the same time on one sound. This is another example of running effects in real time. One effect may be a chorus, one may be a reverb, and one may be light distortion. When running simultaneously, you are hearing what all of them sound like stacked on top of your audio file.

- ✳ **Convert batches.** This is one thing that any sound designer in the video-game business will tell you is important. Batch converters are one of the best friends to the experienced sound designer and all of the major wave editors have them. **Batch converters** allow you to take a folder or a list of sounds and perform up to several small functions on them in one swift stroke. For example, after editing 100 44.1 kHz, 16-bit laser blast sounds, your sound programmer says they need to be 22 kHz and 8 bit. Pulling the files into the batch converter can convert them all at once.

I think you're starting to get an idea why these types of programs are so handy. Wave editors are like Swiss Army knives: They save time and they save headaches. And the more that you work with one, the more I think you'll agree.

❋ Other Wave Editors

While I'm discussing the most popular and useful wave-editing applications, let me mention these:

- ❋ DSP Quattro for Mac
- ❋ SaDiE for PC
- ❋ Wave Editor for PC
- ❋ Wave Creator for PC
- ❋ Wave Editor 1.2.3 for Mac

Sound Forge for PC

Sound Forge, shown in Figure 4.1, is one of the first and most widely used wave editors out there. When you ask most professionals why it's a favorite, stability is one of the first responses. I can remember many a day sitting in front of its light grey background with blue wave files floating listlessly across the screen. I know dedicated Mac users who still have a PC around so they can use Sound Forge.

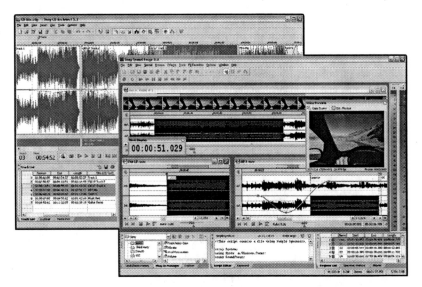

Figure 4.1

Sound Forge has been around for a while, and is still regarded as one of the most stable and versatile wave editors around.

Back in the day, it was pretty much the first wave editor that was recommended, but these days it's got some stiff competition. Some of the new version updates haven't necessarily helped it much. For example, changes have been made to its batch converter, which was one of its major features for video-game work. Sound Forge used to have a dedicated, separate batch converter fittingly titled Batch Converter. The cool thing about it being a separate program was that you could edit different files over in Sound Forge while you were running a batch. Now that it's included, you have to batch within Sound Forge. Sound Forge does not have a batch rename function, either. You'll have to rename files by hand, essentially, or enlist the aid of third-party software.

Some things that are really cool about the newer version of Sound Forge is its ability to use Virtual Studio Technology (VST) plug-ins. Previously you could use them through a third-party wrapper, but now there is no need. I should mention that I keep hearing that the new batch converter is having problems with VST plug-ins. It may be fixed by the time you read this. Another thing that I have to give Sound Forge is its speed. The program processes quickly. It may not be as slick or elegant looking as some of its competitors, but its efficiency is well worth it. Sound Forge's well thought-out interface is a real boon when quickly editing files. Once you have the key commands down, you can edit files in no time flat.

Wavelab for PC

Another old-timer is Wavelab, which has added several extremely cool features over the years, including batch renaming! This new feature makes this a very formidable package (and this is just one small new feature on top of many others). Wavelab, shown in Figure 4.2, is a two-track editor that goes beyond regular conventions and adds multi-track functionality via its Montage mode. Within **montages,** you are able to blend sounds, crossfade, and create ambiences, loops, and so on. Montages also allow you to bring 5.1 surround files into Wavelab. With 5.1 becoming more prominent in games, this is a huge feature indeed. The fact that you can have a video track within a montage running makes this package competition for some of the multi-track editors out there! But for propriety's sake, I'm keeping Wavelab under the two-track status that it's known for.

Figure 4.2

Wavelab is a choice PC editor with features that rival even some multi-track editors.

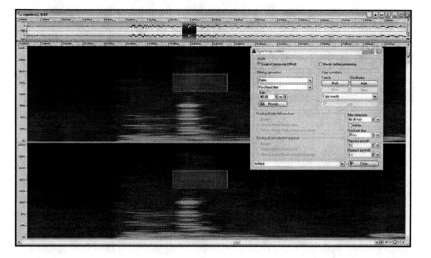

The Master section allows you to have several VST and DirectX plug-ins stacked on top of one another to create a bigger space and more dynamic sound. You can have one reverb going, one chorus going, a little EQ, and some light filtering. For example, you can use the low-end and high-end filters in the included multi-band compressor to shelve off the low and high ends; compress the midrange extremely tightly to get a good enclosed helmet sound, and then add just a touch of the included distortion plug-in on top of it. That's just one example of how you can create some cool effects.

If the amount of plug-ins that are available aren't enough, old-timers might be happy to know that Wavelab 6 allows external FX processors. Time to bust out the old Lexicon PCM-80! Also, spectrum editing is something altogether new. You can edit audio files in a sonogram view showing frequencies and allowing you to edit them as they occur. No other program, up until this point, has allowed you to isolate frequencies in one section and paste them into another section of the same sound.

Try using Wavelab to render complex effect environments on an individual sound or to perform some very creative editing. Beware its batch converter, though: It has been known to lock up with larger loads consisting of non-VST plug-ins.

Peak for Mac

Peak offers two-track editing features at a reasonable price. It's flexible, can batch rename, and has a batch converter with several nice features, including appending a clip to the beginning of each selected file. Peak is shown in Figure 4.3.

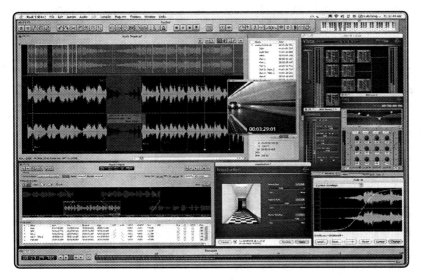

Figure 4.3
Peak offers two-track editing features.

Peak, which is not known for its stability, does offer the ability to use VST and Audio Units plug-ins. Audio Units plug-ins are developed by Apple, for Apple, and work with Pro Tools and other Mac editing programs. The people at Bias have definitely taken an interest in the sound designer community. Another wonderful feature is the Threshold function, which automatically divides files by amplitude. When you are just coming off of a field-recording gig, this is a really useful feature!

Multi-Track Editing Programs

The **multi-track editor** allows most of the artistry to occur. This is where you can blend sounds, create ambiences, and blend music. In days past, sound designers had to rely on reel-to-reel for this kind of complex operation. A multi-track reel-to-reel cost more than a car. These days, a laptop with a program that costs a few hundred dollars can do the exact same thing. Is the quality the same? Some might say no; some won't notice. What we know is that these programs have extensive creativity tools. Only our imaginations and computer are in question at this point.

So what is a multi-track editor? Imagine a program with several tracks of audio lined up sequentially. These tracks span across time horizontally. Within these tracks you can have several tracks of audio playing side by side. One track starts at the very beginning; one track starts three seconds later. Also, within these tracks are lanes for automation. **Automation** allows you to tell the computer to lower the volume at a certain part of an audio file or to change the panning at a certain part of a sequence. Additionally, automation can control more software-specific parameters like the mix of a reverb or the resonance of a synthesizer plug-in. The cool thing about most automation schemes is that you can physically draw where it begins and ends. This makes for precise edits. With these automation tracks, you can tell one track to slowly fade in, while another track slowly fades out.

So what are multi-track editing programs good for?

* **Blending.** One raw sound for a given part may be too thin. You may want to blend the sound to create a bigger and more dimensional sound. (There's more on blending sounds later in this book.)

* **Creating ambience.** There will be plenty of times when you need to make ambiences to suit each game level. For example, a two-track editor can't combine the horns, car movements, wind, and footsteps you need on the level where the main character walks around downtown.

* **Cutting scenes.** These theatrical events in movies are scripted, and usually require several sounds in orchestration. It's just like doing Foley for a movie! (See Chapters 6 and 9 for Foley and cut scene information.) It's the sound designer's job to mix in the music for the cut scenes. You need a comprehensive multi-track program that can sync to video.

* **Composing music and producing audio.** If you are planning on designing sound as well as music, pay attention to this section of the chapter.

Convinced yet? You're probably wondering which is the right multi-track editor for you. Can I name a couple? Of course I can! This whole chapter is here to help you in making decisions. Just like wave editors, there are tons of great multi-track editing packages out there. Some are highly expensive, some are more competitively priced. What do the pros use?

Pro Tools for PC and Mac

Pro Tools, seen in Figure 4.4, is by Digidesign and has been touted as the standard for several years. Most serious recording schools teach it, many big-name recording houses use it, and several big names still use the program. One of the main big reasons to use Pro Tools: If you have to send your session to someone else, if you are working with multiple sound designers, if you plan on collaborating in the future, odds are the other parties are using Pro Tools. It's just that prominent in the industry. It's also compatible with most industry-standard file formats. Even if someone you're working with isn't using Pro Tools, odds are any imported audio and video files will work.

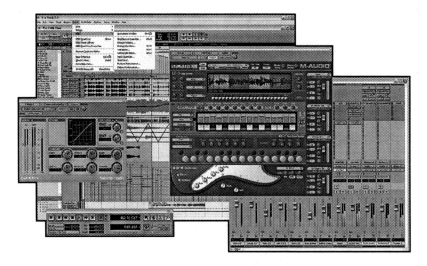

Figure 4.4
Pro Tools has been the longtime champion of the multi-track editors. If you are using a Mac, it's a wise choice.

Pro Tools on a Mac features a very short setup process. Because Pro Tools is geared to work with Digidesign devices, you don't necessarily have to worry about compatibility issues. You are pretty much good to go if you are on a Mac. PCs setup for Pro Tools, however, elicits users' horror stories. One sound designer spent a day and a night as a consultant trying to help a client set up Pro Tools on a PC laptop. He got on the phone with Digidesign, went through the long list of setup instructions, and worked patiently with their customer support. In the end, he turned around and told the guy to buy a Mac. I bet at this point you're starting to see a pattern. I bet you're reading between the lines. If you go with Pro Tools, it might be best to go with a Mac. If you decide to go with Pro Tools on a PC, get the fastest machine that you possibly can.

To run Pro Tools, you will have to invest some money in Digidesign hardware. The Digidesign hardware will perform a variety of services, depending on which piece you buy, but the hardware also acts as a security device that allows Pro Tools to run. The hardware is not cheap (though it's cheaper if you're on a Mac). You can go with one of the lower-end 002 systems. I'd suggest the 002 because you're getting a mixing console along with an audio interface. The 002 is a hardware control surface available from Digidesign. As I mentioned before, it has a built-in audio interface.

Keep in mind even this low-end system will cost a couple thousand dollars. But in the end you're buying some peace of mind.

One thing that I should mention: If you are planning on being a one-stop shop for music and sound design (and quite a few people are), Pro Tools is not known for its strength in MIDI sequencing. If you do go Pro Tools, invest in another program that does have a more elaborate MIDI palette (like some of the other programs listed in this chapter).

Nuendo for PC and Mac

With a very slick arsenal for sound editing, sound mixing, and musical composition, Nuendo is definitely a formidable force. Nuendo isn't reliant on a specific brand of hardware, but can work with essentially any sound device with an ASIO or Core Audio driver, and it can work with any control surface or keyboard.

Duking It Out

While Nuendo may not have the lion's share of business, there is fierce competition between it and Pro Tools. I've met more than a few professionals who switched over from Pro Tools to Nuendo, tired of paying to keep up with what Digidesign offered.

Nuendo, shown in Figure 4.5, supports all the major industry file formats for film and audio. Its PC version also supports VST and DirectX plug-ins. With the number of plug-ins out there—some for sale and some for free—it's difficult to see this feature without salivating.

Nuendo's file-management features are noteworthy. Anything that helps you keep track of your sounds and audio files is extremely useful indeed—especially when you need to quickly mix down a cut scene for a game and need to know exactly what files are what and where. Nuendo even has a batch processor and is very good for MIDI sequencing! Its audio editing prowess is extremely formidable. The interface is smooth and intuitive. Additionally, you can apply effects in real time or process by highlighting an area and indicating what you want rendered. Nuendo is also extremely good for mixing down in surround. It even outputs video to external monitors!

If you think you are going to work with more than one person, Nuendo offers network integration. You can allow other users editing rights or work at the same time. Also, other hard drives available on your network can be set up for use with Nuendo, which is handy if you are limited on space. There's even a chat feature for when you are working with other people on a project.

Figure 4.5
Nuendo has quickly become a preferred choice for sound design and music composition.

Nuendo is a little on the expensive side, but consider that you don't need any specific hardware to run it. Additionally, it doesn't include any kind of hardware, so you need to purchase an audio device. Also, as Nuendo is entirely processor dependant, you want the fastest machine possible when using this program.

❋ **Other multi-track editors**

While I'm discussing the most popular and useful multi-track editing applications, let me mention these PC options:

❋ SONAR 5: Features included reverb plug-ins from Lexicon, as well as the Vari-Phrase Technology created by Roland.

❋ Apple Logic Pro: The choice for many sound designers/composers. It has extensive editing capabilities and is noted as being all-around solid. Part II of this book details Logic.

❋ Digital Performer: A well-regarded choice from way back when for multi-tracking and sequencing. Like Logic, I discuss Digital Performer in Part II.

❋ Cubase: Runs off the same audio engine as Nuendo, so if you're strapped for cash, Cubase SX is a solid option.

Plug-Ins

After you see the hero pull out his main artillery, he tends to go for the smaller things. These tools may not win the battle, but they have their place in the overall scheme of things: You'll see a happy look on the hero's face when he realizes he brought his trusty knife and uses it to cut the ropes that bind him.

Plug-ins definitely fit in to this category. There's no way you could use a plug-in to design sound for an entire game, but you can't live without them in certain scenarios. What are **plug-ins**? Small programs that run in host applications, such as two-track and multi-track editors. Plug-ins, or **effects**, perform specific duties like generating reverbs or choruses. Some are for equalization, some are even used to correct problems in recordings.

In the classic audio studio, you had your two-track reel-to-reel, your multi-track recorder, and your mixing board. The external effects unit was a smaller box or boxes that, when you patched sounds from your track, would make them sound like they were echoing or being doubled. For example, the hero has just entered a large canyon and yells, "Hello!" It's supposed to echo. In the original recording, the hero is yelling through a regular microphone with no effects at all. You use different effects until you get a good echo and patch the voice through. Voila, instant canyon!

Not all plug-ins are compatible. Here are the major formats:

* **VST plug-ins** are probably the most popular. The format exists for both PCs and Macs. They are native to Nuendo and also work in Wavelab and Sound Forge. Pro Tools can use VST plug-ins, but it requires a third-party application to make it work. VST plug-ins rely on your host CPU processing power to run in most cases. Some VST plug-ins run off external processing units.

* **DirectX** is probably VST's biggest competitor. DirectX plug-ins are compatible with Nuendo and Wavelab and run native in Sound Forge. Like VST, DirectX plug-ins rely on your host CPU processing power.

* **Audio Units plug-ins** are strictly for Apple. They work with Pro Tools and several other Mac editing programs. Nuendo does not use Audio Units plug-ins.

* **Real Time Audio Suite (RTAS)** is by Digidesign for Pro Tools LE. This type of plug-in relies on your CPU to run.

By reading through the different types of plug-in formats, you can get an idea what you should be investigating for the multi-track and wave-editor programs. You may also want to investigate plug-ins online.

You'll want many types of effects. Here are some of the main ones:

* A good compressor for maximizing audio output
* A good reverb for emulating open areas like churches or sewers

* ❋ EQ to tweak frequency
* ❋ Boutique plug-ins like SFX machine that process and create sounds

A lot of small, independent programmers put a considerable amount of love and skill into some of these little gems and offer them free online. You never know when you'll find one that will create that certain sound. The other great thing is that you can run multiple plug-ins simultaneously on top of one another to create very rich, layered sounds. You'd really be surprised by what a couple of plug-ins can do to one piece of audio. It can be night and day. For example, I had one sound that was merely a hydraulic lift. Through the use of a plug-in titled simply Glitch, the sound was chopped up and randomized. Adding a slap back delay plug-in on top of it gave it a multi-stage feel. Then adding some EQ using another plug-in gave it a low thud. You couldn't tell the original sound from the beginning. It started off sounding like a lift. Now it sounds like some space-aged robot!

Basically, plug-ins are the spice to be added in to the soup. The paint for the canvas drawing. There's no end of fun to be had with them. Here are a few plug-in packages seeing wide use in the sound-design field.

Waves Platinum Native Bundle for PC and Mac

Waves is one set of plug-ins that you will hear mentioned quite a bit. You might even say that the Waves plug-ins have infiltrated some of the industry language. You'll often hear people mentioning that they "L1ed" a sound to beef it up. They are referring to the L1 Ultra-maximizer, a mastering plug-in.

But the L1 is just one of the plug-ins that come in this sonic arsenal. Plug-ins like the Renaissance Compressor, Renaissance Reverberator, MaxxBass, and Q10 Paragraphic EQ make this a formidable bundle. There's even the Ultra-Pitch plug-in for pitch shifting. This can be handy for creating all manner of effects, from drastic to minute. The price isn't cheap, but you'll be set for a while and you can be confident these plug-ins will be used. The Waves Platinum Native bundle can run as DirectX and VST on PCs. On Macs, it works as AU, RTAS, and VST.

Reaktor for PC and Mac

Reaktor from Native Instruments is a multi-purpose program that can run as a plug-in or as a standalone audio suite. Reaktor has a little bit of everything, from effects plug-ins to software synthesizers (covered later in this chapter). Some of the effects and sound devices found within Reaktor do some things to audio that you just won't find anywhere else (see Figure 4.6).

One thing that is completely cool about this program are the endless plug-ins available online for registered users. You can literally create your own plug-ins for Reaktor and put them online for other people to use. If you have an idea for a certain type of delay, or chorus, or synth, you can create one in Reaktor with all the complexity that you can imagine. Reaktor 5, the latest incarnation of the program, works as a plug-in for Audio Units, VST, RTAS, and DirectX formats.

Figure 4.6

Reaktor offers effects plug-ins, as well as several other handy features like soft synths and sound generators.

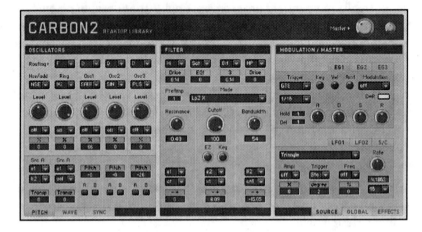

TC Electronics Power Core for PC and Mac

TC Electronics offers a very nice package of plug-ins that perform an admirable job for almost any application. For starters, they include reverbs built off TC's award-winning reverbs. In the past, reverbs such as MegaReverb could really choke your CPU. Not to fear, though: The Power Core is a digital signal processing (DSP) system for either platform.

> ❋ **DSP**
>
> A DSP system is a separate device that contains multiple processors on its own and is connected via FireWire. Your computer uses FireWire's external DSP chips to run. The great things about running a DSP system is that your CPU isn't bogged down with plug-ins and you can run plug-ins that your machine, on its own, might not be able to handle.

The TC Voicestrip plug-in features a really nice panel of EQs, gates, and limiters, as well as a compressor and de-esser. If you're going to engineer recording sessions that include voice actors, this plug-in is highly recommended. It also sports a great distortion plug-in called Tubifex that emulates old guitar amps. But wait, there's more! The TC Power Core plug-in pack can be expanded upon. You can buy additional plug-ins like the DVR2 reverb plug-in. This plug-in is a more elaborate reverb that comes directly from the legendary hardware reverb: the System 6000. In terms of price, Power Core compact is about the same as the Waves bundle. You can also get Power Core as a PCI card intended for inside your computer. Additionally, there's the Power Core FireWire that is a separate rack unit, which has four DSP chips, whereas the other versions of the Power Core only have two. This means you have twice the processing power. That's great if you're really into stacking effects.

❄ **Other Plug-In Bundles**
While I'm detailing the most popular and useful plug-in bundles, let me mention some others:

- ❄ WaveArts PowerSuite
- ❄ PSP Audioware Everything
- ❄ Nomad Factory Blue Tubes
- ❄ Arboretum Hyperprism
- ❄ UAD1

Synthesizers

A **software synthesizer** is a computer program that can reproduce and create sounds. Synthesizers come in many different forms. There are standalone programs, like Reason or Reaktor that act as a suite of synthesizers and audio devices, and they can also be used with other programs, like Pro Tools or Nuendo. They can be controlled by external hardware keyboard controllers and played musically. Additionally, there are plug-in instruments that must exist within a host program like Nuendo or Pro Tools. Once you activate them and select your controller (if you have one), you can play them like a regular synthesizer; they don't require special hardware in most circumstances.

Synthesizers have been finding good use in the sound-design field for some time now. They are responsible for every bleep, whistle, and whir that you hear in a video game title. At times, you might be surprised what was originally a synthesizer and what wasn't. Synthesizers have become capable of reproducing many different real-life sounds. Many carry pre-recorded sounds that can be manipulated and combined with several other sounds. The Hartmann Neuron, for example is a DSP synthesizer capable of modeling sounds with its own oscillators and filters based off a recording.

However, a vast number of these DSP synthesizers ironically choose to emulate the old analog synthesizers. Funny, huh? Synthesizers like the Access Virus are capable of sounding like the famous synthesizers of old, like the Minimoog. They even have filter settings modeled off the Minimoog. Additionally, the Virus is capable of sounding like a very new synthesizer, with far more possibilities than the synthesizers of old. With its built-in, lush effects processors and ex-panded polyphony, the Virus is a beast. There's also the Nord Lead by Clavia. This synthesizer has the vibrant sounds similar to the old Roland. It even resembles the old classic synthesizers with its many control knobs. Don't be fooled by its red shell. You can get some very lush, classic sounds out of this synth—everything from old style bleeps and whistles to gritty basses. That's not to say there aren't several synthesizers out there that attempt to do their own thing. Most tend to be software based, and that's okay; software synthesizers save vast amounts of money. If you look around, you'll find a software synthesizer to fill just about any niche that you can imagine.

One particular form of synthesis that I've found to be seriously useful is granular. **Granular synthesizers** can break a piece of audio down and manipulate it in ways not possible with any other synths or samplers. I used the Malström synthesizer in Reason to take a didgeridoo sample and turn it into a very noisy car engine without expending much effort at all.

But I would be shielding you if I didn't say there is a battle being waged. Yes, just like the old Mac versus PC argument, people disagree regarding hardware versus software synthesizers. I encourage you to turn a blind eye to this particular argument. Sound design is a subjective field and any raw audio in the hands of a creative mind, regardless of the source, can be transformed into something pleasing or cool. Why do puritans believe in using hardware synthesizers? They believe the raw sound is thick and more robust. The old analog monsters have extremely broad frequency ranges. You can filter frequencies as you need to. Soft synths are known for being a little thin. This is changing, however. Software (or soft) synths are getting more robust every day. Several emulate the old synthesizers well.

Then there's ease of use. A software synthesizer only takes a couple of mouse clicks to bring up. A hardware synthesizer takes a little more setup time, unless you've already got it wired in. Ultimately, it's your preference and money. I just want to tell you that either (or both) are okay.

Finally, consider when to use a synthesizer. A few years ago, I would have told you only when you need something sci-fi or electronic. These days, you can get some surprising results from some of the newer synthesizers. Would I use that car engine sound from a synthesizer over the real thing? Not on your life. But if I needed to create a spaceship that was supposed to sound a little like a car, you bet I'd use a synth. In this particular instance, I'm creating something otherworldly that hints at this world.

Here are a couple synthesizer suites that are in wide use.

Reason for PC and Mac

If you want to imagine an entire rack of old audio gear, synthesizers, and samplers, look no further. Reason is probably one of the most versatile audio environments around. Using a virtual-rack styled interface, you can create any number of synthesizers, samplers, effects boxes, or mixers. Not only can you create several instances, you can also turn the rack around to do very elaborate wiring configurations.

Reason sports a granular synthesizer, which I mentioned earlier in this chapter. The Malström (one of the synthesizers in Reason) allows everything from the creation of swelling pads to very noisy, distorted sounds. I have used the AM filter on the Malström to emulate old Army radios and sub-space transmissions.

The NN-XT sampler is one of the easiest samplers I know to configure. It has a really down-to-earth approach to setting up patches. This is great if you need to mix several sounds at once or layer sounds in a complex fashion. It also sports multiple outputs, which is handy if you want several sounds going through several effects units. The Subtractor synthesizer is perfect for little bleep and whistle sounds. It's also good for noisy FM-style sounds, especially when you run it through a Scream distortion unit.

Reaktor for PC and Mac

I am talking about Reaktor again! As mentioned previously, Reaktor comes with a slew of synthesizers that are quite formidable. Carbon has been a staple for several versions and has a robust sound with a very user-friendly interface. Oki Computer is a compact wavetable synthesizer intended for more lo-fi, digital sounds. This is a great choice for creating interface, computer, and robot sounds. Steampipe 2 is an acoustic modeling synthesizer that models air being blown through a tunable pipe. This is awesome for creating steam-built engines, wind, and various hybrid sounds. Spending a little time with a wave editor and some samples from this synth could lead to some very interesting results.

Reaktor also houses basic sound generators as well. These are invaluable for creating soundscapes and atmospheres. Two of the sound generators that are included are Skrewell and Spacedrone. And don't forget, you can create your own synths, samplers, and effects in Reaktor. Additionally, tons of these modules are available on the Native Instruments Web site for registered users.

❈ **Other Synthesizers**

While I'm mentioning the most popular and useful hardware and software synthesizers, here are some others:

- ❈ Native Instruments Absynth offers a highly elaborate sound editing environment with the ability to exist in a 5.1 surround environment. It has synchronizable envelopes that allow you to make very rhythmic or organic sounds at a whim. One great feature is that it can work as a standalone program, as well as a plug-in for programs like Nuendo, Logic, or Pro Tools.
- ❈ GForce Minimonsta
- ❈ If you enjoy synthesizers that are more akin to the classics, Arturia creates several software synthesizers that come remarkably close. One of these synths being the Minimoog V. This synthesizer can work as a standalone or a plug-in. You can increase its polyphony way past what the original synthesizer was capable of; it also has built-in effects, and it has a patch memory!

Samplers

A **sampler** is essentially a musical device that uses raw audio as its source, rather than pure tones (like a synthesizer). For example, once you bring a dog bark into a sampler, you can play dog barks all the way across a musical keyboard. You can even have a different recording assigned to each key!

There's nothing like having several of your own sounds spread across the keyboard when creating sounds or an environment. Samplers accommodate just such a task. Several years ago, samplers were extremely expensive and difficult to program. These days, all you need is a decent computer, a hard drive with an adequate amount of space, a good amount of system memory, and a good soft sampler.

One classic use of samplers is sound manipulation. You have the envelopes and the controls of a synthesizer, but the raw sound of your well-recorded audio right there at your fingertips. You can run the sound through effects, play the sound at a lower speed (or note). It's a very tactile way of working, rather than just playing around with a computer screen.

You can use a sampler for its original use, which is music. Several companies have very large sample libraries of all kinds of sounds. But, they also have recorded material from symphonies, choirs, and other amazing sources that most of us wouldn't have access to from home. Reason and Reaktor have very powerful samplers built in, but there are other extremely powerful software samplers out there, for a decent price, that are a little more dedicated.

Kontakt

Kontakt, in Figure 4.7, has quickly become the sampler of choice for many people. The fact that it accommodates 5.1 surround, as well as multiple sample formats, has made it a must. Kontakt has the ability to do real-time pitch shifting and time compression. This is great when you want to try different speeds on the fly rather than by rendering in a wave editor. Additionally, it sports a very easy-to-use key-mapping system for laying out sounds across your keyboard, a feature I mentioned earlier with samplers. For effects, Kontakt has impulse-response effects that are awesome for creating life-like reverbs or special effects. I can't even tell you how handy this is when you're trying to simulate an environment.

Every sound designer and composer I've spoken with has this program. The number of libraries available to Kontakt are staggering, and this program's abilities make it a must for any studio.

GigaStudio

Hailed as the most successful sampler on the market, GigaStudio (formerly known as GigaSampler) has a huge following and a large library to support it. The library is made up of highly produced sample libraries that can emulate most any instrument. As a rule, GigaSampler is more commonly used by composers to trigger lavish orchestra banks and realistic instruments.

Figure 4.7
Kontakt has quickly become a staple soft sampler for pretty much every sound designer and music composer I know.

But don't let me tell you it can't be used for sound design. In Part II of this book I step into how GigaStudio can assist you in creating lush scores and musical atmospheres.

❄ **Other Software Samplers**

While I'm mentioning the most popular and useful software samplers, let me mention these also:

❄ EXS24 in Apple Logic Pro is a built-in sampler.

❄ MOTU MachFive is a standalone sampler.

❄ HALion by Steinberg runs as a VST plug-in in any VST-compatible host.

If the sampler of your choice is not included in this chapter, it's most likely included in Chapter 12.

5 Sound Design: Basic Tools and Techniques

The sound designer's weapons have been chosen, and the production of the new title is in full swing. There's a fresh database hungry for new sounds, and it's time to start putting some sounds together. In earlier chapters, we've covered database management, project management, and meetings. In this chapter, we're going to focus on the sound itself. This means taking one sound at a time and getting the best results that we possibly can.

When I need to create a sound, I tend to imagine what it would sound like in my head. For example, a sound I just started working on is that of a door opening. The description in the database tells me that it's a plain wooden door in a house. In my mind, I start imagining what it would sound like. I imagine the door knob turning at a regular rate, then the slight click and turning sound of a metallic knob. Then I imagine a slight creak. Granted, not all of the wooden doors out there have a creaking sound. But we're making a game! The sounds need to be slightly exaggerated in order for them to immerse the player in the game environment.

I go back through my field-recorded material and look for the wooden door opening that I recorded. There it is! You can hear the knob mechanism and a slight creak, but the creak is not very apparent. But, this is an easy fix—I bring my door-opening sound into my wave editor and call up a compressor plug-in. I lower the threshold and experiment with my compression ratios until the creak is louder, more up front. Once I apply the compression and play it back, I find that I have the sound I'm looking for.

That's pretty easy, huh? That's the perfect scenario right there, where everything goes perfectly and there are no problems, whatsoever. But is it always that easy? Not on your life!

Go on to the next sound, which is a little more complex than the first. I'm supposed to make another door sound, but the door is not of this world. The description makes this door out to be a mechanical steel airlock that would be found in a space ship. For this kind of sound we have to do some heavy thinking. What does an airlock sound like? I would imagine a sliding mechanical door that works in small stages as it opens. When the seal of the door is initially broken, a huge amount of air is released.

Obviously, this is not going to be as simple as the first door, right? This sound will require several layers of different sounds, as well as some effects, to complete with any form of realism. Hopefully, when we were field recording, we got plenty of different mechanical and hydraulic sounds. It will make putting this together a lot easier. Mechanical sounds add that intricate, metallic, precision audio that we need to make the airlock sound elaborate and well thought out. The hydraulic sounds tend to have a good "hiss" that you want to complete the airlock. But we still have to put them together and make them gel.

So how do we go about it? That's what this chapter is designed to show you: several different techniques for layering different sound, effecting different sounds, and creating different sounds. We'll finally get to see how we can use all of the different software packages we've been talking about. In fact, we'll also get to see what all of those little plug-ins are for as well!

Mind you, there is no earthly way that I can show you every little trick that's used to manipulate sound into award-winning game audio. This chapter will show you the basic methods the pros use to manipulate audio into complex, in-depth sounds.

Basic Tools for Sound Design

In every wave editor and every DAW, you'll find some simple features that make manipulating audio that much easier. We've touched on some of these tools in earlier chapters, and in this chapter we're going to exploit them! At a glance, some of these tools may seem simple and slightly boring. Believe me, they are necessary! Through simple tweaks here and there, you can get some surprisingly cool stuff. . .sometimes even without effects.

The wave editor that I'll be using in this section is Wavelab. Don't worry if you don't have it; these are standard tools that can be found in most wave editors.

Time-Stretching/Time-Compression

If you think about the principles behind **time-stretching**, it's almost awe-inspiring. It's the ability to take a sound that plays at a certain length and sonically stretch the audio within set parameters without changing the pitch. There are several fun things that you can get out of time-stretching.

For example, remember that door-opening sound that I made earlier in this chapter? What if I stretched that sound out to be twice as long? Imagine it: It's got the same pitch as it used to, but now it's a very slow opening door. Heck, it might even sound more mechanical now. Maybe I could use it for a space door if I played with it some more!

Or here's another example: Say I decided to record my printer when it's printing a piece of paper. For one thing, printers, bread makers, blenders, and the like are all electrical devices with small engines that work very rapidly. When you slow down these small engine sounds with time-stretching, you can keep that high-pitched whine but hear more of what's going on in the little engine. From there you can cut certain parts from the initial recording, and then make additional sounds that you hadn't thought of before. Small appliances around your kitchen are great for creating gear sounds for robots, machine sounds for vehicles, and mechanisms for airlocks, like we talked about previously. There's a lot you can have fun with.

So what are some other things that can be done with the concept of time-stretching? What about doing the opposite with **time-compression**? This is where you speed up how quickly a sound plays without changing the pitch. What if you took that printer sound and sped it up to where it's playing 50 percent faster than before? Try to imagine what that would sound like: You hear all of the little hums and clicks, but they are moving more rapidly now. It almost sounds like a magnetic lock that a secret agent triggers when he uses a certain key.

But what about sounds that are a little more intense found outside of this mundane environment? Say you have some recordings of jet airplane flybys. What if you wanted to make the jet flyby sound more like a swoop? You could use time-compression to make it fly faster, right? It might even begin the makings of a good spaceship, once you've done the time-compression.

By now you should see some of the cool things you can do with time-compression and time-stretching—tools that were almost unimaginable 20 years ago. It really gives you a kind of all-powerful feeling when it comes to working with audio. Even outside of actual sound design, time-stretching and time-compression can come in very handy for music. Figure 5.1 is an image out of Wavelab where I'm stretching a song from 120 BPM to 130 without changing the actual pitch of the song.

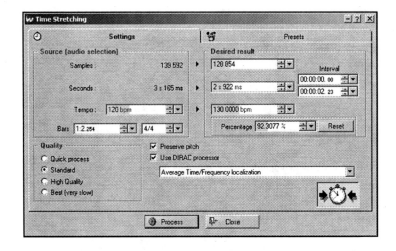

Figure 5.1

Time-stretching in Wavelab.

Realistically, you could spend days time-stretching or -compressing different sounds to achieve unheard of and sometimes impossible audio files. I bet you're probably thinking what you could do with this feature if you combined it with some other features, like. . .pitch-shifting. In the next section, we'll find out!

Pitch-Shifting

Now that we understand what time-compression and time-stretching are, I'm going to throw your brain for another loop. **Pitch-shifting** is the ability to change the pitch of a sound without changing its actual length.

Remember how it would sound when you turned up an old tape deck to a faster pitch? It always changed how fast the song played. With pitch-shifting, that doesn't happen. If you pitch the timbre of a recording up 20 percent, a sound will play back higher, but the speed of the sound will stay the same. How is this useful? Let me recount the ways.

First, say you record yourself growling. You like how you annunciated the growl, but it would be a lot more evil if it were deeper. Additionally, you like the length of the growl, and you need to keep it within a certain time frame. Just pitch-shift it down while preserving the time of the recording! All of a sudden, that growl has the same gravel that you liked before, but it now sounds deeper and a little more evil. It's lower now, and also it's a got a little more bass to it.

Go back to our printer sound. With the time-stretching, we made it longer, more drawn out. Now when we pitch-shift it down (see Figure 5.2), we've got some industrial terror before us! Are you starting to see how these tools can unleash some holy havoc? There's really no end to how much audio manipulation you can do with pitch-shifting and time-compression and -stretching. And do not forget that you can pitch-shift up. Think about recording some car drive-bys. Then take them into your favorite wave editor program and pitch-shift them up. What sounded like a car now sounds more like a motorcycle or some kind of sci-fi vehicle.

Figure 5.2

The pitch-shifting console in Wavelab may look slightly complicated, but it's really easy once you've figured it out.

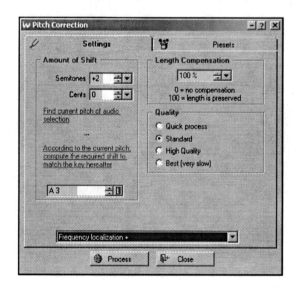

This is definitely another one of those tools that you'll want to experiment with. With pitch-shifting, many things that wouldn't be possible with a regular sound recording are now suddenly possible. You can even use it to fix a singer who is singing slightly off key!

Pitch-Bending

Pitch-bending is what most DJs do with turntables on a regular basis. Pitch-bending allows you to pitch up a sound and have either a gradual or serious upward and downward swing in the pitch before and the pitch after the bend. Say that I've recorded the hum of a car and that's it. The sound that I'm to design is supposed to be a car idling with one engine rev. Granted, there's nothing like the real thing for this. But for a moment, pretend that I forgot to record an engine rev when I was recording the car.

I open up the pitch-bend function in Wavelab (or whatever wave editor you are using). Now, I highlight the area of the audio file that I want to pitch-bend. From here I use the graphical editor in the Pitch Bend window (pictured in Figure 5.3) to draw in my pitch-bend. Notice how I have a rapid pitch up and down?

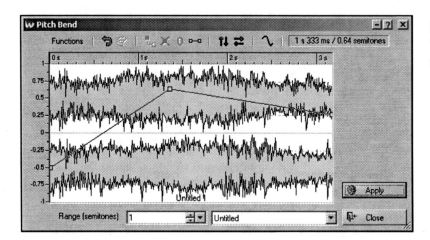

Figure 5.3
You can use the Pitch Bend window to "bend" a sound.

Now, when you apply the pitch-bend and play it back, you hear the engine rev up and down quickly, similar to how a car would. As I said before, it's not the same as a real engine rev, but sometimes you can fake it if you are crafty and know your tools. In all cases, it would be better to run outside and record another car; this is just for the sake of demonstration.

Pitch-bending is also good for using one sound to create totally different sounds. Keep in mind, you can draw all sorts of patterns, or **envelopes**, in the Pitch Bend window. After you've done so, you can always combine this with the pitch-shift, and time-compression/-stretching feature we talked about earlier!

Here's another example: You have a steady stream of white noise. You know that white noise sounds basically like static, right? In the Pitch Bend window, I draw some gradual curves going up and down, pictured in Figure 5.4. After I apply the pitch-bend function, the white noise now sounds like wind blowing!

Figure 5.4

You can draw curves over white noise to simulate wind blowing.

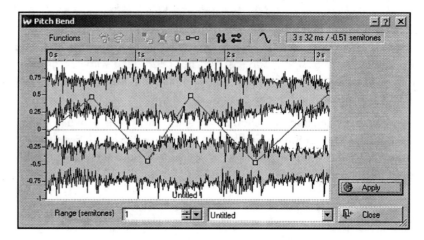

If you have a wave editor in front of you that has the pitch-bend function (be thorough in your search, it may not have the same name as it does in Wavelab), try playing around with it for a while.

Bring in sounds of all sorts and try mangling them in many different ways. Keep in mind that after the file has been mangled with the pitch-bend, the whole file may not be useable, but one section of it might be. The next section discusses what to do if you have a section of audio that is cool, but maybe not the rest....

Fade-In/Fade-Out

I think you probably already know what a **fade-in** or a **fade-out** is. Just in case, I'm going to tell you anyway: It's a gradual volume reduction (or increase) of audio, rather than an abrupt cut in volume. Doing a gradual fade makes a sound ease in rather than abruptly blare out. So why am I wasting a valuable book page with this almost redundant information? Because fading comes in handy in many situations other than the gradual fade out of some of the longest love songs ever.

Often when you edit audio, you are pulling a snippet out of a much bigger file. Much of the time when you record something, you get a long series of various noises, but some of these noises you will not need. And in some recordings, there will be **clean exits** of sound. By that I mean the sound plays and ends without any other outside interference. There will be times, though, when you may not get so lucky. For example, I'm at a race track recording race cars driving by. Tracks are not exactly contained environments; there are a lot of different outside noises going on. When I get back from the race track and listen to my recording, I hear one drive-by that is perfect! The problem is that a guy yells something at the very end.

One way that I can mend this is to try to fade off the tail of the drive-by before the voice comes in. This way it still sounds like the car is whooshing, or fading out, but it does so before you hear the voice. Keep in mind, fades don't have to be gradual. You can zoom in very close with wave editors and make very quick fades. A **quick fade** still sounds much better than a direct cut. A direct cut is highly noticeable, sometimes with a pop or click, and it sounds very abrupt. With a quick fade, there's still some smoothness in the exit of the audio file. Have a look at what I'm talking about. Figure 5.5 depicts a sound with an abrupt cut, both at the end and at the beginning. I know you can't hear, it but it sounds terrible!

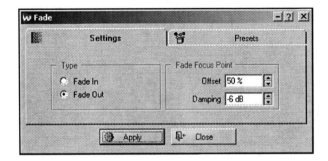

Figure 5.5

You can use the Fade feature to fade out the abrupt cut.

I zoom in at the very beginning of the audio file and do a quick fade in. Now when I play the file back, it's not so jarring when the audio file first starts. Once I do the same for the end of the file, I still have an abrupt sound, but it doesn't sound like it's a mistake or a glitch anymore. It sounds more polished.

Quick fades are also really good for editing voice files that have strange mistakes at the beginning of them. For example, say that we have a vocalist who was supposed to be singing "Ahhh," but at the beginning of the recording there is a slight waver. All we have to do is cut the beginning off where it warbles, and then do a quick fade at the beginning to keep it natural. Now no one will ever know the difference. Or here's another example: What if an actor coughs at the beginning of a voice file, but the rest of what he says is okay? Just cut off the cough and do a quick fade, as long as the words are still intact.

Fading in and out may not seem like the most exciting thing to do in a wave editor, but it actually helps you do some very subtle edits that sometimes save hard-earned recordings. Don't forget how easy they are to accomplish, too!

Silence

Most audio files that cross your chopping block will not be in perfect shape when you first get them. In fact, most audio files will require a certain amount of editing.

Say you are editing a wave file that has a lot of noise between two impacts. This noise is something that you don't want. What do you do? Use the Silence command shown in Figure 5.6. Select the area of the wave file that you want to silence, and then choose Edit, Silence. From here you can select how you want Wavelab to handle the silence. Do you want true silence or do you want to use another wave file's background noise? You decide!

Figure 5.6

Use Silence to get rid of un-wanted noise or to intro-duce some of your own.

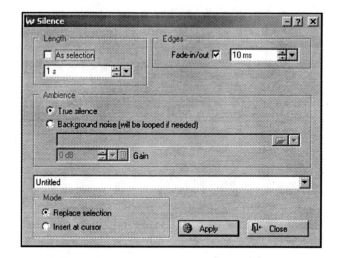

Change Gain

Changing the gain is simply raising or lowering the level of an audio file. This is usually done in decibels, or dB. If you want something to be louder, you will raise it +1 dB or more. If you want the sound to be softer, you'll lower it −1 dB or more.

Many times you'll have a raw recording that is too low in volume or possibly too high. The Gain function will help you get the volume to the level that you want it to be. One important thing to note is, when you're raising the gain, you do not want the total volume to exceed 0 dB. If this happens, you will most assuredly introduce some severe clipping into your recording.

Programs like Wavelab have a function called Get Peak Level. This has the audio program ex-amine the highest peak in the audio file and adjust your settings accordingly. This way you don't have to play a guessing game as to how many decibels you should raise the audio file before it surpasses 0 dB.

Sometimes you may have a recording where the sound you want to raise is mired in a noisy background. As soon as you raise the gain, you also raise the background noise. That's when the next tool comes in very handy.

Reverse

We've covered a lot of the more necessary tools for designing sounds, the kind that clean and spruce and set things right.

Reverse, as it's called in Wavelab and pretty much every other wave editor, causes the selected portion of an audio file to play backward. This sounds pretty simple, but it allows no end of fun. You can come up with some pretty cool sounds this way. For example, take a simple sound like an iron clank in a reverberating room. It's pretty cut and dry—you know what it is from a mile away. Try selecting the sound within the audio file, including the long tail (as seen in the upper part of Figure 5.7), and then selecting Reverse in the Process menu. In the lower part of Figure 5.7 you can see that the long tail is now introduced first in the audio file.

It now sounds like the iron clank has a flying-towards-your-head effect because that tail sounds like it's moving forward instead of decaying, as it once was. You can use this kind of effect for creating all sorts of urgent moments or "in-flight" sounds within a game.

Think about combining this with some of the other tools we talked about earlier in this chapter, like time-compression! You could slow down a car engine, and then reverse it! That would create a totally otherworldly sounding vehicle that you could manipulate in all sorts of ways. You could even slow down the engine enough to where you could hear the individual cycles, and then reverse them. From there you could mute around them, and you'd have an all-new electro-mechanical sound that you didn't have before! What about using creature noises, like dog barks? You could reverse them, and then pitch-shift them. All of a sudden you've got some sort of dark evil creature!

Reverse is literally one of those tools that can have you up all night thinking of all the possibilities. It's one of those tools that make sound design the fun job that it is. You get to experiment like a mad scientist in a lab until you get that perfect sound. If you consider ways that you can combine the Reverse option with some of the other tools that I've mentioned, you can get some stellar results that maybe no one has ever thought of before.

Crossfade

Assume you have two audio files that you want to combine into one file. That's easy to do. Just highlight the piece of the audio file that you want merged with the other file, and then drag the highlighted piece over. Boom, you're done!

Now say that not only do you want these two files combined, you also want them segueing into one another; you want some bleed between the two of them. In this case, you'll do a **crossfade**. Just highlight the area of the audio file that you want to fade into. Next, while holding the mouse

Figure 5.7

You can see what a sound looks like before and after it's been reversed.

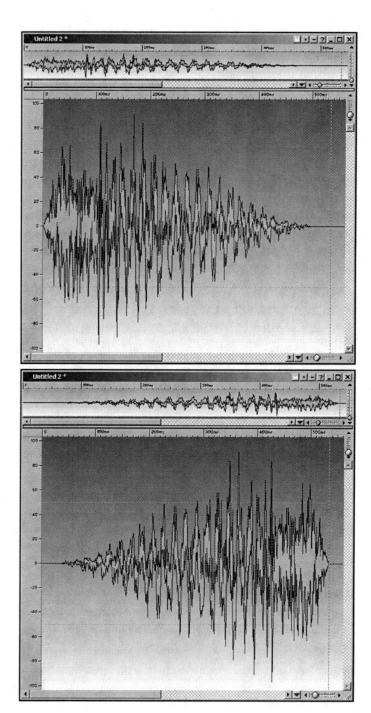

button down, drag the segment of the audio file that you want to blend into the other file over into the highlighted area. You'll notice that, when you're holding the other file over the highlighted area, the mouse cursor changes to a strange waveform-looking icon. Once you drop the file in, the audio file looks dramatically different, as seen in Figure 5.8.

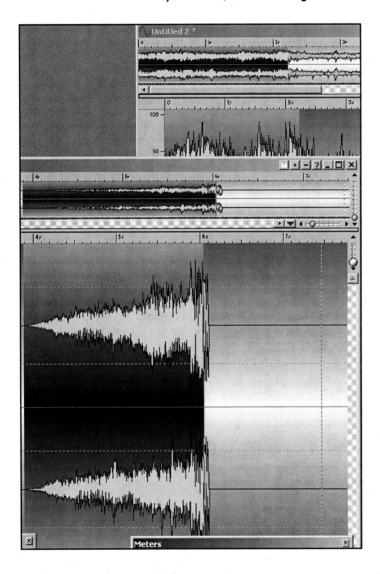

Figure 5.8
A crossfade in Wavelab can be accomplished without the Crossfade menu.

What's happened is this: A crossfade has occurred! The starting audio file will slowly fade out, while the other file is slowly fading in. This can be a nice effect if you're trying to make two completely different sounds seem as if they exist within the same environment.

What if you need more control over your crossfade? You can simply copy a portion of one audio file and then highlight the area of another file that you want to crossfade into. Once you've highlighted the destination audio file, find the Crossfade function within your wave editor. In Wavelab, it's under the Process menu, or press X on your keyboard. A window appears, similar to the one shown in Figure 5.9.

Figure 5.9

You can see crossfading as it happens when you use the Process menu in Wavelab.

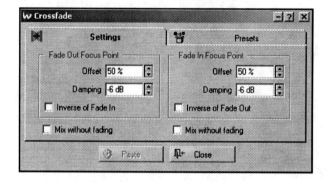

The Crossfade window will let you adjust how the crossfade will occur. These are basically more minute adjustments that will get the crossfade more to your liking.

Effects

Hopefully you've had some fun with the basic tools that I've described. All of these features can be found in any wave editor, and they make up the fundamentals for manipulating audio. In this next section, we'll discuss applying effects that make your audio bigger, bolder, and sometimes more mysterious.

In your wave editor, you may have stumbled upon the plug-in section. This section houses all of these neat little processors, such as Reverbs, Delays, Choruses, and Compressors. You'll even see plug-ins for equalization, or EQ. All of these are basic effects that can do wonderful things to make your audio sound more alive.

When we record audio in the field, some of the environments can be a little mundane. Additionally, some of the sounds can be a little small, to boot. Applying effects in creative ways can help make the more mundane audio larger than life.

For example, what if you are asked to create a sound for a crumbling castle wall? This sound can be accomplished quite simply by recording some tumbling bricks. Okay, that was easy. I have some brick recordings that sound like a house from down the street fell apart! From here you can get creative and use pitch-shifting to lower the sound. Then you can apply a reverb effect to make the bricks sound like they are in a large cavernous area, like castles usually are!

Using effects like this can make your work sound more real and dimensional. It may even save you a little money, too. I mean, it's not like we can all afford to fly out to Europe to record crumbling castles, right?

Here are some effects and how they can be useful in sound design.

Reverb

One of the most widely used effects in the FX lineup is reverb. **Reverbs** are basically echoes that are echoing so fast it sounds like one extended tail on the end of a sound.

A great example of a reverb is when you walk into the lobby of a post office with tiled floors. Whistle inside of one of these places, and you'll hear a tail on the end of your whistle. It almost sounds like an echo, but it's highly diffused.

There are many different reverb plug-ins out there that simulate everything from actual places to older electronic reverb effect units. All of these plug-ins are highly editable and bring a lot to the table. It is true that reverbs are more or less known for giving that big "hallway" sound to effects, voices, drums, or whatever. You can also use them to make sounds more hollow or a little bigger.

There are **gated** reverb settings that can apply a big reverb but have an abrupt ending. Essentially, there's no tail on the end of the reverb, no decay. This gives an effect like a push behind a recorded sound, as if there's a lot of air behind it. Figure 5.10 is an example of a reverb on a Gate setting.

Figure 5.10
This is a reverb in a Gate setting. Gated reverbs are great for adding a little punch and dimension to a sound.

An effect like this can be good for punches in small increments. It also can be good for robotic mechanisms as well as for heavy impacts that occur in more open areas. It's a nice spice that makes sounds a little bigger.

There are also reverse reverb settings. This kind of setting puts a slight delay on the audio at the beginning, causing the release or decay of the reverb to happen at the beginning instead of the end. This effect does not play the sound backward though. It's a neat effect for simulating objects flying through the air or objects moving in close proximity to the player in a game.

One thing to keep in mind before applying reverb is that the game you are working on may be utilizing real-time effects. To give a little more definition to this, the game may apply its own reverbs in real time! It's best to confirm this with the team at the beginning of a project, as I described in Chapter 1, "Meetings."

Real-time reverbs are becoming more and more common as game technology moves forward. But effects like gated and reverse reverbs can still effectively be used because they aren't really adding any kind of decay.

Don't forget the convolution reverbs that are out there! These reverbs are actually sampled "impulses" of actual buildings, places, and equipment. They allow you to apply their legendary characteristics to your dry sounds. Granted, if you are working on a game that has a real-time reverb, you don't want to apply some famous cathedral to your sound. But maybe you could edit the convolution reverb to play without the decay on the end? These are just some of the ways that you could experiment.

You should also be careful using reverb in too many of your sounds. If used too much, your game could wind up sounding like it's being played out in a garbage can. Look at the levels you are designing sounds for and determine whether they would really need reverb in the kind of environment that's being designed. For example, would you really need reverb in the middle of a desert? Deserts are known for being wide open spaces, so reverb probably wouldn't work there.

However, reverb would definitely work in a cave or a long hallway. Taking note of such things can definitely help you in making your game sound the best that it possibly can be.

> ### Favorite Reverb Effects
> In many of the individual sounds that I've designed, I've employed the TrueVerb found in the Waves Platinum bundle. With TrueVerb, you are able to really define the room that you are trying to emulate using its advanced editing features. With very little effort, you can get what you are looking for.
>
> I've also really enjoyed the VSS3 that is an optional plug-in for the Power Core. This reverb uses a stereo source reverb algorithm that was taken directly from the classic System 6000. Despite the fact the VSS3 has an amazing editor that seamlessly controls hundreds of parameters, the shipped presets cover every possible need.

Chorus

Chorus is sort of a strange seasoning that gives audio fullness when used appropriately. It's basically a slightly detuned version of the sound played back a few milliseconds off. This makes it sound like there are two versions of the sound playing back almost in unison. While this is happening, it's also moving in and out of tune in a sine wave pattern. You can adjust how quickly the sound moves in and out of tune and how audible it is as well (see Figure 5.11).

For game sound design, chorus can add fullness to almost anything. Add it onto a car engine to make it sound a little more robust. You can add chorus to an electric spark to make it sound more "electric." Chorus is good at brightening things and making them more full.

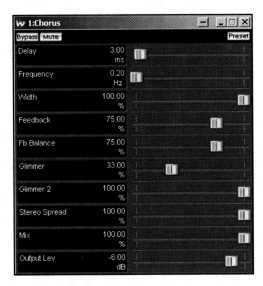

Figure 5.11
The CP-1 Chorus ships with Wavelab. It has a simple editing interface and a nice way of making your sounds more lush.

When the degree of how far the chorus detunes is set higher, it turns in to a flange. A **flange** is a highly detuned, slower chorus that adds a kind of metallic effect to a sound. Try adding it to metal impacts to make them more metallic!

If you're looking for something to widen a sound, look no further. Chorus adds a nice, warm thickness that can really turn a sound around if you mix it in appropriately. Just don't add too much, or it will sound very warbly.

> ❄ **Favorite Chorus Effects**
> I really like the ChorusDelay effect that ships with the TC Power Core. It has a very fat reverb that definitely thickens up a sound. The editor is very simple, and it has a ton of great presets designed by TC.

Delay

Delay, or digital delay, is basically an echo. It's a very specialized effect because you don't need echo on everything. It's just one of those things that you use now and again. If you speed the delay up, though, you can get some really nice psychedelic effects. When I say speed up, I mean adjust how fast each echo is repeated. For example, at the default setting, when I play a tap through the delay, it sounds like tap. . .tap. . .tap. When I speed up the rate of the delay, it's now taptaptapttap.

If you time out a delay with just the right rate and mix, you can make a singular sound behave as if there are multiple repetitions going on in that particular instance. This can be handy if you want a single set of footsteps to sound as if there are a few people walking together, or as if one car driving by is actually a couple of cars.

Like reverb, delay is an effect that should only be used every once in a while simply because not many things actually echo. But as I was saying, it's a good way to make one sound appear to be many.

> ❄ **Favorite Delay Effects**
> I really enjoy using the PSP 608 Multidelay (see Figure 5.12). This comprehensive multi-delay plug-in is extremely tweakable. For example, you can add a high-pass filter to the second delay instance, and then add some drive to the third delay instance. With little effort, you can make one instance sound like quite a few different sounds!

Figure 5.12

The PSP 608 Multidelay is a highly editable delay with a wonderful sound. The fact that it has so many different choices for each delay instance, like a filter for each delay, makes it a joy to use!

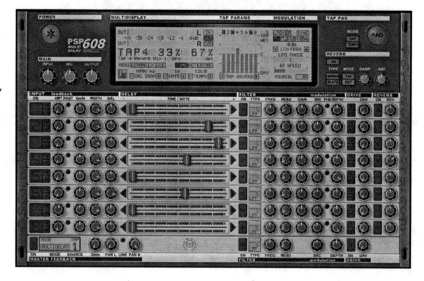

Distortion

There are several situations where you might want a sound to be a little more raw. Distortion is perfect for this kind of effect. To sum it up, **distortion** makes a sound appear overdriven without actually peaking the audio past 0 dB.

Do you know what it sounds like when you turn a radio up really loud? It sounds overdriven, like the speakers are about to burst. This is what distortion simulates. I've actually gotten a lot of use out of distortion for voice lines. I'll use distortion to simulate radio communications. All you have to do is get a bed of white noise. This is pretty easy to come by—some wave editors like Sound Forge will even generate it for you. You mix the white noise with a voice line to make it sound like there's a lot of white noise in the background. Then you apply distortion to the mixed file. Bingo, instant radio!

Distortion in light amounts is great for making a sound a little more ferocious. It's kind of fun to make one version of a sound distorted, and then mix it with a dry version of the same sound. For one thing, it will make it a little more three-dimensional, and it will also make it sound a little more raw. This is cool for impacts, and the like.

Distortion in the right amounts can make your sound set a little more dynamic and raw in some areas. Like most of the effects listed in this chapter, use careful amounts. You don't want people to think you're overdriving your whole sound set.

❈ **Favorite Distortion Effects**

Even though Reason is not a plug-in, I tend to use it a lot to process sounds by introducing them into Reason via the NN-XT sampler. When I do this for distortion, I always use the Scream unit (see Figure 5.13). Scream can make a sound either raging, crunched, or screaming. With its intuitive interface, it's quick and easy to get the sound you are looking for.

Figure 5.13
The Scream 4 distortion unit found in Reason can make any sound go from a nasty beast to a bit-crunched cell phone.

Compression

Virtually every sound in your set can use a little bit of compression. This effect allows you to tighten up a sound so that it will cut through the mix a little more. Compression can be a very difficult thing to grasp at first, but let me see what I can do. I often use the bread explanation. For example, when you first encounter a loaf of bread, it's usually fluffy and light. Say that I want my bread to be a little more dense, not so fluffy. I use a my hand to press down on the bread. After I've pressed down on the loaf of bread, it feels thicker, more compressed. Essentially my hand was the compressor. It's pressed the bread down and pushed some of the fluffiness out.

If you look at a sound before and after it's been compressed, you'll find that before it will have a lot of peaks. After the sound has been compressed, you won't see as many peaks, and the sound will seem more consistent. That's because, depending on your compressor settings, a lot of the dynamics have been pulled out. Compressors essentially cut the dynamic properties from sounds. This can be very helpful if you want to make a sound cut through the mix a little more. In the beginning, a compressor will lower the volume of a sound. Thankfully, all compressors have an added gain to boost the signal after it's been compressed. Once you have adjusted the gain after the compression has been added, the sound will basically sound louder, due the fact that it's not going lower or higher during its play time. It's now consistent.

When designing sounds for games, it's important to make sure that all the sounds are basically at the same perceived volume. You don't want a lot of different volume levels because the game itself will mix the volumes of each sound. With functions like three-dimensional audio, the game itself determines from what speaker a sound plays and at what volume in regard to the player's position. If a player is far away, the sound plays at a low volume. If the sound is close to the player, it will play at a higher volume.

If your sounds are all at different volume levels, the player will not know how far away an object is. Compressors are great for helping you get each sound at similar volumes. You can run a batch file that compresses each audio file, once you're done with a set. The compressor will compress each file and output them at a certain volume. Granted, you do need to listen to each sound after the batch has concluded. Some sounds will need to be manually adjusted up or down.

Remember, compression is your friend, and it's something that may take a while to clearly understand. The best way is to start experimenting. Take a sound file that has a lot of peaks and dips, compress it, and then compare the before and after version of the file. Apply and undo, apply and undo.

Favorite Compressor Effects

I'd really like to recommend the Renaissance compressor from the Waves Platinum bundle. Not only is this a great sounding compressor, but it's very easy to use for someone just starting out. There's an Attack slider, a Release slider, the Threshold, the Ratio, and the Gain sliders. Additionally, it has the Electro toggle, designed to simulate a hardware compressor. There's also the Opto toggle that gives the sound a little more punch.

Equalizer (EQ)

Say you've been given a muffled sound that you're supposed to use as a source for an audio file. It's frustrating because this thing sounds like it was recorded through a telephone book. If there was only some way to bring out the high end to give it a little more air! Well, never fear— there is a way. Just bring out your trusty equalizer, or EQ, plug-in.

In Figure 5.14, you'll notice that I'm adjusting the high end of the graphic EQ found in Wavelab, somewhere between 5 kHz and 12 kHz. I'm only giving it a slight boost so the sound will not be as muffled. This is just one of the handy applications for which you can use an equalizer.

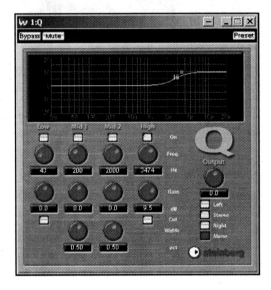

Figure 5.14

Adjusting the upper frequencies of an EQ to give a little more air to the sound.

Equalizers are also good for getting rid of annoying frequencies. Say that I have a sound with this one piercing frequency that is getting on my nerves. In my trusty graphic EQ, I start off by picking out where I think the bad frequency is and boost that frequency all the way up. From there I start sweeping the frequency range around, as pictured in Figure 5.15. When I feel I've isolated the annoying frequency, I lower it all the way down. If it is in fact the right frequency, I will have mostly eliminated it. If it's not, I'll sweep around a little more until I feel like I've pinpointed it.

There are several books and documents online about how to use an EQ properly. It's mostly used for corrective purposes, but it can also be used for enhancing a sound, such as boosting the low end so that it's more bass heavy, or boosting the high end to give it more air. But be careful not to overdo it—you could end up EQing out what you like most about the sound!

Figure 5.15

Cutting a specific group of frequencies from my sound.

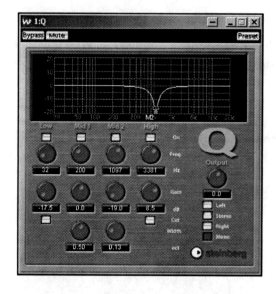

❋ **Favorite EQs**

The Renaissance EQ in the Waves Platinum bundle couldn't be a better EQ to start with. It features filter curves that are based on analog, vintage equalizers, resonant shelves, and flexible controls that make working with it a joy. If you need to boost some low end or eliminate some annoying frequency, this EQ will get the job done.

6 } Advanced Tools and Techniques

Hopefully, after reading Chapter 5 you spent some time experimenting with a wave editor, or at least mentally exploring the possibilities. Knowing your tools is essential to becoming a savvy sound designer. It's kind of like being in elementary school and going over flash cards to learn multiplication tables. The goal is to know the answer instantly when the problem is presented.

Sound design can be a similar process, except a sound design problem usually isn't a one-step solution—it will be several steps. For example, when I'm asked to create a werewolf growl, I will instantly start creating a step-by-step list in my mind of how to put it together. First, I know that a werewolf is part animal, part human. Maybe it would be best to have a human growl and pitch-shift it down? Secondly, once the growl is pitch-shifted, maybe I could use a little chorus to give it that big, other-worldly feel? Third, maybe I could boost the low end just a smidgeon with an EQ plug-in to make it a little more bass heavy?

If you can start this kind of inner dialog when you are presented with a sound design task, you will have most of the work done before you even start. In all reality, it's the ability to plan, but it's also something else. It's imagining how a sound will work before you start. Try it! Think of a sound that it would be cool to create. Imagine what it would sound like in your mind, like that game you used to play as a kid, throwing around action heroes. "I will smite you, you dreadful villain! Take that!" You scream and make hitting sounds. Remember those times? It wasn't really that long ago and you, like most of us, probably made those same sounds with your mouth. I know I did.

I had giant robots walking slowly over to the human fortress: "K-chunk, K-chunk," I would say. When the robot got close, he'd slowly raise his laser gun and fire. A shrill noise permeated my air-conditioned room, but in my head there would be a shrill beam sound reverberating off of the steel walls of the fortress. When the beam made contact with the fortress wall, I'd imagine the impact sound, a laser ricocheting against a metal wall. I even used a synthesizer to make laser sounds to help me with my battles.

Was this ever you? Did you ever wish you could really hear those sounds and see those battles and live those moments? For me, some of those times helped erased all of the awkward moments of adolescence, and I dreamed of something more. Those moments were an escape for me, as I'm sure they were for you.

Sound design is wonderful in the sense that you can actually get back to your childhood by imagining again. It's funny that millions of self-help books tell you to get in touch with your inner child—now a sound design book is telling you the same. It's true though, you have to imagine. If you can let yourself fall back into that old game you used to play when you were a kid, and then just take it a step farther with the tools at your disposal, you have it made.

In this chapter, you make use of the tools that you explored in the last chapter. You combine the tools to recreate playing like a kid, as I mentioned earlier.

Return of the Robot

Now, try to imagine the robot attacking the fortress again, but this time you're an adult with tools for sound design. The robot moves toward the fortress; every footstep has a "K-chunk" sound. I imagine that you could use some sounds from a local machine shop, then maybe combine those with a metal object, like a can, crunching into gravel. But many people don't have access to machine shops or high-quality recorders; maybe you could use something around the house?

You could try recording a blender or the release of a bread toaster. One of these small machines could be manipulated with a pitch-shift and a time-stretch for part of the robot's footsteps. This could be the joint movement. The way I look at it is that the robot will have motors running all through its leg. One motor in its knee, one in its waist, and so on. It would be nice if you could simulate it using some of these small motors like blenders and such.

So that's the beginning of it—you pull several sounds together to make one sound. Not every scenario will be like this. Sometimes you can find one sound to take care of one request. Sometimes it takes more. Really, there's no set way to create a sound; everyone has his own way of doing it.

Back to your robot. Shoot for a simple device that you could start off with. For the leg motor, try an electric drill. You can start with variable speeds so it sounds like the motor spinning up and slowing down. You can also hold the drill down to get one continual pitch. Later, you can use that continual burst of drill for any number of things.

So now you need an impact sound. As I was saying, you're working with things from around the house. I bet you could find something metallic, like a hammer. Instead of hitting an object the way you usually do with a hammer, hold it upside down and jab it straight down into some gravel or some dirt. Later on, you could pitch that impact down to make it sound like a really big object walking on rocks.

I suppose with this you've moved pretty far from the simple way kids make robot sounds. They just use their mouths. But when it comes down to it, this is reminiscent of what you did as a kid: You imagined! Coming up with solutions to sound requests using common methods is what makes sound design so fun. Take a moment now and ask yourself, "How would I have made a robot footstep?" I bet you can think of something completely different from the way I did it. Stop and imagine what you think the footstep should sound like. Play it over and over again in your head. Break the sound down into small pieces, or think of a sound you've heard that resembles this sound. Now that you've got it, try it on your own.

And no, I'm not trying to skip out on you. I will finish the sound that I've begun. Now it's time to start manipulating the sounds.

Manipulating the Robot

So you've assembled a few sounds for the robot at this point, and the big question is what to do with them? The most important thing is to bring them into a multi-track program like Nuendo (which is what I'll use here) and arrange them in a way that sounds cool. Keep in mind: You don't need Nuendo to do this; it's just the program I have. Pro Tools, Cubase, SONAR, or something similar will work.

So get cracking! I'm going to open up a new arrangement in Nuendo, then start importing some of my drill and can recordings. This way I can move the ingredients around, so to speak. In Figure 6.1 you can see an example of my different sounds spread out.

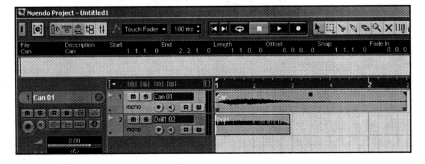

Figure 6.1

All the sounds I will be using to assemble robot steps are placed on individual tracks so I can mix and arrange them.

Now I'm going to start placing the sounds where I think they should go. It would make sense that the leg motor would be the first thing heard in the sound file. I'm kind of shooting for the, "Whrrr, k-chunk" scenario. So the first thing I do is place the drill motor at the beginning of the time span, at measure 1 (see Figure 6.2).

I'm going to press Play in Nuendo so that I might hear what things sound like so far. So that I don't have to keep hitting Play and Rewind, I set up **loop points** so that it will play my little mess over and over. Simply playing a loop over and over again, I find, is a really quick way to get to

Figure 6.2

After the sounds are all imported, you can start arranging them in the order that you want to hear them.

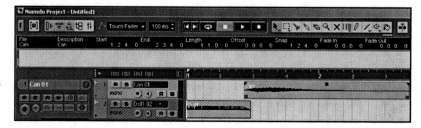

what you want. You can arrange while the sequencer is playing, and, as you arrange the sounds, it will get closer to or further from what you want to hear. Also while the loop is repeating itself, you can get an idea of what kind of effects might sound good on the dry sounds. Additionally, you can tell if you should apply some rendering effects, like time-stretching, and so on. Think of it like a painter: You take a look at the painting and add a couple of brush strokes to modify the face on the painting. You take a step back and see how it looks from a distance. Standing back, you notice that the sky needs to be a little more blue. You make another couple of brush strokes. You whittle away in small increments, making slight adjustments as you go along.

After listening for a bit, I've decided that the drill motor sounds a little too much like a drill motor. I think I'm going to try pitching it down to make it sound a little more massive. I mean, if you are going to create sounds for a giant, killer robot, you want him to sound menacing, right?

Pitching down in Nuendo is easy to do. You'll notice in Figure 6.3, if you right-click the sound file within the arrangement window and select Process, a submenu appears. I'm going to choose Pitch Shift. If the program you are working in doesn't have the same options, just consult your Help manual; it should point you in the right direction. I'll go ahead and preview the pitch-shifting until it sounds like what I'm looking for. Once it's suitably low enough for my purposes, I press OK and Nuendo renders the audio accordingly.

Now it sounds like I have a motor attached to a small tin can. That's not going to work at all. Obviously, you're going to have to do some processing on our gravely tin can as well. I try pitch-shifting the tin can down a little bit using the Process menu again. With this sound, I decide to pitch it down a little more. I want it to sound really big and ominous when it hits.

Now that I have both of the sounds at a pitch that suits my taste, I'm going to try out some different effects to see if I can join the sounds a little better. Currently, both sounds don't exactly sound like they belong together. By adding just a little bit of reverb, it can make them sound like they both exist in the same environment.

Nuendo, like most multi-track programs, allows you to **group** tracks. This means you can send the outputs of both of your audio tracks to one track. After you have set this up, you can effect both channels as if they are one (see Figure 6.4). Once I've grouped my tracks, I can apply effects, EQs , and so on, and they will affect both of the sounds identically. This keeps me from having to copy EQ and reverb settings to both channels every time I make a change.

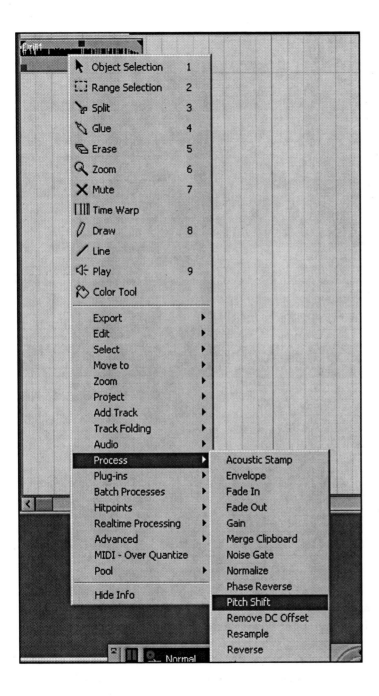

Figure 6.3
You can use the Process menu to pitch-shift your sound.

Figure 6.4

By grouping tracks, you can globally effect everything assigned to that group. Essentially you're creating a sub-mix.

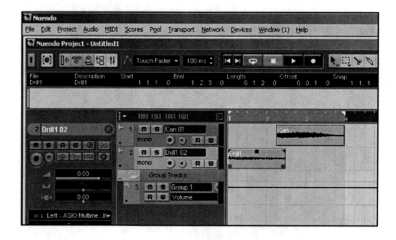

I start looping the sounds again to hear what I have. I remember that I still need to add some reverb to the two sounds to make them seem as if they are in the same environment. To do this, I click the Inserts tab in the Channel Inspector on the left side of the screen.

Figure 6.5

An insert effect affects the channel directly, rather than going through an auxiliary channel, like an effects track.

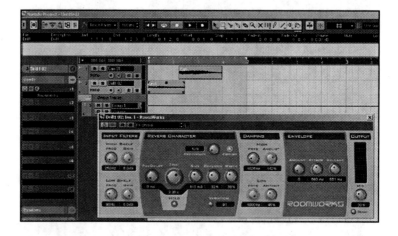

As you can see in Figure 6.5, I've chosen the RoomWorks plug-in that comes with Nuendo. As I shuffle through the various presets, I listen for one that works for me. While I'm doing this, I'm watching the Mix knob in the lower corner of RoomWorks. You really need to keep an eye on this when you are using effects as inserts—if it's too wet, it will sound like a tin can. I usually check out each of the presets and jog the Mix knob around to make sure I'm giving every preset a fair chance. Once I've gotten a setting that I'm comfortable with, I stop the looping and take a moment to rest my ears. When I return from a my small sojourn, I push Play to hear what I've got. It's definitely metallic and it's definitely big, but it still seems like it's missing something.

❋ **Take a Break**

There's one thing I recommend when doing any kind of audio work—take frequent breaks. Give your ears a rest. When you hear these noisy sounds playing over and over again, you can really lose your objectivity. Taking a break for a minute or two will let you come back with a refreshed outlook.

One effect that I use pretty often when I'm doing robot sounds, and I should say one effect that has been used extensively for droid sounds, is a small chorus. I bring one up and shuffle through the various presets. When I find one that I like, I turn the chorus on and off to see if it's really helping the sound at all. In my opinion, it isn't. So what is this sound missing? I start to imagine what my childhood alter-ego might think. What did he say it should sound like? It was sort of a "whrrr, k-chunk." After remembering my original idea and listening to my current work, I notice that the K in the k-chunk is missing. Thankfully, there's an easy mend for this.

❋ **Handy Voice Recorder**

A voice recorder can come in really handy. You can make some mouth noises to convey your original ideas. I offer a word of warning: Never let this voice recorder fall into the hands of someone else. It could be a very embarrassing moment if someone listened to you making laser noises.

I select the can sound, hold down the Alt key, and then drag the sound into another area. Instead of dragging the actual sound, however, I create an entirely new copy of it, as seen in Figure 6.6. The reason for this is simple. It makes sense that the foot of the robot will hit the ground in two parts, like your feet do when you walk. This would explain the k-chunk. I'm making a sound for the different part of the leg.

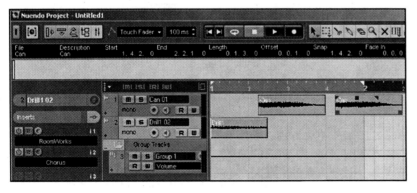

Figure 6.6
Isn't it good to know that you can create multiple copies of the same file and use it in different ways?

I decide to pitch-shift again, but this time I pitch up. As soon as I select Pitch Shift for my new copy, I'm greeted with a dialog box, as seen in Figure 6.7. If I choose Continue, I am processing both the original and the new version. If I click New Version, only that version is processed.

Figure 6.7

A warning comes up when you process a file that is a copy of another file. It keeps you from processing more than you intended.

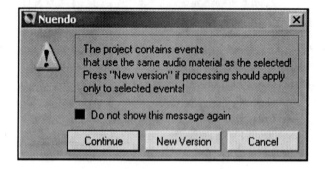

After I get through with the processing, I decide to position the new sound where it will fall a little closer to the beginning of the file, giving a little separation. Now the sound has a segmented feel—it actually has the k-chunk. The only problem is that the lighter sound has the same length as the lower sound. You can't really differentiate between the two. But there's an easy way to fix this: In Figure 6.8, notice that I've circled the end of the audio file. See the little triangle in the upper-right corner of the sound file? When you move your mouse over it, arrows appear. If you move these arrows over, you initiate a fade out. Remember fades from the last chapter? In Nuendo, you don't even have to render it. You can do it on the fly.

Figure 6.8

You can put your mouse cursor on the upper-right triangle and create a fade. Most multi-trackers have this functionality.

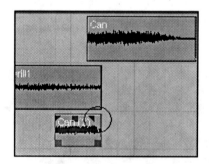

Now the file slowly fades out, but it's still too long. I decide to take it a step further. In Figure 6.9, I've circled the box in the lower-right corner of the audio file. When you move your mouse cursor over the box, the arrows appear again. These arrows allow you to scale the size of the audio file. If you scale the length of the audio file, the fade remains, but it fades out earlier.

Now that I've got the length and the fade right, I decide to move the file closer to the beginning of the file while the loop is playing. As I slowly move the file forward, the sound slowly starts

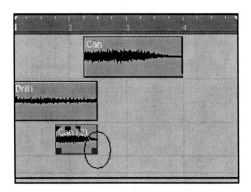

Figure 6.9
See the squares in the lower corners of the sound file? These allow you to scale the length of the audio file.

sounding like my childhood fantasy. But there's still something that isn't quite right .... Ah. I forgot to put the new file on the new audio channel into the group I set up with the reverb. Once that is set, it sounds like I've got a piece of precision, robotic machinery that's ready to blow up some humans.

There's only one thing left: Render all of these audio files as one single file. First you set your loop points. Every multi-tracker has loop points, so consult your manual to see how to set them up. In Nuendo, to set the left loop point, Ctrl-click where you want it to appear. To set the right loop point, Alt-click where you want it to appear.

Figure 6.10 illustrates the way that I've set mine up. Notice that I've added some space after the file ends. There's a good reason for this. Real-time reverbs you've set up on your sounds do not show up visually. If you set your outpoint or your right locator before the reverb tail ends, it is cut off in your final file. I always like to overcompensate. Later on, you're going to edit this in your multi-tracker, anyway.

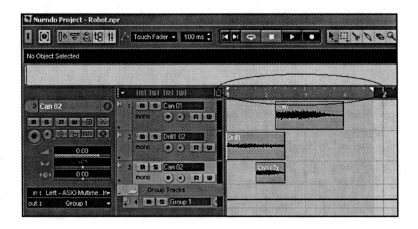

Figure 6.10
I've highlighted the loop points for you. Loop points serve many purposes, including rendering.

I go ahead and double-check my sound now to verify that everything is the way I want it between the locators. Once I'm positive, I click the File menu, as shown in Figure 6.11, and choose Export > Audio Mixdown.

Figure 6.11

Choose File > Export to open up the Audio Mix-down window in Nuendo. Every multi-tracker has a function like this.

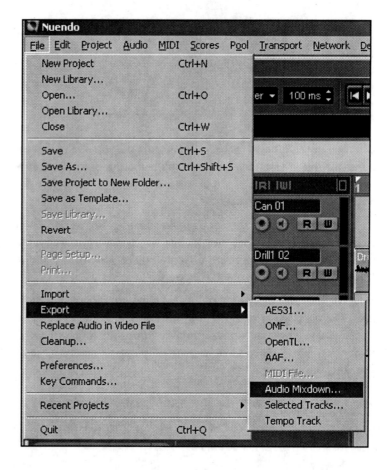

Once this has been selected, a new window comes up, as shown in Figure 6.12. The Export Audio Mixdown window lists all the different ways that you can export your audio file. I decide to name my file Robot_Leg. As you can also see, I've circled the area where you can change the file types. The reason I chose the standard wave file is just for compatibility's sake. Other people on the team may not have a program that can audition wave 64 audio files. This is almost a redundant move. Audio files of 44 kHz/16-bit are never used in game audio because they are way too large. They are commonly down-sampled later to a smaller format, like 22 kHz/8-bit audio. Granted, every game has different requirements of its audio file. Who knows, maybe they're using 48 kHz/24-bit audio by the time you've gotten around to reading this book.

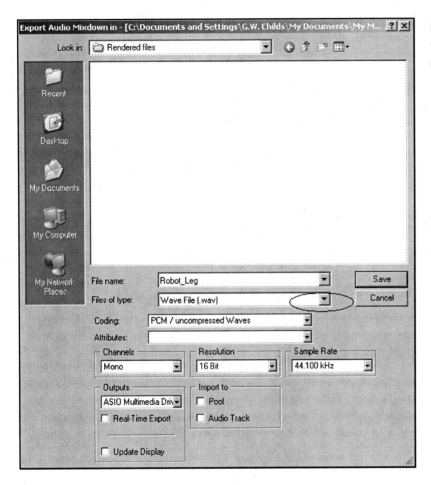

Figure 6.12
Click the down arrow to see other file types.

Once you click the Save button, you have finished up this sound file. Now it's time to trim it down in your wave editor.

The Robot Thus Far

The previous exercise is a simple method of combining a few sounds to create another sound. It's a common way of creating a larger complex sound with smaller, simpler sounds. Here's what I've done:

❋ Imagined the sound and deconstructed it into parts to find individual parts to recreate it.

❋ Gathered two sounds from entirely different sources. Combining the sounds from different places helped create a more diverse and dynamic final product.

- ❋ Imported the sounds into a multi-track editing program (Nuendo) to arrange and edit them as needed.

- ❋ Arranged the sound files in a manner that closely resembled the imagined sound.

- ❋ Using the Pitch Bend function in Nuendo, sonically manipulated each sound to resemble the imagined sound.

- ❋ Created fades and scaled the lengths of each file to play for the appropriate amount of time.

- ❋ Using Nuendo's Group Track function, sub-mixed sounds into one channel. This was helpful when applying global EQs and effects over all of the sounds.

- ❋ Used effects to create a small environment for the sounds. This gave them more of a metallic/mechanical feel.

- ❋ Moved loop points into the appropriate positions for continuous looping.

- ❋ Talked about the need for taking small breaks when producing audio.

- ❋ Used the Ctrl-drag command in Nuendo to create a clone of another sound to use in another part of the sound we're trying to create.

- ❋ Applied more pitch-bending to the clone to make another part of the sound. When pitch-bending the clone, Nuendo asked if I'd like to create a new file or affect the old file as well.

- ❋ Using Nuendo's Export function, exported the final mix as a single audio file.

This may appear like a lot of steps to create one small file, but it actually goes pretty quickly once you've gotten the idea of how it works. I think you'll find after spending some time creating various sounds that you'll start to automatically know how to devise certain sounds. Basically, as soon as you're presented with a task, your mind will start to work on ways of creating just such a sound.

And this same exercise can be applied to any type of game, not just making robots. Say you want to create the sound of a bat hitting a baseball that ends with the crowd cheering. All you need to do is get the impact of a ball hitting a bat, and then add in a small bit of a crowd roar at the end of the arrangement with a small fade out at the end. What if you want to create the sound of soldiers marching with hints of military gear jangling at each step? Then you get some footsteps and combine them with some metallic rattles. Of course, each of these small scenarios for different types of games could be more elaborate. In fact, they can be as elaborate as you want them to be. Just keep in mind, however, that game schedules are often very tight and, while it's great to experiment, you're on a deadline.

Combining sounds is an easy way to create a small scene in audio that immerses the player in the visuals. Don't get me wrong; you don't need to combine every sound. Sometimes having a simple sound, like an empty bullet shell hitting the ground, is enough to immerse the listener. For example, say you want to create the sound of a door knob turning. That's pretty straight forward, right? There's really no need to combine the sounds in this instance. But what about creating a sound of the door knob turning and then creaking open? That would be a perfect opportunity. Combine a door knob turning with a door creak, and you're done.

And you don't have to use Nuendo to perform this exercise. I prefer Nuendo, but you may have another program that fulfills your needs.

When You Need Inspiration

Everyone hits a brick wall when doing this kind of work. But it can be especially hard when you are new to it. After you've had plenty of time experimenting and creating, you start to get a good idea of what something sounds like when you take a certain path. At the same time, you get an idea of what doesn't sound good.

✳ Movies can be a wonderful source for inspiration when designing sounds. With a DVD or a VHS player, or even if you're playing an MPEG on your computer, you can listen to a sound over and over. You could even record it for reference.

✳ Video games themselves can be an excellent source of inspiration. You don't even have to buy a game to check it out; you can rent some and just listen. With a video game, it's a little easier, too. In almost every video game there is an audio Options menu in which you will usually find a Volume slider for sound FX, music, and voice. If you want to focus on just the sound FX, turn the music and voice down. Now you have all of the sound FX isolated.

✳ Your environment is rife with inspiration. I like to bang on different surfaces, walk around new areas, and just enjoy different places. It can become a game that you play with yourself and other people. You can make a collection of different sounds that you've picked up in various ways and through various means. Have fun with it!

Canned Sound

What if you still can't find what you're looking for? What if you don't have access to the kind of source material that you need to complete a certain sound? This kind of problem can come up for plenty of us. After all, not everyone has access to several guns or machinery or animals. Thankfully, there are companies that have gone to the trouble of making extensive libraries of all manner of different sounds. There are even Web sites where you can buy certain sounds from the comfort of your own home, right over the Internet.

That may lead you to wonder what's the point of your job. I'm not necessarily suggesting that you use these sounds as is. I recommend thoroughly investigating your options first. Surely there's a gun range around where you live or work; surely there's a machine shop somewhere! Desperate times can call for desperate measures, however. Sometimes using **canned** (or purchased) sounds for source material is a great option when you're slammed and don't have time for a quick field recording.

One Web site—www.soundrangers.com—has a really great selection of sounds that you can preview, and if you like a sound, you can buy it direct. This alleviates the need to buy an entire pack or CD of sounds, which can be very expensive. There are certainly several different online libraries to choose from. I just found the interface of this Web site to be quick and easy to move through. Great inspiration.

Existing Sound FX Libraries

If you don't have access to the Internet, or you just want a huge arsenal of royalty-free sound FX at your disposal, purchasing an existing library might be a viable option for you. These libraries are anything but cheap, but you can use them as source material for creating your own sounds and rest assured that you are using quality audio in making them. Some recommended libraries follow.

Sound Ideas General 6000: Basic Set

This is a comprehensive library, offering a full range of different categories for everything you could ask for in sound effects. Some of these categories include Animals and Birds, Construction, Crowds, Fire, Household, Industry, Military, Office, Sports, and Transportation. Crazy enough, this only covers a small part of what this set offers. On top of tons of basic sounds, it also includes ambience tracks from around the world. It even has Foley sound. If you're looking for a good library to build off of, this set could be a good match for you. You can find more information at www.sound-ideas.com.

Hollywood Edge Historical Series

This sound library is brought to you from the award-winning sound designer, Nigel Holland. Holland is responsible for the brilliant audio heard in the movie *Braveheart*. In fact, the library actually includes audio used in *Braveheart*!

As the title suggests, this library is geared toward historical reenactments. It includes sounds from infantry, cavalry, horses, churches, castles, city ambiences, and some fantasy sounds, like dragons, sea serpents, and trap doors. Considering that many video games take place around wars and old world environments, this might not be a bad library to have around. After all, how easy is it to get a small army together to record? For more information, check out www.hollywoodedge.com.

Universal Studios Sound Effects Library

Cooperation between Universal Studios and Sound Ideas made available a large collection of sound effects that come straight from some of Universal's classic pictures. It's like getting access to Universal during the shooting of some of the greatest pictures ever made. The library is made up of several different types of sounds that include everything from airplanes to animals, space doors and space guns, grenades, rockets, sword fights, machine guns, and steam trains. In fact, it even has Indians and Western battles for the cowboy (or cowgirl) in all of us. You can find more information at www.sound-ideas.com.

7 } Software Instruments and Samplers

The last chapter focused on putting together one sound out of multiple sounds using software as it was intended. In this chapter, you take a slightly different path.

As I've mentioned before, sound design requires a lot of experimentation. With that being the case, a lot of fun can be found from experimenting alone. A favorite pastime of many a sound designer is thinking of new ways to create new sounds. This pursuit has led to most sound designers having very carefully guarded secrets in their recipes for certain effects, like chefs.

Take a moment and examine how chefs work: There are some who enjoy cooking just using recipes alone; however, I'm not talking about this kind of chef. I'm talking about the good ol' Southern chef that will taste his way to creation. I'm sure you know the type. These guys or gals will gather several ingredients together and taste what they have, and then add a little more spice, and then taste a little more. The bottom line is—there is never an exact recipe. You just need the main ingredients and experimentation.

For the sound designer, software instruments and samplers are your ingredients, and the recipe is how you use them to manipulate or create your sounds. These tools are important because they allow you an unimaginable creative outlet in a small and compact container. You can bend sounds, shorten sounds, extend sounds, and mangle sounds. It's truly a wonderful time to be in the business because you can pretty much do whatever you want with any sound.

I have a few tools that I really enjoy working with. I don't always get the exact sound instantly every time I use them—I have to tweak it a little until it's right. But eventually I get there. The tools I use may be completely different from every other sound designer's, but it's my way of working and that's the way it goes. One tool that I enjoy immensely wasn't initially intended for sound design. Reason has been a tool that I've used for years, and I can usually come up with a closely matching sound with very little effort.

Do I use Reason and nothing else? No. It's usually a cross between Wavelab and Reason. I'll take raw session files from the field, cut the sounds out of the session that I'd like to use in

Wavelab, and then load up those sounds in the Reason sampler, known as the NN-XT. From there I tweak the sound until I get it exactly the way I like it.

Why do I prefer to do it this way? Reason's modular system of different pieces of hardware equipment allows an infinite amount of routing. You can create an unheard of signal chain that can do amazing things to audio with very little effort. For example, you can have unlimited EQs that resemble and sound like very expensive hardware pieces. Additionally, you can filter your audio with one of the filters in Reason, add two, three, or seven expensive-sounding EQs into your signal chain, add a very expensive Reverb, double the sound with a Spider Merger/Splitter, and then A/B between several signal paths of the same sound. As you can see, Reason allows you to be as creative as you want in a one-stop shop. You can route cables as you need to and find endless ways to enhance and destroy audio.

Is Reason the end all, be all? Not by a long shot. But it's a tool that I've gotten really comfortable with, and I know how to do things quickly in it. It's a preferred kitchen of mine. My point in telling you about it is this: Don't be afraid to try something new in creating any sound. Try new programs, try new systems, try hardware—have fun!

Allowing yourself to be stuck in one type of program ends in stagnation. With the number of plug-ins available to most audio programs, however, you'll have a tough time exhausting all the ways to create. There are simply tons of free tools just dying to be used. A Web site such as www.kvr-vst.com is one that can show you many different free VST plug-ins, and it even has a rating system.

In this chapter, I'm going to show you how to use Reason in a sound design environment. You don't have to use Reason, of course, but because I'm so comfortable with it, it's what I'll use to show you some techniques. Hopefully, while you're following along, maybe you can think of a different program that you really enjoy using, and then come up with a way to use it outside of the box.

Using Reason for Sound Design

This chapter assumes that you have Reason when going through the exercises. If you don't have it, you can always download the demo from www.propellerheads.se.

Before beginning, let me shoot back again to why I like using Reason for sound design:

* Reason allows you to work in a virtual environment that resembles hardware.
* You can get creative, and thus generate all forms of new sound with imaginative wiring within Reason.
* Reason has an excellent set of effects, EQs, and filters that can really make a sound interesting.

- ❄ You can run multiple points of automation during any sequence, allowing you to really manipulate audio.
- ❄ There is a wonderful mastering tool in Reason to help you beef up your sound.

As you can see, this "simple" music program is suddenly a lot more complex than it initially appears. There are several tools available that enable you to manipulate the holy hell out of a sound. Take for example the Scream device found in Reason. It's a distortion device, but it's also a bit cruncher, a ring modulator, and an EQ all rolled into one. See what I mean? Even one simple device in Reason can be used for many different things.

Another device that can be used in several different ways is the Subtractor. I use this synthesizer for its white noise generator, and to output LFO pulses to another device. Additionally, I'll use it for random bleeps and whistles when I'm trying to create some interface sounds.

Really, I could go on and on about all of the different functions Reason is capable of. That's why the program is so cool—when it comes to sound you can always find something new in the program.

The Malström

So you've heard me blather about how cool Reason is; now let me show you. Go ahead and boot up the program now. If you don't own it, and you haven't downloaded the demo, go ahead and grab it. I'll wait. ... Done? Great!

If you haven't used Reason before, when you first boot up the program, the default demo song will be loaded automatically. While I think it's great to check out demo songs for their routings, this is far from the purpose of this exercise. You want to work with a clean slate. Set this program up so it gives you an empty rack every time you create a new file.

1. In the upper-left corner of the Reason window, click the Edit menu and select Preferences. The Preferences dialog box appears.
2. The dialog box should start with the title General Page in the menu bar. If this doesn't appear automatically, click the down arrow next to the page and select General from the drop-down menu.
3. From the General page, select Empty Rack inside the Default Song box.
4. Close the Preferences dialog box.
5. Go back to the upper-left corner of the Reason window and select File > New. An empty rack appears. You can close the window that opened with the default demo song.

Now that you've got your empty rack, you will see mostly blackness, as shown in Figure 7.1. From here, you're going to check out the synthesizer known as the Malström.

Figure 7.1

Starting off with an empty rack or work area in Reason makes it easier to keep track of what is going on.

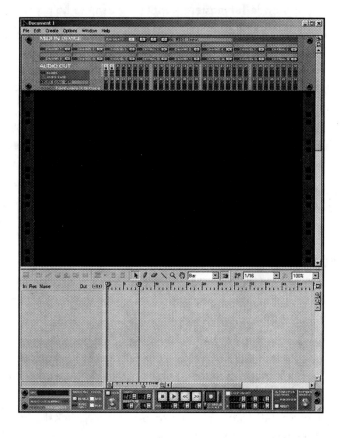

First things first: You're going to need a mixer before you bring anything in, right? Go ahead and right-click in the black area, or click the Create menu and select Mixer 14:2, as pictured in Figure 7.2.

The reason you need a mixer is simple: You may decide to add other devices to the process at a later time. There is only one main set of stereo outputs coming out of Reason into your computer. If you'd like to see what I'm talking about, turn the rack around by pressing the Tab key. You'll notice on the back of the Reason hardware interface up at the top, there are a lot of Audio In plugs available. Two in particular have a grey area around them, which are inputs 1 and 2, shown in Figure 7.3. If Reason is not running through another audio application, then channels 1 and 2 are your main inputs. If you unplug these inputs, you will get no more sound from Reason. Basically, these inputs are the link between the virtual world of Reason and the physical speakers on your computer.

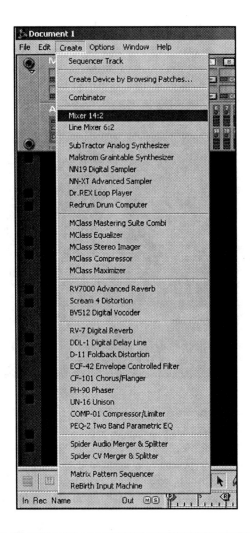

Figure 7.2
Creating a mixer, or anything in Reason, is easy. Just go to the Create menu.

Figure 7.3
Even though Reason is software, it's designed to work like hardware. For example, it even has inputs for how it interacts with the audio hardware present in your computer.

A mixer comes in handy for several reasons. The main one is that, without something to mix the sound together, you wouldn't be able to get several instruments or hardware devices outputting through just two tiny inputs. In Figure 7.4, you see the back of the mixer as it's connected to the hardware device. Notice that several inputs are available now, and the way the mixer is outputting to the hardware interface? Hopefully, it makes more sense now why you want the mixer around.

Figure 7.4

Mixer 14:2 is a great tool for creating audio in Reason's virtual environment.

Go ahead and turn the rack back around by pressing the Tab key again. Now you will see the front of the mixer with all of its pots and faders. You're going to add something to the virtual studio to make some sound move through the mixer. Go up to the Create menu and select Malström Graintable Synthesizer, as pictured in Figure 7.5. Immediately the Malström appears in your rack. It's big, and it's green, and it has a lot of knobs. (That's probably your first impression of this piece of hardware.) But don't be intimidated!

> If you're running a PC, you can access the Create menu by right-clicking in the black area of Reason. If you are using a Mac, you can access this menu by pressing Control and then clicking in Reason's black area.

First, I should explain why the Malström is cool for what you're doing—designing sounds. A Graintable synthesizer works by manipulating real audio, much like a sampler. Inside of the Malström, there are hundreds of different audio files that have been specially processed for use with this synthesizer. What separates the Malström from a sampler is that you can manipulate the

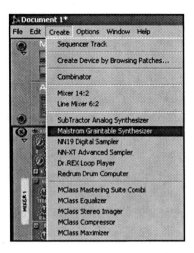

Figure 7.5
You can use the Create menu to access many of Reason's virtual instruments.

audio in the Malström down to its smallest part, or **grain**, of sound. This allows you to do some pretty wacky things to the sound that you have in front of you.

Unfortunately, you cannot import audio into the Malström; it's just not an option. But as you can see in Figure 7.6, there's plenty of sound to work with for all manner of tasks, and you never even have to break out your field recorder.

Figure 7.6
Malström has plenty of different raw sounds available for manipulation. Click in the LCD window to see a list. Remember, you can have up to two sources of audio per instance of the Malström.

Now don't get me wrong, I think it's important to capture your own audio when you can. But sometimes you need something quick and different. Synthesizers like the Malström are great for helping out with just such an endeavor.

Do you see where it says Sine in the OSC A box? Go ahead and click Sine, and a menu of several different sounds will pop up. You'll notice arrows both at the bottom and at the top of the menu. You can click on these arrows to scroll up and down in the menu. When scrolling, you'll notice a ton of different sounds that are categorized as different things, including FX, Synth, and so on. Go ahead and select Wind: Didgeridoo.

Most likely you don't have any kind of controller keyboard at your disposal, especially if you are new to Reason. But that's okay. A controller makes Reason a little more fun and easier to explore, but it's not necessary. You can easily draw in the notes that a keyboard would play.

On the Sequencer toolbar (located at the top of the Sequencer window with an arrow, a pencil, a line, and a magnifying glass), there is one button in particular that toggles Reason in between the arrangement view (that it defaults to) and the editor view (used for editing notes, automation, and so on). You can see this button in Figure 7.7. Click this button and you immediately switch over to Edit mode. You should currently be editing the Malström because that's the only thing added thus far. Click the In button to select what you're editing in Reason, shown in Figure 7.8.

Figure 7.7

Pressing the button lets you edit automation or small parts.

Figure 7.8

When you press anywhere in the In field, you will see a little keyboard appear. This lets you know what instrument you're currently working with.

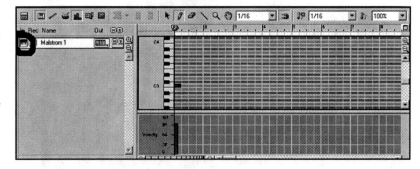

You'll notice that a little keyboard is currently residing in this spot. Once you add more instruments and devices into Reason, you will be able to move this keyboard to any of those instruments, which will allow you to work with them. The keyboard can only reside in one track at a time, however.

Now that you are in Edit mode, go ahead and add your note. Up in the toolbar, you see the small picture of a pencil, as shown in Figure 7.9. Click this button.

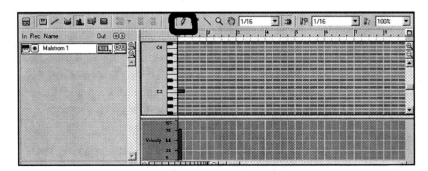

Figure 7.9
The Pencil tool in Reason allows you to enter note and automation data.

Now you should have a floating pencil that you can drag anywhere. With the Pencil tool selected, draw in a note on the key of C3, just as you see in Figure 7.10. With this note in place, you will be able to hear the Malström now. Go ahead and click the Play button or press the spacebar to check it out.

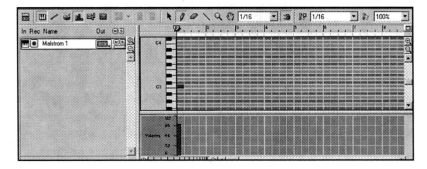

Figure 7.10
Once you've added a note, you are actually triggering one of Reason's instruments. If you have a controller keyboard, you can bypass this step.

Now that you are listening to the Malström, you are probably noticing a few different things. The first is that your sound isn't playing very frequently and, secondly, that it doesn't play for very long. It isn't playing very frequently because your loop points are set very far apart. Drag the right loop point a little closer in to the note that you created. You can see an example in Figure 7.11.

Figure 7.11

If the Loop button is on, which it is by default in Reason, you only hear the portions between loop points.

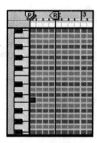

Once the loop points are in place, you're ready to begin modeling a sound. The Malström offers several different ways to manipulate its raw sounds, as I've mentioned earlier. The first area that we'll concentrate on, however, is going to be the OSC section, which is short for **oscillator**. All synthesizers have an oscillator section, though the classic synthesizer does not have a granular oscillator, like the Malström. This is one of the things that makes the Malström such a unique instrument.

In Figure 7.12, you will see the oscillator section as a whole. Go ahead and try adjusting the Motion, Index, Shift, and Octave knobs. While you're at it, adjust the envelope section as well. Those are the knobs labeled A, D, S, R. These knobs stand for Attack, Decay, Sustain, and Release. The envelope section determines whether the sound will fade in, fade out abruptly, linger, and so on.

Figure 7.12

This section has two oscilla-tors, which are great for creating sound combina-tions.

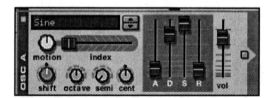

So as you're playing around with this sound, are you getting any ideas? I would hope so. The reason that I pointed you first to the Didgeridoo sound is because it is an organic sound, unlike what you usually hear from synthesizers. Many sound designers feel that electronic instruments don't completely crossover as believable. This is especially hazardous when it comes to video games because it wasn't so many years ago that all you heard from these games were blips and beeps. In recent years, video games are meant to be more of an immersive experience, where you are meant almost to believe that you are filling the role of the hero or heroine.

As you can hear, you can really get some noisy sounds with the Malström, or you can get some pretty natural-sounding pieces of audio with careful manipulation. What's more, with Reason, you can stack several devices like this to make all manner of noise.

If you select the Browse Patch button (shown in Figure 7.13), the Reason Browser will pop up. Select Reason Factory Sound Bank over in the left-hand window and in the Search field up at the top, type in **SciFi Vehicle**. This patch is a prime example of the sound effects you can get out of the Malström. Try extending the note in Edit mode to see how it plays out. Feel free to play around with the patch as well.

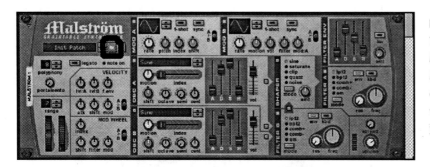

Figure 7.13

The Browse Patch button brings up the Reason Browser, which doubles as a small sound database, where you can organize your sounds and so on.

Enter the NN-XT

While the Malström is a great synthesizer for getting some quick results, often times you are going to want to import some of your own audio. Reason is not really designed to be a wave editing or audio multi-tracking program, but it is possible to do it with ease. But why would you want to? Easy—Reason has great FX processors and other assorted devices that allow you to do some very twisted things with audio. And in reality, samplers have been used for sound design for several years now, so why couldn't you use one in Reason?

That's where the lovely NN-XT comes into play. This is Reason's sampler, and while it's not the only sampler in Reason, it's the one worthy of mention. There is the NN-19, but it is very limited; so you're going to focus on the NN-XT for this exercise.

One of the oldest tricks in the book for sound design is to set up a sampler with several different sounds attached to several different keys. Once all of the keys are assigned, you play the keys in different combinations to create different sounds. You can create several different zones, and you can create different layers. The NN-XT even allows you to output in several different ways, thanks to its multiple outputs.

For this next exercise, I would like to mention that you will need the full version of Reason 3.0 or higher. Additionally, it's recommended that you have a keyboard controller for this exercise as well. I'll write this as if you don't, but you'll get more enjoyment out of it if you can push the keys.

In Figure 7.14, you'll notice the basics of the NN-XT. At a glance, it looks like a pretty simple device, with only a few knobs for things like the volume and the envelope areas.

Figure 7.14
The basic NN-XT, when it's first "created," looks very simple. Don't let this fool you.

This is actually quite deceptive. The NN-XT has many functions, and this is only the "closed" view of the device. In Figure 7.15, you'll see a circled arrow button at the bottom left of the NN-XT. I'd like for you to click that button now.

Figure 7.15
Click the small arrow button to reveal the entire NN-XT.

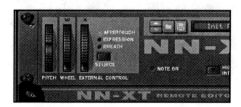

After you have clicked the small arrow button, you will see that the whole page has been taken up by the complete version of the NN-XT.

As you and I will not have the same sounds available, it will be better to work from sounds that I've created especially for the book at its companion Web site, www.courseptr.com. This way you're working with the same sounds, and you can hear what I'm doing. After you have downloaded the sounds, place them in a folder called Book Sounds on your desktop. Click the Edit menu, then scroll down and select Browse Samples, as shown in Figure 7.16.

After clicking Browse Samples, the Reason Browser appears. Select Desktop over in the Locations section, and then click the Book Sounds folder, as depicted in Figure 7.17.

After opening the Book Sounds folder, check to see if the Autoplay function in the Audition area is selected. You can actually listen to each sound as you pass over it. Give it a try! Once you've finished listening to the different sounds, go ahead and choose Mechanical 1 and click OK. If you don't see it, I've highlighted it for you in Figure 7.18.

After you've opened up the sound effect, you are free to play around with it if you have a keyboard controller. If you don't have a controller, there is an easy work around: Just repeat the steps that you used in the chapter's previous Malström section.

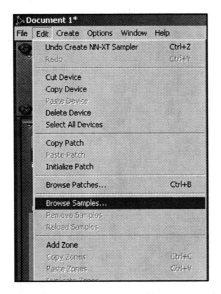

Figure 7.16
Go up to the Edit menu to find the Browse Samples function. Remember, the NN-XT must be selected for this option to show up in the Edit menu.

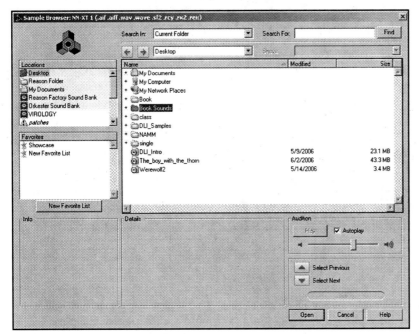

Figure 7.17
Use the Reason Browser to find the NN-XT sampler patches. Make sure you highlight Desktop > Book Sounds.

Figure 7.18

As you can see, there are many different sound FX to choose from in Reason. Go ahead and choose Mechanical 1.

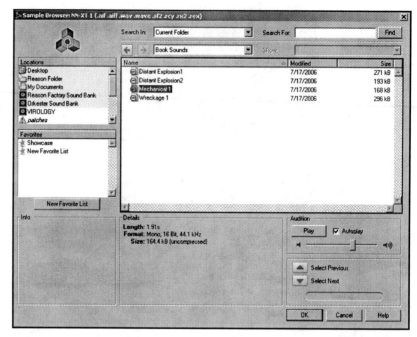

As you can see, it's fun to play the sound at different pitches, and so on. I'm sure you're getting ideas, but make room for some other samples. You'll notice in Figure 7.19 that I've circled a long blue rectangle. This rectangle spans the key range that is currently assigned to the sample. If you were using just one sample, this would be fine, but you want to eventually add more. Fix this.

Figure 7.19

When you initially load a single sample into the NN-XT, it gives a very large key range. Slide this bar around to change the key range.

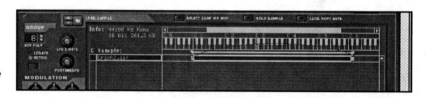

On each side of this long triangle you notice small blue squares. Drag the square on the right over to the middle, and then drag the square on the left over to the middle until it matches Figure 7.20. Now the sample only plays off one key: C3. As you can see in the figure, it's right underneath C3.

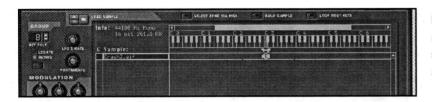

Figure 7.20
Drag the small boxes over to the middle where the sample only spans one key.

Now that this has been taken care of, you can import another sample. With your mouse cursor, click anywhere in the blue region of the NN-XT until the Mechanical 1 sample is no longer high-lighted. Now go back up to the Edit menu and select Browse Samples again. This time I want you to choose Wreckage 1, as shown in Figure 7.21.

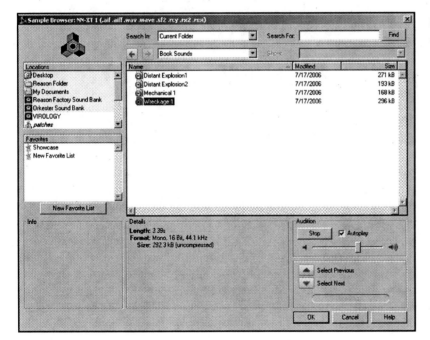

Figure 7.21
Choose the Wreckage 1 sample.

Once you've chosen the Wreckage 1 sample, go ahead and decrease the key range as you did with the Mechanical 1 sample until your NN-XT looks like Figure 7.22.

If you try playing your keyboard now or clicking Play (if you set up a note in the Sequencer), you will hear two samples, one on top of the other. Wouldn't it be better to be able to play the sounds independently? This is an easy fix. If you click on the key range, you will find that you can drag it to nearly any key on the keyboard at the top. Go ahead and drag it over to D3 so that it looks like Figure 7.23.

Figure 7.22

Now you should have two samples that have different key ranges.

Figure 7.23

Now that you've created two samples that play on different keys, you can trigger them independently.

Once you've separated your key zones, you will be able to play both sounds independently. With just these two sounds alone, you should have some ideas already. But imagine the ability to mix several!

Now that you know how to zone these samples, you can do what sound designers have been doing for years: mixing on the fly. This is even a cool method for creating sound design for cut scenes, as you are able to ReWire Reason to applications like Pro Tools or Nuendo and trigger them as you go along with the cut scene that you are scoring. Go ahead and try adding some more sound effects to your sampler and splitting the key zones on your own using the method that I showed you.

Now try adding a reverb to your sampler. First, click the Create menu up at the top. This time, I want you to select the RV7000 Advanced Reverb, as shown in Figure 7.24.

Figure 7.24
The RV7000 is a great way to add some dimension and mood to your sound FX.

Once you've created the RV7000, take a listen to what your FX sound like now. They should sound like they are being played out of the end of a tiled restroom. The reason the reverb is so intense is because the mix, by default, is set all the way up. Turn it about midway, like what I've done in Figure 7.25.

Now that the mix is down, the reverb should be much more moderate and way more natural. At this point, you should try browsing through some of the reverb patches. This is easy to do! Click the Browse Patch button on the RV7000. Immediately the Reason Browser will pop up. Make sure that the Reason Factory Sound Bank is selected, and choose RV7000 patches. Inside this folder, you will find a slew of different presets that will make your FX sound very interesting.

Figure 7.25

Turn the mix down on the RV7000 so the reverb isn't so intense.

Remember, you aren't limited to the sound FX that are supplied in Reason. You can import your own sound FX very easily. Reason will play .wav files and .aif files from 16 bit to 24 bit. Just think what you could do with some of the sounds that you recorded yourself.

After you've found some sound combinations that you enjoy, record them in the Reason Sequencer. In fact, record several variations. Once you have some cool recorded sounds, go up to the File menu and then select Export Loop as Audio File. From there you can create an audio file of your work that you can later edit in your wave editor.

If You Don't Use Reason

What's been performed here in Reason can easily be created in any other sampler. All samplers allow you to create multiple key zones, allowing different keys to be assigned to different samples, and so on.

The important thing in this exercise is to fill the keyboard with a cool palette of sounds that complement one another. After you have found some great combinations, sequence some of these key combinations and play them back; see if they are what you are looking for. If they work, export an audio file of the combination.

In your soft sampler, research how to create different key zones and how to assign sounds. Once you have learned your sampler's method for doing this, download the sounds from www.courseptr.com.

Now take some time to try out different key combinations between the different sounds. Also, try timing the sounds in different ways. Have one sound play slightly before the other. You can even try broadening the key zone of a specific sound so you can play lower and higher versions of it across the keyboard.

Once you've accomplished some sound combinations that you really like, record them in your sequencer. After the sequence has been recorded, look for an option in your sequencer called

Export Audio. All sequencers have this feature, including Reason. After the audio file has been created, bring it into your wave editor and trim it to taste.

✳ **No Reason**

I've only covered a couple of the devices found in Reason. This leaves you many other devices left to explore on your own. If you'd like to learn more, several online resources offer great tips:

- ✳ www.reasonstation.net
- ✳ www.peff.com
- ✳ www.propellerheads.se

Additionally, several books are available for learning Reason, should you so desire. One great book is *Power Tools for Reason 3.0* by Kurt Kurasaki. Course Technology, Cengage Learning also offers a complete range of books on Reason, including Skill Packs, Power, and Overdrive books. You can see them all at www.courseptr.com.

---

8 } Batch Converting

When you're working at a video game company, life can move along in one of two ways: Things can move at a snail's pace because there isn't much happening, or you can find yourself working so hard, so quickly, and so much that you won't have seen your loved ones for weeks. Most of the time it's the latter. Things are usually moving quickly, and you just don't have much time for anything. I'd love to say that this doesn't affect the quality of the sound in a game, but often it does.

When you have an insane deadline to get several hundred sounds together, you will find that you'll let more slip by. You don't have the time to make every sound you create into an audio masterpiece. A sound becomes just another sound sometimes.

Occasionally, you will have projects where the schedule has been carefully planned and everything just falls into place. This is usually due to having a producer that is extremely on the ball, but you can't attribute it all to the producer. It may also be a really talented development team, and they're just staying on schedule, thus making things easy for everyone.

For now, pretend that you're on a project where everything is behind and that all of your sounds were due yesterday. Assume that you've been at work for nearly two days straight without being able to go home. You've just submitted your first delivery, and you made the scheduled date. You're tidying up your office a bit before you go home, taking the night off in celebration of your hard work. Suddenly an e-mail pops up. It's one of the associate producers letting you know that the files you delivered are not in the right format. The game engine that's being used requires 11kHz/8-bit .wav files. The .wav files that you delivered are still at 44kHz/16-bit. Additionally, the e-mail states that the files need to be shaved off a little bit because there's a lot of silence at the end.

Well, there goes your night off! It's easy to beat yourself up at this point. You even find the e-mail where they asked for 11kHz/8-bit files. What were you thinking? Considering you delivered several hundred files, you know that it's going to take some time to convert them, unless.... What if you could automate the procedure? What if there was a program that could convert all of the files you delivered at once? What if there was software that could trim the time off of the end of your files? Such a program is called a *batch converter*. Yeah, I know I've mentioned it in other parts of this book, but now the batch converter is finally getting its moment! This chapter is entirely on batch converting. I'm going to focus on the way batch converting can save you time and energy.

In the predicament above, the solution is really simple. Most batch converters can convert file types easily. Also, they can trim the ends off of the files, add time on to the ends of files, create gaps, and so on. In game development, time is of the essence—when you know shortcuts for problems that are presented, not only do you save yourself time, but you make yourself look good in the process.

Granted, the problem that I presented above was your fault because you didn't follow instructions. You missed a vital part of the request. You'd be surprised how much you forget, though, when you haven't had a day off in weeks and have been leaving work at 3 A.M. on a Sunday!

What Is a Batch Converter?

First, start by learning what a **batch converter** really does. Essentially, it's a simple, small program that can be directed to process a group of audio files in various ways. It can basically do everything that your wave editor can do but to a group of files, instead of one file at a time.

For example, if you need to add reverb to every file in a certain set, you would simply drop them into a batch converter, tell the batch converter to process them with reverb, and then tell the batch converter what reverb setting to use. In about a minute, the batch converter will spit out several copies of the same files (or overwrite the files, if you prefer), but now they will all have reverb! This seriously beats the hell out of having to apply reverb individually to every audio file in a set. That can just get messy and ugly.

Batch converters tend to ship with most of the wave editors that are available these day. In fact, if your wave editor doesn't have a batch converter, you might do well to move on to one that does. Wave editors that I know have batch converters are the following:

* Wavelab (Steinberg)
* Peak (BIAS)
* Sound Forge (Sony Digital)
* Barbabatch (Audio Ease)

Other programs do have them, but these are the big three wave editors. For this chapter, I'll be focusing on Wavelab.

❄ **Batch Converters Need Fast Computers**
Batch converters actually work faster and more efficiently based on your machine's processor speed. Essentially, the faster the computer, the faster the batching. If you're currently in the market for a new computer, don't skimp on the processor speed!

Batch File Renaming

Wavelab has recently (version 6) been updated with some features that make it truly helpful for video games. One of the newer features that I'll discuss is the Batch Rename feature. At first this may seem like one of the most boring features available, but, believe me, you have no idea how often files may need to be renamed.

When creating a video game, there is usually a naming convention set up by the development team. This is an easy way for them to know what is what, who it should be assigned to, what level it plays on, and so on. There's really no consistency in how the naming structure is set up from project to project, but I can give you an example. Say you're on a fictional team that wants you to label sounds by the first three letters of the character name, the number of the level that he appears on, and a short description of the sound that the character is making. So maybe the file name will look something like this: ROB02LASER1. The name is mapped out like this: Robot, level 2, the first variation of laser fire that the robot makes. This is pretty cut and dry, and it tells the person that will be wiring the sound where to assign the sound within the engine, and so on.

Now suppose you find out that all of the file names are supposed to be lowercase. Yeah, it sounds stupid that something so small could affect how sound files play, but it does occur! What do you do? Back in the day, I can tell you what I would have been doing—renaming every file one at a time. This tedious work could sometimes take an hour or so of precious time, and it also ran the risk of introducing human error. For example, what if I mistakenly gave one of the files the wrong name while I was in a hurry?

Using a tool like the one available in Wavelab lets you avoid having to do something as tedious as this and lets you move on with your job, possibly avoiding some serious mistakes later on. For this exercise, if you don't have Wavelab, you can simply read along or check to see if your wave editor has a similar function.

Fix those files! I'm going to open up Wavelab, click the Tools menu shown in Figure 8.1, and choose Batch File Renaming.

Once you've selected the tool, the Rename screen will pop up. This is the interface for the actual tool. It looks surprisingly simple doesn't it? I'll go ahead and describe the options on the first page, shown in Figure 8.2.

Figure 8.1

Finding the Batch Rename tool is easy—just look under Tools.

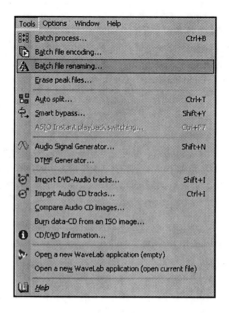

- The first field at the top is the area where you tell the tool what directory you want it to work in. In my case, it's the Robot Sounds directory.

- The first checkbox underneath is the Scan Sub-Folders setting. This tells the tool to not only relabel everything in the current directory but also the subfolders.

- The next box, Rename All Files, indicates whether you want to rename all files or only certain files. If you deselect this setting, the options below it will no longer be un-selectable. As you can see, I've checked this section because every file in the folder will be affected.

- Only Rename Files with This Extension allows you to change the file names that have differing names from one another—if you only want to rename .aiff files and leave the .wav files alone, for example.

- Skip Read-Only Files tells the tool not to mess with files that have been marked as Read Only.

- Set New Extension allows you to change the files to any file extension that you want. They can be .wav, .aiff, and so on. Keep in mind, it's usually better to use a regular batch converter for this, unless the extension is highly uncommon and you don't need to change the sample rate, and so on.

- At the bottom, you will notice a small drop-down menu. Here you can save your Batch Rename process for later, in case you think you might use it again.

- When you hit the Next button at the bottom, you will be taken to page 2 of the Batch Rename tool.

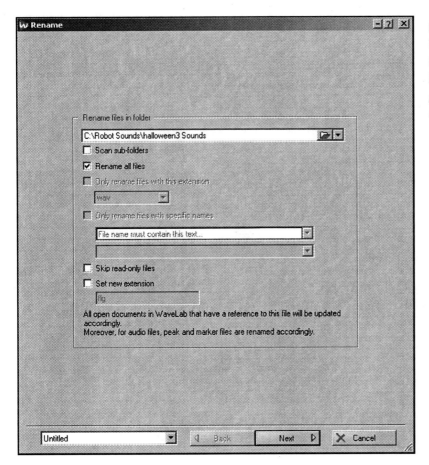

Wow, that was a lot to cover in the first page, huh? Well, wait until you see the next page! As you can see there are several more options. You'll notice in Figure 8.3 that I've set the operation Type to Convert, and in the drop-down menu below, I've set it To Lower Case.

On the right side of the screen, you can see that there is one task in the Convert list for this batch converter. You can, of course, add more tasks for the Batch Rename tool, but you're going to keep it simple. Underneath this list, you'll notice the Preview area. This handy feature allows you to type in a name, and then it will show you an example of how your Convert list choice will rename your files. Pretty handy, huh?

It looks like you have everything set up properly, so click the Preview button. Instantly, a list pops up like the one shown in Figure 8.4.

Figure 8.3

Page 2 of the Batch Rename tool gives extensive options for renaming your files. There's something for almost every situation.

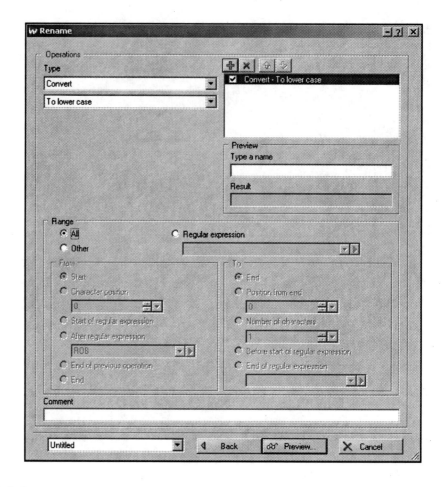

Look over the list a little bit. Do you see any errors? Me either. Go ahead and press Apply.

What happened? The page just disappeared? I guess the creators of Wavelab aren't much for small talk! They obviously don't plan on giving you a Task Completed page. Oh well, see if it actually worked. Navigate to the actual directory where all of the files are stored. In Figure 8.5, you can see that they are all perfectly lowercase now.

The last exercise may not have seemed like it was that interesting or worthy of your attention, but believe me, it's nice to know how to perform a task like this. Situations like this will occur! You may not have even been the person who named all of the files in uppercase; it could have been another sound designer. All of a sudden, you may have your lead racing into the room and asking you to convert all of these filenames.

If you don't use a batch converter, believe me, you will be cursing life when you have to do the manual steps in Windows or the Mac OS, converting one file after another. You'll be pleased to

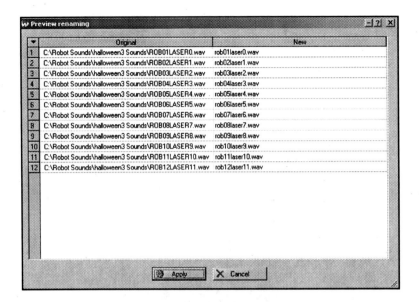

Figure 8.4
Wavelab's Preview Renaming option will show you what all the filenames will look like before it actually converts them!

know that the Batch Rename tool in Wavelab does several other tasks. You can add numbers sequentially after each filename. You can have it look for filenames that say something in particular and replace them with something else. You can even have it import and insert items, like dates and sample lengths, at the end of each file.

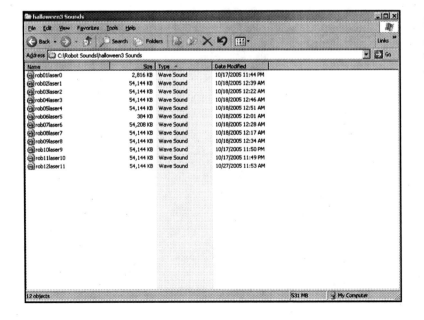

Figure 8.5
As you can see, all of the files have been converted to lowercase. Boy, did this save some time!

Again, these things seem like some of the most boring features known to man, but you never know when they will come in handy.... And they will!

Batch Processing

Batch processing is different from batch file renaming. In the earlier exercise, you were just changing the filenames. Now you're going to change the files.

Say I have a situation like the one shown in Figure 8.6. I'm using more than one effect running on a sound that I plan to render onto the file once I've tweaked the settings where I want them.

Figure 8.6

I'm using more than one effect on my sound in the Wavelab Master section. How will I batch process this?

When I click the Render button, the file is burned. Later on, though, I decide that I want to put this effect on several files. Something about this effect combination just brings out something cool in the sounds.

Believe it or not, you can actually save your effect combinations within the Master section of Wavelab! What's even more cool is that you can bring up these effect combinations in the batch converter later on. Don't worry, this feature is not unique to Wavelab. To my knowledge, Sound Forge and Peak both allow this. They may just go about it in different ways. Go ahead and see how this works.

The first thing I do is open the batch processor in Wavelab. Go up to Tools and select Batch Process, as shown in Figure 8.7

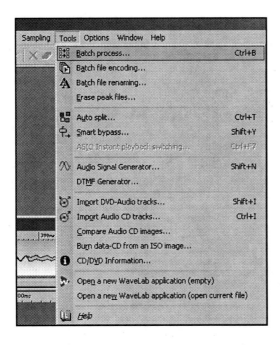

Figure 8.7
Thankfully, the batch processor is in the same spot as the Batch Rename tool, which makes it easy to find.

After I select it, the batch processor pops up. At the moment it's blank, because I haven't started anything yet. But this will soon change. Check out Figure 8.8 for an example of what the batch processor looks like when you first open it up.

Once I'm in the batch processor, I call up the directory of the robot sounds I was working on renaming in the previous exercise. After I admire their lowercase splendor, I drag them into the batch processor.

If you look in Figure 8.9, you'll see that the batch processor has changed significantly. There are now plenty of files in there to work on, and it looks as if they are in some kind of folder.

Figure 8.8

Like the Batch Rename tool, the batch processor looks amazingly simple. It can get as complex as you want it too, however.

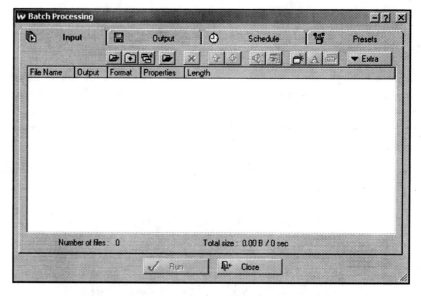

Figure 8.9

When sounds are added to the batch processor, they are added to a batch folder. There can be several batch folders depending on what you need the batch processor to do...and how good you are at programming it.

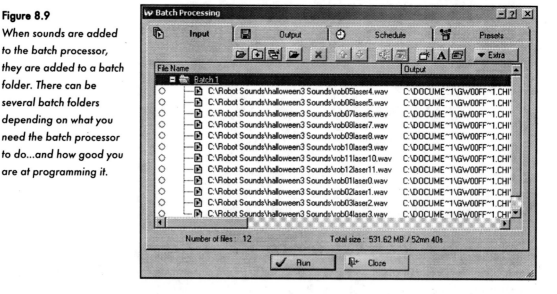

When sounds are added to the Wavelab batch processor, they are placed inside of a batch folder. The batch folder isn't necessarily a real folder within the operating system. It's more like a project folder for your files while they are being used within the batch processor. Additionally, these folders contain the instructions for what you want the batch processor to do to the files.

You may have several folders in the batch processor at a time, each folder containing different instructions and different files. In reality, you could program the batch processor to do your entire days worth of work! When I double-click the folder called Batch 1 in the Batch Processing screen, the Processor List window pops up, like what's shown in Figure 8.10.

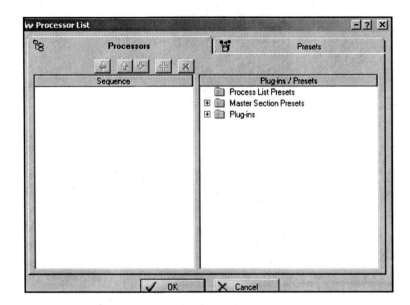

Figure 8.10
When you double-click the Batch 1 folder, the Processor List screen appears. This screen allows you to add in the instructions for what is supposed to be done to these audio files.

Again, like the main Batch Processing screen, the Processor List screen is empty until you assign instructions to it. But first, how do I assign all of those plug-in settings exactly the way I set them up in the Master section? To answer this, go back the Master section before proceeding any further.

In the Master section shown in Figure 8.11, I've circled the Presets button, which allows you to save and load presets that you've created for the Master section. You can save pretty much any combination. You can have up to eight plug-ins with their settings saved within each preset. This feature really comes in handy when you've done more than a couple of things to make a sound.

For example, say that my source audio file is a footstep. What I really need is an ethereal footstep in the netherworld, however. First I add a reverb to add a little ambience to the footstep, then I add a chorus to give it that washed kind of effect. After I have the effect right, I decide to EQ it a little bit to give it a little more low end.

I remember later on that I have other characters that are going to need footstep processing like this as well, so I end up making a preset in the Master section by pressing the Presets button. Immediately, the Master Section Presets screen pops up, like what you see in Figure 8.12.

Figure 8.11

The Presets button in the Master section allows you to save combinations of effects and settings that you used to get a certain sound.

In the Master Section Presets window, I'm able to save my preset. In the upper-right corner is a field for me to type in the name of my preset, which I've named Ambient Footstep. You can see an example in Figure 8.13. Once it's named, click the Add button. Immediately, the name shows up in the Presets list (see Figure 8.14). Additionally, all of the previously grayed out options are now available.

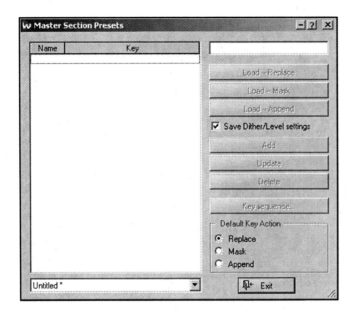

Figure 8.12
The Master Section Presets screen allows me to save my Master section preset. You'll notice that there's plenty of room for more presets!

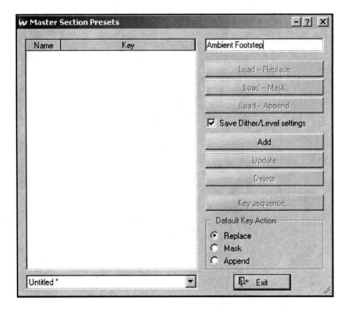

Figure 8.13
Adding a preset to the Master section is extremely easy, and the Master Section Presets screen has multiple uses.

With the preset added, I click the Exit button. I return to the Batch Processing window that I left open earlier. Again, I double-click on the Batch 1 folder and the Processor List opens again.

Figure 8.14

The name shows up in the Presets list.

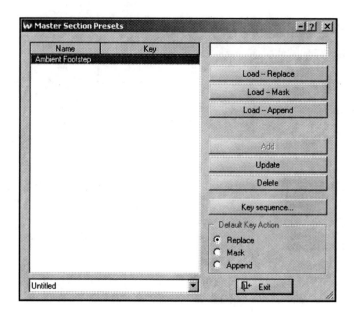

On the right, you'll notice a list of folders in the Plug-Ins/Presets area. Open up the Master Section Presets folder and my Ambient Footstep patch is available within (see Figure 8.15).

Figure 8.15

Now that the Master section preset has been saved, it shows up in the Plug-Ins/Presets area of the Processor List.

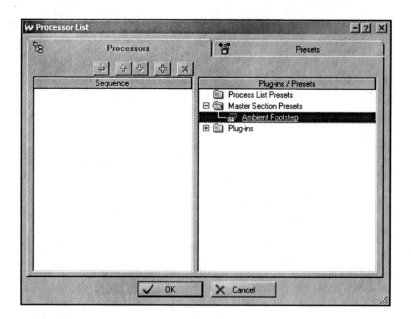

Once I double-click the Ambient Footstep patch, the preset is loaded into the Processor List. Don't forget to double-click. I remember a few times when I started an extensive batch process that was processing several files and later came back to discover that nothing happened because I forgot to load the preset!

After loading the preset, you'll notice in the Sequence area all of the different plug-ins that were used to make the preset, as shown in Figure 8.16.

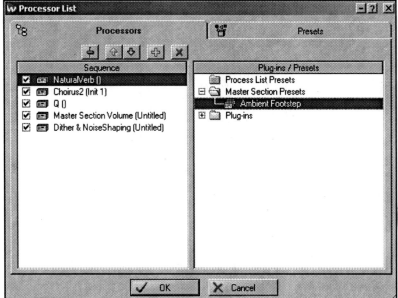

Figure 8.16
Once you've loaded the Master section preset, the Sequence area will display all of the plug-ins that were used to make the preset.

After loading the preset, click the OK button at the bottom of the Processor List screen. Now the batch processor is locked and loaded! But you're not quite ready yet. At this point, you need to know where the batch processor is going to put the files. There are many different ways to do this. You can find those options by clicking the Output tab at the top of the Batch Processing window.

In Figure 8.17, you can see what the Output page looks like. The most important part is the Output File Names section. This is where you tell the batch processor which destination folder to place your files in. You can either type in the location, or you can click the File button that I circled for you. This button will allow you to use a browser to select your preferred location.

Figure 8.17

On the Output tab, you are able to tell the batch processor where it should put your files.

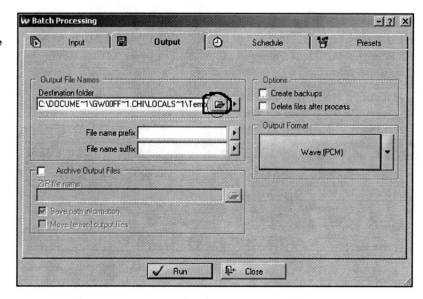

❄ Choosing Formats

On the Output tab, you also can tell the batch processor how to save your files. In the Output Format section, you could choose .aiff instead of .wav.

I decide to use the browser to select where my file will be saved. I push the button and the Browse for Folder dialog box appears. It can be seen in Figure 8.18.

Figure 8.18

The browser allows me to choose where I want my file to be placed. I can even create a new folder from here if need be.

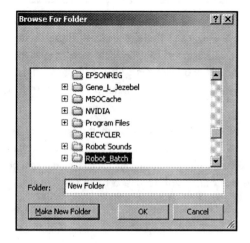

I decide to make a new folder called Robot_Batch, as you can see in the last figure. Basically, I'm good to go now. But before I start of the batch processor, let me go over some of the things on the Output tab because you will undoubtedly find them helpful later on (refer to Figure 8.17).

Within the Output File Names section, you can also elect to add a prefix or a suffix to your saved file. This may be helpful if your project has special naming conventions for files that you may have to put up on an FTP, for example.

In Figure 8.19, I've circled the Archive Output Files area. When this section is enabled, you can output your files within a ZIP file. This is another handy feature if you have to store your files on an FTP site or e-mail them to someone. Granted, it's only a small bit of compression, but every bit helps. You also don't have to worry about the files being separated. Additionally, you can have the path information saved within the ZIP file. This just retains the file hierarchy if you are processing multiple files. As for the Move (Erase) Output Files option, this will eliminate the un-compressed version of the files. I'd elect to leave that option alone. You can always delete the output files later, but you never know when you might need them.

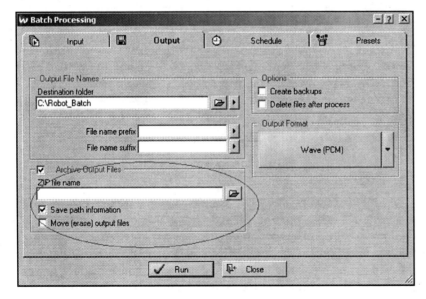

Figure 8.19
Wavelab even allows you to export your files in a ZIP file. Pretty thoughtful, huh?

The next section to cover is the Options area circled in Figure 8.20. This section allows you to have the batch processor Create Backups or Delete Files After Process.

Figure 8.20

The Options section can be very helpful or very hurtful if you aren't paying attention to what you're doing!

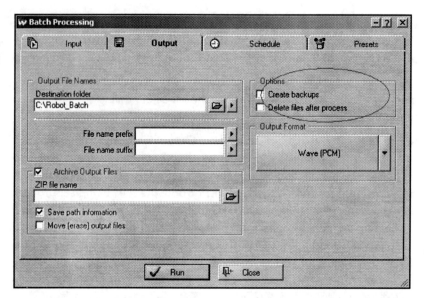

> **❋ Keep Your Original Files**
>
> Do not use the Delete Files After Process option. You never know if the batch processor, no matter how stable, is going to glitch or if you put in the wrong settings while eating your morning donut. If you opt to delete these files and there is a problem, you are stuck. There is no going back.
>
> I tend to keep one backup on my personal computer and another on the network. Other people burn regular DVD backups. This is a personal preference, of course, but it's not a bad idea. Perhaps I'm living on the edge a little?

I've had a few moments in my career when the blood has drained rapidly from my face, and, usually, it had something to do with a batch processor. Always create backups before you batch process! One time I had 1200 voice lines that needed to be processed with reverb within a very short amount of time. Even with a batch processor, it still takes a little time to process that many files. The batch processor glitched during the process and ruined my files. I had to retrieve a very early backup that our IT department had to dig off of the server. It almost set us back a week.

Finally, as shown in Figure 8.21, there is the Output Format area. This is a wonderful section that allows you to choose what file type you want to export as. Wavelab has an extensive amount of file formats to choose from (see Figures 8.21 and 8.22).

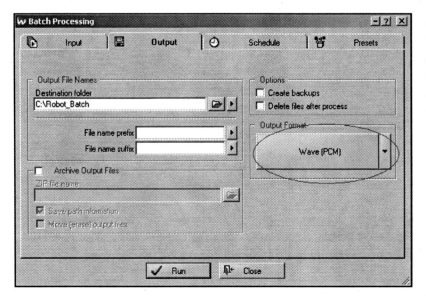

Figure 8.21
The Output Format section allows you to choose what format the final files will be saved as. There are many different formats to choose from.

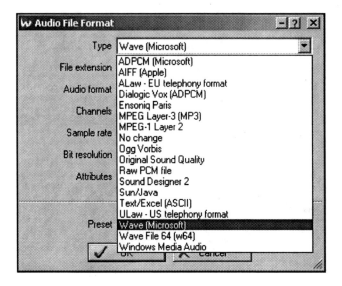

Figure 8.22
The Presets list shows the name.

Now that we've gone over all of the different export options, I think you're able to finally batch process! I know you're excited, so I won't embellish much more than I need to. At the bottom of the Batch Processing screen, go ahead and click the Run button. Immediately the Monitor window appears, showing me the progress bar of each file as the batch processor goes through all of them (see Figure 8.23).

Figure 8.23

The Monitor window is a handy screen that tells you how much time is left to batch each individual file.

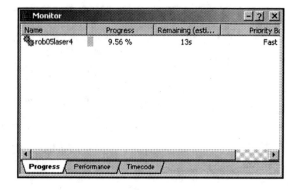

In Batch Processing window, you can not only see a list of all the files, but also which file the program is currently working on. Wavelab does a great job of letting you know "if we're there yet." This is particularly handy when your boss is breathing down your neck and asking if those files are done! See Figure 8.24.

Figure 8.24

You can monitor how many files are left to process from the Batch Processing window. This is handy when those files were needed yesterday.

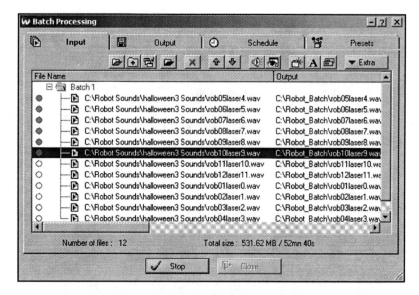

Quick Keys

There's another program that I've made great use of out there called Quick Keys. You can use this program to make all sorts of key commands that do multiple functions. When I've thought of something that I could automate, but it wasn't in my batch processor, I use this program. You can find out more information at www.quickkeys.com.

9 Mixing Cut Scenes

A **cut scene** is either a pre-rendered movie or a scripted scene where a major plot point unfolds. These scenes are usually designed to impress the player and help tell the story. Here's an example: You've been battling your way through thousands of zombies. You get up to the altar that rains a holy fire down on the undead minions. Immediately a movie starts, showing you sitting down next to the altar and a thousand ghosts rising up. A voice booms, "You have saved us from a lifetime of servitude throughout the ages as undead! Please accept this token of our gratitude." A gleaming sword appears and your character begins swinging it around and smiling. He thrusts it up in the air and the spirits rejoice! The scene fades out and the scrolling credits let you know that it's the end.

That end scene is a cut scene. It gives the character an ending and lets you know what happened to the hero. It's the piece of cheese that you are running through the maze for. Without it, it's almost like you're doing it for nothing. Players can't accept that. Stories have become a major factor in how games are graded these days. When people begin playing a character for even a short period of time, they tend to bond with that character. Additionally, players just need a break! Games are challenging and it's nice to stop and catch your breath before going onto a harder level.

How do cut scenes affect you? Players have come to expect these scenes to be audibly, as well as visibly, exciting and interesting. Sound and music play a pivotal role during these scenes, and composers and sound designers are expected to really show their stuff. Gamers have nice audio systems at home these days, and they want to play games that sound great on their systems.

And really, it goes beyond wanting to reward the players. Most people work nine-to-five jobs: get up, go to work, and repeat it all over again the next day. Games are the escape for many people. They are a way to feel like the hero you always thought you were (until you figured out that you weren't seven feet tall and bullet proof). So when you get a chance to play the hero in a game, you want to be completely immersed. You want the explosions, the gunfire, and the glory ... and most of all you want some recognition for your efforts. You want the parades and the undying gratitude of an alien civilization. You want to get the girl! You'd also like to taste the winning side of grasping power.

This chapter focuses on adding sounds and mixing down cut scenes so that they really do add to the performance that the artists have put in. We're going to focus on adding in ambience, we'll focus on blending in Foley tracks, we'll mix in a little music and we'll add some gunshots and explosions! Sounds fun, right? Well it is! It's where video games meet the movies! It's where you get a chance to be really theatrical and get creative with your mix. And this is definitely the time to do it.

During cut scenes you have a captive audience. This means that you can pan things the way you want, automate volumes, and totally control the mix. In other parts of the game, the player can move around and, as he does, the mix changes around him. Not here! This may seem like a very intimidating exercise, but in actuality, it's a way to show that not only are you a sound designer, but you're also a hero!

The First Cut Scene

In this segment of the book you add the music and mix the cut scene together.

I'll be doing it in Nuendo. If you aren't using Nuendo, don't worry; just verify that your host application has the ability to play a movie file. I recommend starting out with any old .avi, .mov, or .mpeg file and importing it into your host application. You can always kill the audio and add your own.

You'll be mixing this movie for surround. Every cut scene these days is mixed in surround and then later encoded as a stereo audio file that plays back as a surround file (as long as the consumer's system has the proper encoder).

> ❖ **Are You Surrounded?**
>
> This chapter assumes that you do have a surround speaker system because, in reality, I couldn't walk you through mixing a surround cut scene without one.
>
> If you do not have a surround speaker system, practice putting together a cut scene in stereo format. There's a slight difference, but it's worth getting the editing and mixing time in.

The Stage

The stage where all the actors, creatures, and environment will be seen and heard consists of a small screen on your computer and six speakers. In Figure 9.1, I've made a diagram of what the speaker configuration will look like. As you can see, the setup has five smaller speakers and one large speaker in the middle. The large speaker is the **subwoofer**, or **sub**. This speaker emits only the low-frequency effects, also commonly referred to as the **LFE**. You feel the low-frequency impacts through the sub, which picks up where the other speakers can't go. The sub cannot play sounds above a certain frequency.

Figure 9.1
This is a standard 5.1 surround speaker setup.

When you listen to all the speakers at the same time, most of the action occurs in the front channels, but certain sounds will be mixed in the back to create the feeling that things are going on in the back. Additionally, the person mixing usually separates certain tracks to make the audio more dimensional. In all reality, she's setting up a sonic stage and the listener is placed smack dab in the middle of it.

Imagine yourself in the middle of this diagram. Four speakers are in front of you. Behind you, there are two speakers. You hear the music fade in on the back left and back right. The music is stereo, so it's low in the back and takes up a little bit of both speakers. Now imagine the ambient tracks filling up the front speakers in stereo. You hear rain, lightning, thunder. Occasionally, a little bit of thunder goes off in the back speakers. Suddenly you hear footsteps in the front, somewhere between the left and center channels. The main character is walking into the picture. While he's walking, his footsteps move slightly from the left to the center speaker. As he walks, you hear a leaf rustle to the right and some birds chirp on the left. The music is still playing low in the background. In the distance, gunfire goes off low in the left channel. The sub gives off a slight thump as the character hits the ground. You hear the gun being pulled in the center speaker and then fire slightly between the center and left speakers. A bullet round pings in the right speaker.

It's pretty cool to imagine, huh? Imagining ahead of time, while you're watching the movie, is a great way to get an idea of what you're going to need before you start. You can basically assemble your palette before you begin, so you aren't throwing stuff in willy nilly. Now that you've visualized, start assembling!

Music

Adding the music is one of the first steps in gathering elements for a cut scene. The music lets you know immediately how much "room" you have for the rest of the audio in the cut scene. For example, say there's a fast-action sequence. This means the music is going to be very big and fill up a lot of space. You can add the must-have sounds like gunshots, explosions, and so on, but it might be tough to fit in some of those subtle sounds, like breathing. Well, at least the whole way through.

Make a point to have parts of the music die down—for instance, when the hero ducks behind a wall before giving his second round of butt kicking. When the music is at a minimum and the drums are light, bring up the breathing and movement, or **Foley**, sounds for a moment. Then, when the music kicks up again, pull back the lighter movement sounds (you won't be able to hear them anyway) and focus on the action sounds, like gunfire.

Who prepares music for the cut scene? That would be the composer! It's her job to make a music track that works perfectly with the cut scene. The composer

* Creates music and times it to perfectly match the cut scene.

* Upon using existing music, cuts the music to perfectly match the cut scene. This includes making a good entrance and exit.

Why am I mentioning this in the sound designer section of the book? Because the sound designer is in charge of mixing in the music for the cut scene. She determines the level at which the music plays.

In Figure 9.2 I've brought an audio file into Nuendo and it matches the movie that I will mix. This is what the cut scene mix looks like at the beginning. At this point, I find a suitable level for the music, somewhere a few decibels below – 12 dB. I want to make sure to give it plenty of headroom for when I start adding the rest of the sounds. I absolutely cannot have the volume go above 0 dB. If that happens, it could introduce digital distortion when it's being played back after the final mix.

Another thing is, the music should be around the middle of a surround mix so you can create a scene. This way you can have most of the action going on in the front channels and the music low between the middle and back speakers to give some dimension. The music is still present, it's just low in the center of the stage. It's a support element, the way it should be.

Thankfully, Nuendo has a limiter that you can add over the entire mix. This allows you to work without having to constantly watch the meter.

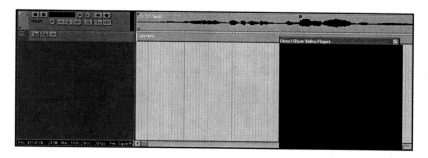

Figure 9.2

I've brought in an audio file and a movie file. From here I match the two up and continue.

Ambience

An ambient track is good for the beginning; insert something that sounds like the environment the cut scene is taking place in. If your character is next to a waterfall, have a waterfall going in the background. If your character is in a jungle, have birds chirping. If your character is in a spaceship, try some white noise and sci-fi sounds. Maybe your scene is a very windy city? Have some wind blowing with some chatter going on here and there. The main thing is to immerse your listener and help him believe in the environment that's being shown.

Ambience should be in any and all channels. It's recommended to use four-channel surround. This means having ambience in the front left, front right, back left, and back right. You can see in my cut scene (in Figure 9.3) I've taken two ambiences. The two ambiences are similar and are both stereo, creating a true surround environment. One ambience is positioned toward the front speakers and the other toward the back speakers.

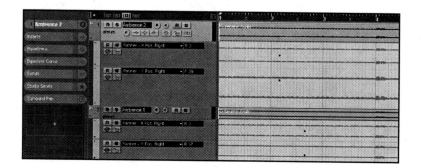

Figure 9.3

I've taken two stereo ambiences and positioned one toward the front speakers and one toward the rear.

Assume for a moment that you don't have some sort of ambient environment track to use for your cut scene. They really aren't that hard to create. Try to put yourself in that place. Watch the video and imagine what it sounds like there. From there you get some ideas for where to get sounds to make an ambient environment.

If you're in a crunch, you could always try going to a Web site like www.soundrangers.com to buy individual sound FX. If you do a search for "ambience" on that site, a slew of backgrounds come up. You can buy these backgrounds for a small price. When purchasing, ensure that it's stereo. You don't want a mono ambience that's in the center channel or panned to the front left or right. What if you find the perfect background ambience, but it isn't long enough for your cut scene? That's simple. Just make a copy of the ambient background and repeat it. You can always dice it up a bit too; this way it's not repetitious.

Foley

The next step in adding sound to our cut scene is adding Foley. **Foley** refers to the natural sounds like footsteps, breathing, opening a door, and the like. Because of how much space music takes, Foley should remain at a minimum in a cut scene. It should be kept to the amount of sound you know you can hear naturally (depending on the camera angle and how close it is to its subject).

For example, say your main character is in a dark alleyway with some very low, moody music playing. Know those suspenseful scenes when you realize something bad is about to happen? That music consists of a couple of notes without anything else. It's acting as ambience. In a part like this, it's easy to add some footsteps and maybe some breathing (if the camera is really close to the character). Say the character accidentally kicks a bottle; throw in the sound of breaking glass, too.

Suddenly, monsters swarm! The music becomes very big and theatrical. The character starts shooting like crazy at all the monsters around him. With everything going on, you can't really hear the footsteps or the low growls. All you can hear are the loud roars, screams, and yelps as monsters are maimed. It's at this point you have to evaluate what *needs* to be heard compared to what you *may* hear. If the music is suddenly huge, you're going to have a hard time making your Foley cut through. You'd have a hard time hearing things like bullets hitting the ground, unless there is a close-up of bullets falling on the ground. If the camera is up close to your hero, you should be able to hear his every breath. If the camera is above him, you should be able to hear his footsteps.

Where do you get Foley material? I mentioned this library in an earlier chapter, but I'll mention it here, as it truly pertains: The General 6000 package from Sound Ideas. If you don't have access to a Foley pit, this is an excellent choice. Because there tend to be a lot of cut scenes when you are working on a game, creating Foley material for every cut scene is probably not the best idea, unless you have the time.

The Pits

Major recording studios have sound stages with several small trap doors in them. These trap doors open to reveal several surfaces and what appears to be pieces of junk. These items create different footsteps, scrapes, scratches, and all other manner of Foley work. Do you have to use one of these **Foley pits**? Absolutely not! You can use a microphone at home.

Foley is basically in the center front channels left and right unless action is happening in the rear. Technically, Foley can be anywhere and should be, depending on what's happening onscreen. It's just nice to keep it mostly in the front, where it gets the most attention.

The cut scene in Figure 9.4 shows three Foley tracks. I've panned one toward the left/center. One is toward the right, where I've added some automation to pan it toward the left. The last only occurs once in this shot; I've kept it mainly in the center.

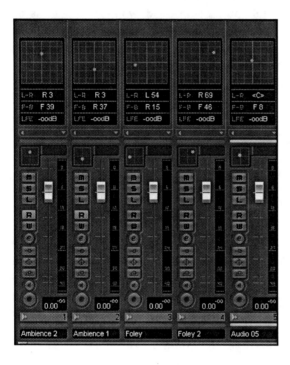

Figure 9.4
For Foley, you should always pan your tracks in a way that makes sense with what's happening onscreen.

Make sure that you have the right kind of footstep first. Is the character walking on grass, brick, tile? Is she outdoors or in? All of these things matter. Imagine a character walking through a grassy field, but whose footsteps sound like she's walking on cobblestones. Would that make sense at all? Nah, not at all.

❈ **Matching Footsteps**
What about footsteps that are moving faster than the character is moving? Cut the footsteps to match what's happening onscreen! Using the Scissors tool in Nuendo (or the Cut tool in your audio program), simply cut the footsteps and arrange them to match what's happening. In Figure 9.4 I've cut footsteps and coordinated them with onscreen steps. It can be a little tedious, but you'll be happy with the results once you get the hang of it.

Sound FX

Now that we've laid a nice sonic foundation, it's time for the fun part: sound FX. Bring out the big guns, the explosions, the flame, and fire. You're going to blow something up!

Sound FX consist of gunshots, explosions, swoops, and other assorted sounds. This is generally the fun part, but like Foley, it does take a little work to match what happens onscreen. For example, assume a machine gun is rattling off bullets in burst. If the burst is too long, cut and fade the burst until it sounds natural. I am not saying that you should slow down the video frame and match every bullet fired. Just get the bullet spray close enough to be believable. No one will be slowing down the video to double-check your work. Another example is a pistol. Finding single bullet shots is easier, but you still need to match them. What if your character runs out of bullets and needs to replace his clip? Match that, too.

Where can you get sound FX? Try these sources:

 ❋ Sound Ideas General 6000 bundle. Chock full of worthy gunshots, explosions, and reloads. Check them out at www.sound-ideas.com.

 ❋ Online. Just one example is Soundrangers at www.soundrangers.com. This company has many sound FX that you can purchase individually online.

 ❋ Your personal sound library.

 ❋ Sounds in another sound bundle that you have permission to use.

Sound FX are generally placed in the front channels: front left, front right, and center. Sound FX should be panned all over by the listener, so here you get to have some fun. I strongly recommend automating your panning in this particular part of the process. There's nothing cooler than hearing certain sounds moving left to right, and sometimes front to back. I'm not saying every sound should be automated. If you do that, no one's going to notice all your hard work. Just automate the panning of a few sounds here and there to spice things up a bit.

Sound FX that go on in the background should be kept to an extreme minimum and occur only when it makes sense. For example: A mortar round flies over and lands out of screen and behind the character. Add a few sounds in the back to create dimension, but try to reserve this area for ambience and music. In Figure 9.5 I've added some FX tracks to my cut scene and applied bits of panning automation here and there.

Figure 9.5

Automation on your sound FX tracks applies movement and simulates reality.

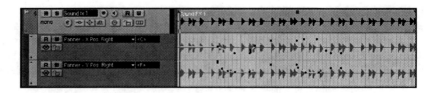

Voice

Voice is one of the most important elements in a cut scene. Voice lines tell a major part of the story and give the game humanity. Voice makes a game immersive. Granted, graphics have improved enough to convey emotion on characters' faces, but the voice really helps you empathize with the character.

How much could you relate to *Pac-Man* back in the day? When he got hurt, did you feel bad for him? Did you ever tell yourself, "Oooh, that must have hurt!" Compare *Pac-Man* to today's *Medal of Honor*, where you hear soldiers screaming. I do not mean to glorify destruction and death; I mean to illustrate how much you are drawn in when you hear that human element calling out. It scares you. It mortifies you.

When adding voice to a cut scene, take special care to match the voice with character lips. Sometimes characters aren't onscreen; you can work around it. Sometimes the character is wearing a mask; the head will move, however.

The voice must always be audible and present in the mix, especially when it comes to dialogue. Dialogue drives the scene and tells the story; if the player misses what's being said, it's unforgivable. However, be careful. Any extremely loud screams need to ride the levels and possibly be pulled back so they're not out of control. Have them audible, but not overwhelming.

If many deaths or similarly dramatic events are occurring onscreen, only a few should be heard. Hearing them all can make it overwhelming. I generally have a different track for each character within the scene. In Figure 9.6 I've labeled each character and each has its own track. Try to organize yours this way as well. Separating them lets you know when one character is too loud, where in the scene he is too loud, and so on.

Figure 9.6
*Give each speaking
character a track.*

❈ **Try a Compressor**
Try adding a compressor to a track within a cut scene. Any track that has a wide dynamic range will work, including a voice track. A compressor helps keep the volume from going all over the place and helps you avoid the very tedious entering of automation points all over your work.

Effects—Adding Plug-Ins

When putting together the audio for your cut scene, consider creating an FX track if your environment would actually merit it. I don't mean sound FX—I mean FX like reverbs, echoes, flanging, and so on. For example, if your cut scene's environment takes place in a forest or desert, you might not want to add FX. If your environment is a dense valley with lots of rock formations, you might want to add some reverb or echo. Reverb and other FX help flesh out the cut scene's audio. It makes it sound more real. Try adding some to yours and see how it adds to the experience.

The Final Mix

Now that you've added all your sounds , matched them up, and performed some light automation, it's time to go ahead and mix it! After all the sounds are in, it's good to play what you have and see where you are. It might even be better if you take a break and later listen to everything back to back. Go ahead and take a break; I'll wait.... Now that you're back with fresh ears, take a listen to what you've assembled. During playback, you may be tempted to start editing while it's going. Instead, I suggest taking notes. When you've listed everything that bugs you, you can go back and make your edits.

After playback has finished, you'll probably notice that the cut scene audio is more like a big wall of sound that just hits you at once. It's normal for your first cut scenes to sound like this. You may find sounds you don't need at all; some seem redundant or don't fit in. Don't be afraid to remove audio. By going through and removing unneeded audio, you are actually improving your mix. You're getting things down to the bare essentials. The important thing is to have sounds that matter. If you see the character taking a deep breath, there should be a breath there. If you see a character cocking his shotgun, there should be a cocking sound.

What you want to avoid is having too many small things. What are the odds of you being able to hear the material movement of a character's pants? Would you even want to?! Would you want to hear the character's every breath? The players can fill in the gaps with their imaginations. It's your job to supply the main elements.

It's also important to make sure that the character's main actions are up and audible in the mix. If you notice a character clearing his throat, that noise should be very audible. If two characters fire a gun within a scene, you should hear those guns firing. There may be guns firing offscreen, but the most important ones are those the camera is showing. And don't forget voice! Voice stems have to be audible. Try to keep them near the middle of the stage.

Now check the music level. Is it interfering with the action? It shouldn't be above –12 dB. How's the ambience? It should be audible but definitely in the background. The Foley tracks should be up front enough that you can make them out, but aren't too obtrusive. For example, if the character lights up a cigarette, should the lighter be louder than everything else onscreen? No. It should be seamless so players notice the sound, but don't exclaim, "That is the loudest lighter I've ever heard!" It just comes down to common sense. Again, try imagining that you are there with the characters. What does it sound like?

When loud occurrences like explosions start happening, they should definitely stand out; but are there too many? If a huge music track takes up a lot of space, are the explosions competing? Pull some back so it sounds like there's action, but the music is still there, along with all of the rest of the Foley and sound FX.

Once everything is automated and ready to go, it will look a lot like Figure 9.7. Everything is where it needs to be and it's ready to be bounced out as an audio track.

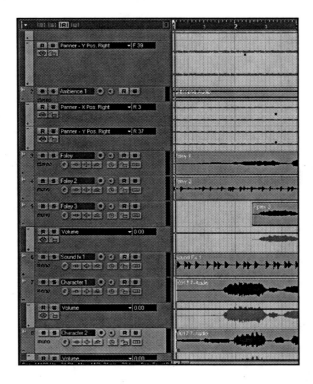

Figure 9.7
This is the final mix. You're ready to export it as an audio file.

To export, I go into Nuendo's audio export page, shown in Figure 9.8, and set up the proper parameters. I know to export it as a stereo interleaved file, and I choose the DTS format so the surround channels are folded in. When this file plays back on a DTS decoder, all the channels will play back accordingly as a surround mix.

Figure 9.8

I'm exporting a surround session as a stereo interleaved file.

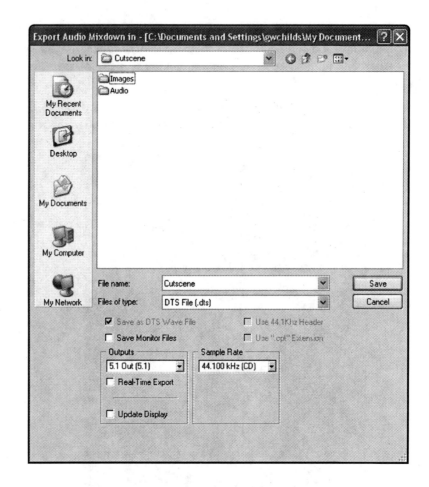

10 } Composers: The Game Design

Composing music for video games is without a doubt one of the most desired fields in the game industry. Every time I meet someone new, and I happen to mention that I have a background in the video game industry, if they are musicians, one of the first questions asked is, "So who do I talk to about getting my music into a video game?" Their eyes are full of hope and enthusiasm. And what's my usual response? I usually just say, "It's not easy."

Why do I say that it's not easy?

First, just think about the music industry itself for a second. Right now, music is in high demand, and it's really easy to get a hold of. Piracy is at an all-time high, and that's made music sales slump for many artists. Record labels have to get more and more creative on a daily basis to stay afloat. I talked to one record executive the other day who is with a reputable record label. He mentioned that not even a day after they released a new CD, it was up for free download on some pirate Web site. And why would someone want to buy something that they can get for free? The bottom line is, it's hard to be in the music industry today.

So knowing that piracy is still causing so many problems, you might wonder what record labels are doing to make money. The answer is simple, and considering what the topic of this book is, you're probably going to guess.... Record labels are now actively promoting their artists' materials for licensing in film, television, and, you guessed it, video games. This is now the gold rush for all record labels. And not only labels are doing it. There are also talent agents that specialize in this. And don't delude yourself into thinking it's just the small-time musicians trying to break in. It's all the musicians. There are big-name bands, with great reputations and big followings, looking just as hard as you might be. Most big-name bands and musicians worked hard to get where they are...and they want to stay there. But as I said before, record labels aren't making the same kind of money that they used to. If the record labels aren't making money, then you can bet the musicians aren't either.

So why am I talking about how hard it is in a chapter that's supposed to be about learning the game design? There are two reasons. First, if you are currently in the running to have your music in a game, I'm here to tell you how lucky you are. Second, even if you aren't there yet, the next part of this chapter describes an important part of learning the game design that you might not know about—it will definitely determine whether you get the composition gig in the future or whether you lose it altogether.

The Audition

You're probably a little worried right now. You're probably reading this section's title and thinking to yourself, "An audition?! But I'm not an actor!" No, you're not an actor. You're a composer. You're the one who's supposed to write the music. But there's one way that you're similar to an actor. You're a talent that uses a medium to convey atmosphere and emotion through your craft.

Well, let me put some fears aside. When you are asked to audition to compose music for a game title, you aren't being asked to dance around in a swimsuit or perform an act. Instead, you're being asked to listen, understand what the design team has in mind for the music of the game, and then create some music that you think matches their goals.

Usually, before the composer even comes onto the scene, the design team has already talked about what they have in mind for the game's music—what kind of style they want and what kind of atmosphere that they want the music to convey.

When you get an audition for a video game, you are essentially being asked to write a piece of music (or a demo) that you think will fit, based on the background information and reference material for the title. The background information is usually the game story, information about the characters, and what the game is supposed to be about. The reference material is usually audio files, or a couple of movies that have a certain sound the design team hopes to emulate. There will also be concept art that you can use for inspiration as well.

How would movies be of any assistance with composing for a video game? Believe it or not, movies tend to influence people in the game industry just as much as they influence the rest of us. Even if the game is an original title that's not affiliated with any movie at all, I can guarantee you that the creator has a few movies that he's drawing from. The main character may be a little bit of this action hero mixed with a little bit of this other action hero. The world where all the action takes place may be similar to a recent sci-fi movie. Additionally, a designer, music director, or a producer will have to think of what type of music they want. Usually, they'll want music that emulates whatever movies they're being inspired by. This is great for you because you can take some time, watch some movies, and relax a bit before you get started.

During the audition phase, you are essentially expected to do a lot of work for no money. There will be stiff competition, you can be sure, and only a small amount of information will be given. Most composers spend an average of a week of full-time work on a music demo for a game.

During that time, you can usually talk back and forth with either the title's producer or music director. This way you can ask questions and sort of feel them out in terms of what they want. The end result is this: The design team will turn on the game and play the game to your music, listening to see if it works with the title.

But I'm sure you want to get back to the real problem here. You're going to be working a whole week for nothing. A good friend of mine and a well-known composer named Peter McConnell summed it up this way: "You have to be willing to work for free in order to work for money." McConnell mentioned that a lot of the younger, more inexperienced composers will turn down work because they aren't getting paid or it isn't a sure thing. This is a mistake. Yes, you are gambling your time and energy, but you're also getting a chance to be heard, and a chance to do something that few get the opportunity to do. This should also tell you that, if people tend to turn down working for free during this phase, you have a better chance of winning the position just by process of elimination.

But don't make assumptions! A game could appear to be more dark and brooding, when it's actually a comedic title. You can totally lose the job based on huge misconceptions. Remember, the game is still in raw form at this point. Sometimes the game may not even be playable, and that makes it hard to tell what the game is actually going look and play like.

Music in Video Games—A Small Bit of History

Music has been an important element in video games since the 1970s. Back then, music was based on MIDI (Musical Instrument Digital Interface), and it sounded very quirky and electronic. Back then, there was no recording that took place for any particular piece of music within a game. All the music was coded into the game. Games like *Pac-Man* are a very good example.

In the last 20 years, video games have gotten much more sophisticated. With the advent of digital recording, it became possible to implement digitally recorded music into a video game, rather than programming it through MIDI, as in days past.

I still remember the first time I heard a recorded symphony being played in a video game, expressly *for* a video game. It was Blizzard's *Diablo II* expansion pack. It was amazing to hear a full orchestra with the dark snowy backgrounds and evil characters tromping around trying to kill me. *Diablo* was even a two-dimensional game, yet somehow the dark somber tones of the strings gave the game new life and energy. In fact, it gave the game a new level of mystery.

Now it shouldn't be said that MIDI or programmed music isn't still being used for video games. Quite the contrary! There are several uses for programmed music with platforms like the Nintendo Gameboy, the Nintendo DS, or video games for cell phones. In this day and age, most of the music is done in the studios of professional composers using digital recording mixed with MIDI sequencing. Composers rely on sampled orchestras to fill in for the real thing. They rely on sampled drums to fill in for the real drummer. Composers have more freedom, in terms of creativity, that couldn't even be imagined 20 or 30 years ago. You can summon choirs at will, even if you can't sing. You can bring in guitars, even if you can't play.

And now, video games benefit from current technology. The action game can use the harsh metal guitars that have been so loved in past action movies. The sci-fi games can use the lush fantasy orchestras so prominent in the big sci-fi block busters. In games like the *Sims*, you can have a more personal, adult-contemporary sound one minute that can be changed to jazz with the flip of a switch. This allows the player to customize the game and feel like he's really running the show.

There are also new features in interactive music provided by game engines that weren't possible before. Music can be filtered to match what the player is doing. Music can now be directional to add a new dynamic to game play. Music can also be in complete surround to match the movies, if need be.

I think you'd agree that as composers for video games, you have a huge palette at your finger tips. Only the schedule of the project, the budget, or the programming power can really stand in your way. Unfortunately and all too frequently, these elements do.

The Team's Needs

Now assume that you've won the audition stage of the game. You've earned the title of Composer, and you've just been given a new game to compose for. It's definitely not the time to rest on your laurels. It's time to get a move on. It's time to start composing. What do you compose first? It may be a good time to ask the team what their most immediate need for music might be. For the moment, say that the team is working on a playable demo.

Demo for E3

At the beginning of any major video game, there's usually a lot of secrecy surrounding the project. Competition is fierce in the video game industry, and letting another company know your launch schedule could jeopardize your whole project.

Another thing that is carefully planned is how and where to launch the title. This is frequently done at trade shows. All the media are there, and they are eager to report on any upcoming titles. Additionally, all eyes are usually on the show at this point, as well. Hardcore gamers avidly watch the announcements during trade shows, whether they actually attend the shows or not.

The main trade show that most game companies are concerned with? Electronic Entertainment Expo (E3). This is presented every year by the Entertainment Software Association (ESA). The ESA is dedicated to serving the business and public affairs needs of companies that publish video and computer games for video game consoles, personal computers, and the Internet. Formed in 1994, the association members include the nation's leading software publishers.

The first E3 was in 1995, and it still is today what it was back then—a showcase of what's up and coming in computer and console game titles. But don't think of this trade show as a bunch of blinking video game screens. I mean, there are a lot of video game screens, but there's a lot of other stuff to see, too. You'll see huge booths with life-sized recreations of characters from your favorite games, like what is pictured in Figure 10.1.

Figure 10.1
The teeming masses of people moving through the E3 convention. You can really get feel for how big this convention is!

You'll see beautiful women and rugged men dressed as game characters. When there are games that tie in with movies, you may see movie characters walking around. You'll also see celebrities walking around in an effort to promote up-and-coming games that they appear in. Heck, you'll see celebrities walking around that are just into computer games. If you love video games, or even just like them, you'll be completely blown away by E3—a whole convention of things to see, and very little time to see it all.

So, how does E3 affect you?

Most of the time, companies are eager to have something to show and announce every year at E3. The way companies usually do this is by releasing a **game demo**, or a video trailer, highlighting a very, very polished movie depicting the game overview. Regardless of whether a company releases a video trailer or a demo, either one will need music. This is a chance for the composer to come in with guns blazing, showing the team what he or she can do.

A demo usually depicts one level of the game, usually the first level. Why? Because the first level is usually best at establishing what's going on in the game. The first level also usually has a tutorial to help the player understand how to play the game and what to do in the game.

It is crucial for the game demo to be flawless and action-packed because the whole game is riding on the success of the demo. Therefore, it is critical for the music to be as perfect as it can be. Sometimes the team will want to implement some of the features of the sound engine and how it uses music. So it's really a good idea for you to understand how the engine uses your music. This will be discussed later in the chapter.

The demo is a great place for the composer to shine. Not only is the team that you're working for seeing what you can do, you are also getting free publicity for other publishers that may want to hire you at a later date. If the music is impressive, people will ask, "Who's doing the music?" This is a great time for you to be standing around with your business cards. E3 is extremely good for networking, and nothing makes you more marketable than having a brand new demo at E3 with your music playing in it. In Chapter 15 I discuss some of the tricks you can use to make the most of your networking.

One thing to keep in mind is that sometimes the composer of the trailer, or demo for E3, may not be the same composer who does the music for the entire game. This isn't necessarily a bad thing. I know people who make very good money scoring trailers and demos expressly for E3 alone. This is another reason it's a good thing to be around with a nice stack of business cards. One demo this year could mean two demos next year. Two demos next year could mean one major title the year after that. But what if you aren't composing anything for anyone yet? Then it would still behoove you to get to the next E3 with some business cards. Information can be found at www.e3expo.com. Now that you're finished with the demo, you've got a whole new goal to accomplish: composing music for an entire game.

Portable Recorder

Composing music for an entire game, whether you know it from experience yet or not, is a daunting task. You have to provide music for every level of the game in several stages. You have to provide music for every cut scene of the game. You have to create music for the opening menus. There are a lot of holes to fill, with very little time to do so.

At the beginning of the game's production, you're going to have tons of reference material, movies, and artwork to organize. Every time you watch something, look at something, and read something, you're going to have ideas. This is a great time to start documenting those ideas as they occur. But what's a way to do this without destroying your flow? What's a fast way to do this where you can get the entire idea down safely without possibly losing the idea by booting up your computer, having the phone ring, and getting distracted? A small hand held recorder, like the one pictured in Figure 10.2, is a brilliant way to store your ideas for the future, with all their original intention, spirit, and influence.

Imagine that you are plowing through concept art for the main character of the game. As you flip through each page and see the different range of emotions and outfits that the character wears, a theme or a melody starts to form in your head. Immediately, you run over to the computer and start its boot sequence. Impatiently you hum the theme to yourself.

Suddenly, there's a knock at the door. It's the postman. He wants you to sign for a package. You smile, and sign for the package, and then you bid the postman a good day. As quick as you can, you run back over to the computer. You boot up your favorite music program. Instantly you bring up a piano sound to start playing, only to find that you forgot the melody!

Having a small portable recorder around can help you capture your ideas quickly, even with descriptions. I carry one wherever I go. Many times I've been driving around in the car humming

Figure 10.2
A voice recorder can help you keep all of those ideas intact that appear throughout the day.

to myself, and all of a sudden I'll realize that I like what I'm humming. At this point, I'll pull out my trusty, handheld digital recorder. I'll turn it on and start humming the theme or melody in my head. If need be, I'll add verbal instructions about reproducing certain properties about the production that I'm hearing in my head.

The same principal can be used when you are constructing the music of your game. Looking over concept art, you might see sweeping vistas that are drawn in with bright colors. You might find yourself humming something beautiful yet slightly mysterious. This is a good time to record your thoughts.

You find yourself looking at the concept art of the game's key villain. You begin reading his back story and find out that even though he is now an evil villain, at one point he was a child that never got a pony and still feels sad and misunderstood because of it. This might lead you to hum an ominous theme that, at certain times, will play a very evil, child-like melody. Turn on that recorder!

Here's another scenario: You play through one of the new levels that involves a car chase. Although it's a regular city car chase, the buildings are designed in a more cartoonish fashion. This may lead you to hum a quick energetic melody, with playful tendencies and some fun trills that hearken back to the Keystone Cops. You got it. Put it on your handheld.

Sometimes, when you are working with certain producers or music directors, they may be open to hearing raw versions of your melodies before you've begun. Heck, they may even encourage it. For whatever reason, they may just be good at recognizing raw potential. Who knows, maybe they are musicians themselves who chose to get into production for whatever reason. This is a rare boon for the composer. You are able to give your producer source material before you begin painstakingly programming and producing it. This is great because you can turn one of your recorded hums, or a quick piano melody or a whistle, into an MP3, and then quickly shoot them off to see if you are moving in the right direction.

So, with that in mind, it wouldn't hurt to ask around the team to see if someone leading may be musically inclined. It may save you some work, as well as some heartache.

Proactivity

Much like writing a book or working on a commissioned painting, you have to be very proactive in scoring a title. When you think about a video game team, you would think from a distance that there is equal consideration in regard to every element of a game. You would think that the artwork is just as important as the story, that the sound is just as important as the music. You'd even think that the game-play mechanics are just as good as the programming.

Unfortunately, I can tell you that it doesn't always happen like this. As it occurs in every walk of life, some things tend to fall by the wayside if the person leading the cause isn't proactive. It's in our nature as human beings to take more notice of things that we see, rather than things that we feel and hear, and this becomes especially true in video games. To quote another saying from Peter McConnell, "They always think about audio last and music very last." With this saying in mind, it should definitely prompt you to stay on top of your game.

When many game projects start, they are usually very ambitious. They are usually claiming that there will be innovative new game features, a set amount of game-play hours, a bold story, and so on.

As the game goes into development, certain features fall by the wayside. For whatever reason, the programmer may not be able to make it work. Additionally, as time gets slimmer, pieces of art get cut, certain characters get cut, and then levels get cut.

It's not that there was anything wrong with any of the ideas, features, or characters; sometimes, there's just not enough time. One character may be really cool, but his or her existence may ultimately have no real affect on the story. A certain level may be really fun, but the story can still go on without it and no one would be the wiser. Additionally, the level may have some serious crash bugs associated with it that could be holding the title back from shipping.

Also, as a title gets closer to shipping, music that didn't matter a week ago for one level, may now be hot on the producer's mind. In fact, a level that may have been cut, (along with your music) may now be planned as a secret mission that ships with a bonus CD as a special promotion.

On a game team, there can be up to ten artists at a given time working on a project, 30 video game testers, seven level designers, and three sound designers. But one thing is for certain: Usually there's only one composer at any given time on a project.

One tried-and-true method for keeping on top of things is to keep a bulletin board, or a white board, where you can chart the status of each level. Every time you get a phone call asking you what your status is on a certain area of the game, you can simply look up and say, "This is where

I am." Additionally, this can be done with a spreadsheet just as easily, and I highly recommended you do both. It's just convenient to have a white board as a visual reference within your studio.

An additional suggestion when composing is to stay ahead of what the team is asking. For months, your work may not seem to be of any concern at all. But don't be fooled by this false sense of bliss. Your work is extremely important to the game. Just because one area of the game may not be ready for your music at the moment doesn't mean that you can't be ready for it.

How the Game Uses Your Music

In some titles, music just plays in the background. The music goes on and on. It gradually moves from song to song, and seems composed to always fit. In other games, you hear music that is entirely interactive. When a door opens, you hear the music take on an eerie quality; when a fight occurs, the music is fast-paced and exciting.

When some games are created, certain people are aware of what can be done with music in a game, and features are implemented at the start. They want the player to have the full experience, as they would have in a movie, and they recognize that music is a part of that experience. As soon as you jump on a project like this, you need to ask how you can compose music in such a way as to make the best interactive experience. This can mean creating several short segments of music that can segue easily from one to another. It can also mean creating some shorter musical cues that identify something has changed for the player or that a goal has been achieved. There are even some in-house engines that can cause the music to be interactive, fading in and out when a character does a certain action or filtering when certain actions occur.

Then there are other times in which the design team is lead by a very visual person, he or she tends not to think about the audio aspects of the game. They are more concerned with creating the most beautiful visual experience that you can imagine. When this occurs, it's not that the design team utterly doesn't care about music or sound. It just means that it's not one of the main goals of the game. Of course, this team will know the importance of music, they just won't make it their priority. When this occurs, you'll want to start making friends with the sound programmer, which anyone in game audio should do anyway. The sound programmer can tell you what the game engine is capable of doing with your music, even when the leads on the team can't.

Internal Looping in the Game Engine

You should ask either your sound programmer or team whether the game engine is capable of internal looping. **Internal looping** is when a piece of music starts over when it reaches the end of a piece of music or at a certain point within the music. But instead of restarting at the beginning of the song, it will restart somewhere in the middle, hopefully without it being obvious. This is a good way to make a piece of music appear to be much longer than it really is. The player hears the beginning of the track when he starts the level, and he hears the ending when either he dies or completes the level. But for the rest of the time, he is hearing a piece of music continually play, over and over. This is equally helpful when you are at the main menu of the game or in Options menus.

This is usually a standard feature, but you'd be surprised how often it's not. When I was working on a title several years ago, the engine was having a severe problem looping the music within any given level. In fact, the loop points weren't syncing correctly, so there was an obvious gap, or glitch, at certain points in the level when the loop point would occur. This was eventually fixed, but this is an example of when an obvious feature should be in place and working...but isn't.

Editing Prerecorded Music

In Chapter 13, "Editing Prerecorded Music," we'll talk about setting up loop points in your compositions so they are ready to go for engines that support internal looping.

Cut Scenes

Another question is, "How does the game handle audio within the cut scenes?"

Much of the time, cuts scenes are **pre-rendered,** meaning that there is a movie not being played from the game's graphical engine. This movie was played using a more sophisticated graphical program, usually a program expressly intended for high-resolution graphics, more appropriate for telling a story at times because of the intricacies that can be incorporated. When I say pre-rendered, these engines will render a scene over a period of time using the computer to do rigorous number-crunching. The visualization of the graphics are therefore not done in real time but over a period of time, and then turned into a movie, like an mpeg, that can be played quickly.

Some of the time, the audio will be burned into the mpeg; other times, the audio will be played separately by the game engine itself. It's good to know the answer to this because you don't want the music stopping abruptly or fading out at an irregular moment. Therefore, if the music is not rendered with the cut scene, you'll probably need to spend some time with one of the programmers to tweak the ending so it's not cutting out abruptly. In some cases, you'll want to spend extra time, timing the music to verify that the length is just long enough to fade out after the video has faded. Music always goes out last. (For more information about cut scenes, refer to Chapter 9, "Mixing Cut Scenes.")

Interactivity

As mentioned before, it's important to know how much interactivity the game's engine will provide with the music. One method of interactivity is the **sideways crossfade.** The sideways crossfade is the ability to crossfade from one piece of music to another, seamlessly, during the game. Why would you want to do this, though?

Well, one reason is to change the mood in the game. Remember how I was talking about the slow, melancholy music that plays during a level? Then that music suddenly becomes fast-paced to emulate what's going on within the level? This is a good example of the sideways crossfade.

Essentially, what composers will do is this: They will create one piece of music that is mellow within their host sequencer (like Logic, Cubase, or Performer), then in muted sections of the sequencer, they create other tracks that go along with that mellow piece of music to make it more intense. When the music is done, the composer delivers two pieces of music from one music sequence. Figure 10.3 is a visual example of what it looks like in Nuendo.

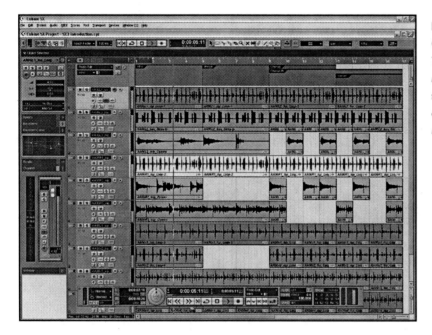

Figure 10.3

Certain sections are muted. Those are the action elements of the music. While they are muted, the piece as a whole is much more mellow.

One piece of music is slow and matches the mood of the level. The other sounds very similar to the original level music, but it has some fast-paced music that sounds more intense. Both pieces of music are intended for use in the same level, but one piece of music signifies the downtime and the other signifies the action. One plays when nothing is going on, and one plays when something is going on.

Beat-Synchronous Instructions

Another feature to ask the team about is beat-synchronous instructions. This feature allows the composer, with help of a programmer or level designer, to introduce instructions within a music track. These instructions tell the game's audio engine to transition at a musically sensible location, like a measure.

Why is this even needed? Well, you don't want a sideways crossfade to happen out of tempo, do you? It would be highly audible to the listener, as well as to you. There's nothing more agonizing than hearing a beat out of step. It reflects poorly on the game and on the composer!

11 } Composers: Tools of the Trade

Now that you've got a bit of insight as to what goes on inside the world of the video game composer, let's talk about the available tools, programs, and weapons of choice.

The composer definitely has a weapons chest that he pulls from for each and every mission, similar to the "weapons" that sound designers use. Composers need multi-track programs, the same as sound designers. Composers also need software synthesizers, audio plug-ins, and video capabilities. The only real difference is what the composer will do with these programs. Composers are not usually concerned with making sounds; they're concerned with making melodies. Also, composers won't be mixing a cut scene, but they will be scoring a cut scene.

As you can see, there are differences and there are similarities. It's not a big surprise that there are a number of sound designers who also work as composers. I really have to extend my admiration to these men and women. Neither of these jobs is easy to obtain, and to obtain both is certainly an accomplishment.

But before we begin, let's have a little state-of-the-nation talk. I mentioned before that back in the early days of video game music, it was all about programming music played off electronic wavetables generated by the game's engine. These days, it's all about the best possible digital recording you can get, sounding as close to film or radio as possible, and within a budget. As mentioned previously, some game publishers in recent years have actually licensed music from different artists. Games like *Grand Theft Auto* feature a variety of different artists to appeal to different tastes.

So if games are moving in the direction of simply licensing different tracks, then where does that put the composer? Obviously, it doesn't put the composer in a very good state at all. With that in mind, it pays to be on top of your game!

One of the first traits that seems to benefit many composers is *versatility*. Being able to jump from composing an epic, orchestrated piece to a hard rock piece definitely helps you out. When you're shopping yourself around to different clients, you never know what they may want musically for their game. The more versatile you are, the more easily you can adapt to the criteria of whatever a producer may have in mind for his project.

But what if you've only worked in one genre of music? What if you only know one style? With the amount of software that's out there these days, it's never been easier to explore new styles at a whim. Programs like Reason have several demos included that embody or merge different styles. If you find one style that fits what you are looking for, Reason takes it a step farther and has many different loops categorized into styles that you can examine and implement into your own sound.

Additionally, there are several companies like East West that sell comprehensive sample libraries, including sound sets, drum sets, and loops, or even instruments and orchestras. Some of these libraries are even sold as orchestra sample libraries that have been produced by famous composers, such as Hans Zimmer or Miroslav Vituous.

In this chapter, we're going to take some time and really explore the tools of the composer, much like we did for the sound designer. As I said before, you're going to see a lot of similarities, but keep in mind, some functions that are appealing for a sound designer may be completely worthless to a composer, and vice versa, of course!

So let's start by moving into the programs that composers spend the majority of their time with—the multi-track program.

Multi-Track Programs

The tool that's used first and foremost in the arsenal of the composer must be the tool that he uses to compose, right? And most good multi-track programs these days are comprised of audio recording and sequencing, all in one package.

Now, we've examined audio recording in multi-track programs in the sound designers portion of the book, but we haven't examined sequencers at all up to this point. This book assumes that you have some prior knowledge of the principles of sequencing and audio. But we'll do a quick refresher, just in case.

A sequencer is a lot like the player pianos of old, pictured in Figure 11.1. I'd like for you to imagine a player piano in action. You see the keys moving around as if a ghost were playing, and up in the middle of the piano you see a brass reel moving slowly. If you look closely as the reel moves, you can see little tick marks all over the brass reel. These tick marks are what cause the piano to play. The brass reel of the player piano essentially carries coded information made up of tick marks that mechanically trigger the piano keys. If you slow down the reel as it moves, you slow down the speed of the piano as it plays. If you stop the reel, the piano will stop playing all together.

Figure 11.1
Notice the reel centered above the piano keys. That reel has coded information that tells the keys what to play. It's a mechanical forefather to modern-day sequencing.

A sequencer works in much the same way, although, it doesn't use a mechanical reel. Instead, a **sequencer** uses computer-recorded impulses to reproduce the events and music of a composer. Sequencers are capable of playing a melody back with the appropriate instrument at the appropriate velocity and volume, with all of the recorded controller information. This is made possible through MIDI, which is mentioned in Chapter 10. The Musical Instrument Digital Interface format has been around for several years and has made it possible for a composer to become a one-person orchestra.

When you record into a sequencer from a keyboard controller, you are sending MIDI data to the sequencer from the keys that you are playing. When the sequencer plays back the recording, it's sending MIDI pulses to whatever musical device you were previously triggering to reproduce what you were playing. Essentially, a sequencer is like an audio recorder, except it's recording MIDI information instead of audio.

But why wouldn't you just want to record the audio of what you're playing? The cool thing about recording the MIDI information instead of audio is that you can go back later and edit how you played the instrument. You can adjust the velocity of one key within a melody; you can also edit the timing to get a piece of music, or **sequence**, to get each note to fall exactly where it should.

And let's face it, there are quite a few of us who can't exactly play with perfect timing! Having functions like quantizing at our fingertips saves a lot of editing. To **quantize** something is to have the computer take every note within a sequence and adjust each note against a time grid set to the appropriate beat based on the note you quantized with. For example, if I played a sequence that was primarily made up of 16th notes, I'd want to quantize later with a 16th-note quantize to tighten up what I played.

There are several functions and features out there that are covered extensively in many tutorial books that you can peruse if you'd like to know more about MIDI sequencing. Course Technology, Cengage Learning, for example, offers books on every sequencer I mention in this book As a composer, the more you know about sequencing, the more your career will benefit in the long run.

So take a moment now and go over some multi-track/sequencing programs that are widely used by many different kinds of composers.

Nuendo/Cubase SX for PC and Mac

Earlier in the book, we spoke about Nuendo as a recording program with extensive features that are useful for the sound designer (see Figure 11.2). Nuendo as an audio platform is a very solid package. It has risen quickly to the top of the heap, and for good reason—it delivers on its promises. It also has a lot of bang for the buck! A lot of its success can be equally attributed to its sequencing functionality.

Several years back, when Steinberg (Nuendo's developer) began creating Nuendo, they drew from many of the same functions that were available in the original Cubase, but they created an entirely different engine—the Nuendo engine! A lot of the visuals between Cubase and Nuendo are different, but the arrangement windows, as well as some other functions, are very similar. This is great because Cubase has been a well-known workhorse of a sequencer for many years. Building upon its knowledge, while developing the many extra Pro features found in Nuendo, has definitely helped its success. Cubase, in its high-end incarnation, is known as Cubase SX. This version is the one that we'll be comparing with Nuendo.

But why would a composer choose Nuendo when he can easily pick up many of the same features in Cubase? This is a very important question, one that can save you some money if you fall into the Cubase category. Cubase and Nuendo, as mentioned before, are built off the same engine. So when you see them both back to back, they look very similar. However, as Nuendo is Steinberg's flagship sequencer, Nuendo has more features than Cubase.

What kind of features? Well, both programs have elaborate surround capabilities, but Nuendo has a lot more to offer on this end. Cubase also has surround capabilities, but it's limited in how many channels it can handle. Nuendo can handle all of the standard surround formats up to 10.2!

Additionally, the Nuendo mixer is quite a bit more elaborate than the Cubase mixer. It offers several different views and configurations. Cubase has been limited in its surround recording capabilities, which is fine for the composer in most situations. But, as mentioned before, if you're planning on delving more into sound design, and possibly movie mixdowns and some serious audio engineering on top of composing, Nuendo may be a better choice.

Figure 11.2
Nuendo is both a powerful recording program and a versatile sequencer.

In terms of MIDI sequencing, both programs are on equal footing. They both offer the same great Arrangement window, extensive quantization options, and cool editing features like Dissolve Part (which breaks the sequence down by pitch or key). You also can do beat slicing within the each program.

Additionally, both programs can import video for scoring, and both programs also have a great marker system that helps you keep track of where you are in the sequence. You can even create folder tracks in Cubase and Nuendo that allow you to drag several tracks into one folder track and collapse it. This is great for keeping your work area organized. Notation is also the same in both programs. This is of huge importance to the composer, and it hasn't been skimped on in either program.

In conclusion, Nuendo and Cubase SX can both be of great assistance. If you don't see yourself using some of the extensive audio features, I'd definitely recommend saving yourself some money and going with Cubase SX. It's a solid program with a sturdy sequencer and a great sounding audio engine. However, if you see yourself growing in your audio pursuits, or you are working in an environment that would benefit from the networking and file-sharing capabilities of Nuendo, it may suit you better to spend the extra money.

Apple Logic Pro for Mac

If you talk to any composer or musician these days who uses a Mac, odds are, they are using Logic Pro. First developed by Emagic, the company was bought by Apple a few years ago. Since then, Logic Pro has become the sequencer of choice for many Mac users. It could be partly because Apple customers tend to stand strongly behind the Apple product line, but also because Logic is a formidable sequencer that contains a fine array of tools and instruments. Logic, pictured in Figure 11.3, is a multi-track recording and sequencing program that has received a lot of polish over the years from people who really know what they are doing.

Figure 11.3

When it comes to the Mac, Logic Pro is one of the most talked-about audio sequencing programs out there!

Logic offers advanced notation features that allow everything from guitar tablatures to drum notation. This feature has been used by many a composer I know who has had to get scores ready for live players. Why is this so important? As a composer you may find yourself working with many musicians once you've written the initial score on your own. If a live drummer is coming in later, you want him to know what to play, rather than spend countless hours getting him up to speed. Additionally, if you are working with an orchestra, it's very important to have sheet music for every player involved. Remember, many musicians only work from sheet music.

Since Apple has taken Logic under its wing, it's incorporated some of its own fingerprints into the package. There are now Apple Loops that can be used in Logic. Apple Loops were originally implemented in Soundtrack and later in Garage Band, both designed by Apple. Logic also supports ACID loops, the most popular PC loop format, and REX loops, a format from Propellerhead Software.

Originally, Apple Loops were produced for the novice musician or film guy who didn't have any musical ability, per se. Now that Apple Loops have been implemented in Logic, these loops can be put through some serious abuse with Logic's vast array of plug-ins and editing features. Users can also make their own loops into Apple Loops directly within Logic.

A solid library of loops at your fingertips is a very nice thing for the composer to have. Nothing fills in empty spaces or adds dimension quite like them. Literally, you're adding another musician on the fly, as well as some variety that you may not have thought of on your own. Loops push song creation along a little more quickly, in my opinion.

Logic Pro includes a startling number of nine synthesizers. This is a lot in comparison to any other package out there today. One of the synths, known as Structure, is a modeling synth capable of reproducing sounds like flutes, strings, and xylophones. This is awesome because, in scoring games that require more of an orchestral score, you can really benefit from something like this.

Logic also includes a powerful sampler known as the EXS24mkII. This sampler will play back up to 32-bit samples, and it has its own effects processor that can be used on all 16 of its outputs. EXS24 is also the most CPU-friendly sampler available, which lets you use many other plug-ins and instruments without running out of power.

Logic is also widely applauded for its sound processing abilities. It includes standard plug-ins, like reverbs and EQs, to incorporate as some of your more obvious effects. Surprisingly, it ships with a nice guitar amp that provides 12 amp models, 8 cabinets, and 4 EQs.

Logic Pro also ships with distortion plug-ins, filter plug-ins, modulation plug-ins, reverb plug-ins, and delays. These are great for getting some of those more unconventional effects for those pop-like scores. These also are effective if you're doing sound design.

One feature that should seriously be noted is Logic's ability to mix down up to 7.1 surround with automated control of mastering parameters. With audio engines in games getting more and more robust and the media that houses the game getting larger and larger, you can expect a demand for more surround compositions and cut scenes.

I would be remiss if I forgot to mention the audio capabilities of Logic. It allows recording and editing of up to 244 audio tracks at 24-bit/192 kHz resolution. It also houses a large array of editing tools that includes a sample editor. Logic Pro as an audio platform is definitely formidable in comparison to other packages on the market. Logic Pro is difficult to pass up if you're a Mac user and looking at composing or sound design. Because it's owned and supported by Apple, you can rely on their reputation for service and customer satisfaction. Among many composers and musicians I know, Logic Pro is consistently touted as one of the best audio packages in the industry.

Digital Performer for Mac
Like Cubase and Logic, Performer has been around since the beginning of computer MIDI se-quencing. Performer is still going strong in its current incarnation as Digital Performer. From day

one, Digital Performer has been one of those programs that many composers have preferred. It's designed with film scoring, studio production, and live performances in mind.

Like many other programs of its kind, its current version has unlimited un-dos, unlimited tracks (based on hardware), and surround sound support.

One thing that's really cool about Digital Performer is that its interface adapts to your work style. Windows can be moved around, and views can be saved so that when you start a new track, all of your tools are in place.

One option that's great for scoring is the Find Tempo feature in Digital Performer. You can set up a master list of cues or import a cue sheet, then choose the type of hit for various markers. This is great because you can assign a level of importance to each hit. After you're done with your list, you can let Digital Performer search your markers and suggest a tempo that hits the critical cue points. This is a great feature for the composer, especially when scoring cut scenes. You can use this feature to really have your music flow between the different cuts.

One new feature in the Digital Performer is its ability to superimpose streamers, punches, and flutters over a QuickTime movie. Steamers, punches, and flutters are visual cues that help composers to anticipate visual hits. This is very helpful in synchronizing your music to what is happening onscreen and is helpful when you are scoring a cut scene for a game.

One feature found in Digital Performer was used creatively for a video game score a couple of years ago by a good friend of mine. He decided that he was going to make some disco music to go along with the level that featured a disco villain. He tooled around and put together a groovy piece, but something was missing. Yeah, a female voice singing some embellishments would be nice. The only problem was, he didn't have access to a female vocalist. What he ended up doing was recording himself singing the parts using Digital Performer's Gender Bender feature. With this feature, he turned his own voice into a female voice. It sounded really good—I didn't even notice until he told me about it!

There are literally tons of features in Digital Performer that have been created over years with the composer in mind. I could probably write a book on these features alone because there are that many. I would encourage you to visit Mark of the Unicorn's Web page (www.motu.com) and check out Digital Performer for yourself.

SONAR for PC

One audio/sequencing package gaining a lot of ground with many musicians and composers alike is SONAR. SONAR was created by Cakewalk a few years ago as a high-end version of their existing Cakewalk Home Studio software. When they created SONAR, they certainly borrowed things from the existing program, but they also added and refined several features that made SONAR a more formidable program than its older brother.

SONAR, pictured in Figure 11.4, is a PC-only program like Nuendo and Cubase, in which audio and MIDI sequencing work together as a team.

Figure 11.4
SONAR offers a slew of plug-ins in its Producer's Package, like a Lexicon reverb and Roland synthesizers.

SONAR offers many of the same features that are found in Cubase SX or Nuendo, giving you great ways to organize your material and maintain it. Where SONAR tends to differ from other PC programs is that it has been endowed with a ton of plug-ins and technologies from outside companies, like Lexicon and Roland. SONAR has actual Lexicon reverb plug-ins included with its Producer edition. It's the only audio/sequencing solution of its kind that can make such a claim. For some time now, Lexicon has created some of the most sought-after reverbs in the industry. You still hear and see quite a bit of PCM-80, a fine example of a great reverb from Lexicon. Pantheon Surround is the Lexicon reverb included with SONAR.

SONAR also incorporates synthesizer plug-ins that are actually made and endorsed by Roland. Additionally, it has the Roland V-Vocal Vari-phrase technology in it that is highly useful for pitch correction, vibrato, and dynamics dealing with the human voice. Hey, you never know when you might have someone doing some "oohs" and "ahhs" for your composition, right?

A few years ago a small company named rgc:audio (www.rgcaudio.com) made a big splash by releasing some very robust synthesizer plug-ins. They were simple in their design, but the sound was huge, and they greatly resembled some of the old Roland synthesizers. Well, when a good thing is created, others take notice. Cakewalk bought the fledgling rgc:audio. Now synthesizers like the Pentagon I vintage analog synth can be found in SONAR. Additionally, the minds behind these plug-ins are working on other plug-ins made available from Cakewalk.

Handy for scoring, SONAR can import a range of video and audio files including MPEG, Quicktime 6, and Windows Media Video. It's also capable of exporting formats such as these with 5.1 surround. Not too shabby!

SONAR has an abundant supply of features, like all of the packages mentioned in this chapter. One of the things that keeps me going back to SONAR is the great names that have contributed to making it what it is today, a pro choice. Do yourself a favor and check out www.cakewalk.com if you would like to know more about SONAR.

Pro Tools for PC and Mac

Pro Tools, seen in Figure 11.5, is an often-used package for scoring and composing. As mentioned in previous chapters, it's been the standard package for years for sound designers and musicians alike.

Figure 11.5

Pro Tools is a well-known solution for audio recording. MIDI sequencing, however, is not one of its strong points.

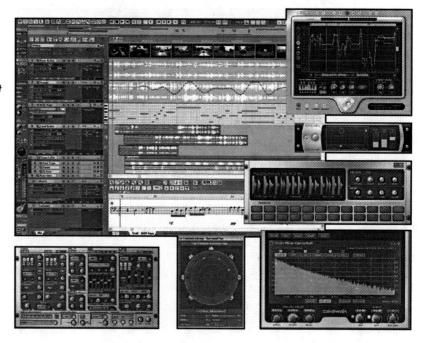

The one thing Pro Tools doesn't do as well as other programs is MIDI sequencing. Sure, the program has MIDI, and it works; but it's better known for its audio features than its MIDI features.

To work around this, there are programs like Digital Performer and Logic Pro that can use Pro Tools' hardware. Additionally, Pro Tools has ReWire technology, allowing it to work seamlessly with Reason and its horde of synthesizers, samplers, and drum machines. Pro Tools is capable of working with almost all of the major soft synths. With a wrapper supplied by FXpansion, Pro Tools users can run VST plug-ins, including instruments. It has intuitive MIDI editing, as well as standard editing for velocity, after touch, and most regular controller properties. There is also a great marker system in Pro Tools for labeling parts of your song, and you can import video thumbnails to score along with your compositions.

Many composers love Pro Tools for their audio needs and do all of their mixing in Pro Tools, but they turn to other programs to handle the actual music composition, like Logic, Digital Performer, and Nuendo. Granted, we can't all afford to go out and buy a Pro Tools rig, as well as an expensive music production package on top of it. So if you're planning on doing sound design, I strongly recommend looking at Pro Tools. But if you want to compose, you should seriously look at some of the other packages listed earlier.

Wave Editors

Just like sound designers, composers also need wave editors. Once you've completed the composition and mixdown of a piece of music, you usually have to export it as an audio file. Most of the time, when you export an audio file that is intended as music, you are exporting it as a stereo .wav or .aiff file. If you are going to burn this audio file to an audio CD later, you would export it as a stereo .wav or .aiff recorded at 44 kHz/16-bit. This is the appropriate resolution for Redbook audio. After exporting a mix, however, you're going to want to do some more detailed editing and perhaps some mastering. Wave editors are designed for this type of pursuit.

Let's say you want to export a mix from Logic as an .aiff file. You set up your loop points in Logic at the beginning and end of the track, then you tell Logic what you want it exported as. Logic does the work, and immediately you have a stereo .aiff file waiting for you. When you play this file in QuickTime, you notice it's got a little too much lead time at the beginning.

So what do you do? You bring it into your handy wave editor and quickly slice off the beginning (see Figure 11.6). And while you're there, you go ahead and slice off some of the end time because there's a lot left over. And right before you're about to save your audio file, you notice that the waveform looks a little thin. It's time for a little mastering, courtesy of the wave editor. You open up your favorite mastering plug-in, which allows you to do a little EQ and some compression. You render the audio file with the mastering plug-in. Instantly that file is looking a lot bigger and sounding a lot bolder than before. You know that no matter what this track is played on, it's going to sound good.

Granted, mastering is a fine art, and it usually takes a LOT more time and energy than the flagrant pass you just witnessed in my five-minute guide to mastering. Mastering alone could take up several books, and it is really done best by a professional mastering lab. But sometimes you just need some quick work to impress a client, and you can't afford the thousands that it costs just to master a quick demo. Wave editors are great for this as well!

Figure 11.6
Wave editors like Wavelab are great tools for those quick edits that are cumbersome in multi-track editors.

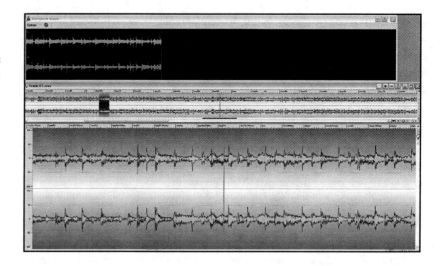

Wave Editors

In this chapter, I'm not going to spend a lot of time on wave editors. These are covered in Chapter 4.

The main wave editors that the composer should be aware of are the following:

- Wavelab
- Peak
- Sound Forge

Each of these editors are highly effective, from the basic maintenance of audio files all the way to fixing acute EQ problems. Wave editors are also highly effective at converting all manner of files from one file type to another.

Batch converters also play a role in the life of the video game composer (refer to Chapter 8 for more information). To give you a refresher, batch converters can take an existing set of audio files and perform a list of instructions on each audio file via programmed automation. Working in the fast-paced world of video games, getting things done with the utmost expediency is very important. Sometimes, things come down the pipe quickly, and you have to get things together a lot more quickly than you had originally intended. Batch converters can help you with these unforeseen events.

Imagine that you delivered a set of music audio files to the video game team that you are working for. They listen to the files, and everyone is happy. Later on that night, you get a message saying that everything was great, but they need the files at a different resolution than what you delivered. Granted, you followed the instructions exactly as they were originally given to you, but the lead programmer is having problems implementing them in that resolution at the moment. And the team really wants to hear them with the game in order to see how they work.

This is an easy fix for the savvy composer who knows how to use a batch converter. All you have to do is go into your wave editor, open up the batch converter, and program it to change the resolution of the files. A few seconds go by as you watch the sliding progress bar, like the one pictured in Figure 11.7. Ding! The little bell goes off announcing the completion of your work. You upload the converted audio files to FTP, and your team is ready to go!

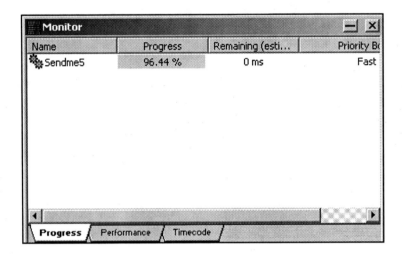

Figure 11.7
There's nothing like seeing that completed progress bar after hundreds of your files have been converted.

Each of the wave editors listed previously has features in their batch converters that are designed to save you time. Too much lead time at the beginning of all of your music files? Use the batch converter to trim the beginning and end of the files. Your team for some reason now wants your music files as mono files, as opposed to stereo files (heaven forbid, but it's not unheard of)? Batch convert them from stereo to mono.

Another handy feature that a composer can always use the wave editor for is the almighty MP3. You never know when you're going to hit a spark of creativity that can transform what was once an agonizing musical piece into one of the best pieces of music ever imagined for a certain part of a game.

❋ **Immediate Feedback**
When inspiration hits and you do something great, it's always nice to get some feedback on your work from people on your project. Having the ability to convert a track to an MP3 and send it via e-mail to someone whose opinion you value is a wonderful feature that many composers have used from time to time. However, you should clear this with the person ahead of time.

Certain audio engines, whether the sleek in-house or third-party audio engines (such as Miles Sound System), also support MP3s. You never know, you may need to deliver all of your music as MP3s.

There are also times when a game company's marketing department will want to feature music on the game's dedicated Web site. This is your moment to shine! Convert the requested pieces to MP3 and get them online. Then every time people visit that site, they will be hearing your music. What better way is there to get your music heard?

MP3 conversion is also great for the fledgling composer who hasn't got a gig yet. You can set yourself up with a Web site that streams your work. You can have the MP3s broken down into subcategories depicting genre, mood, style, or you name it.

There's one last thing that we shouldn't forget. Portable MP3 players are a wonderful way for you to take your work with you on the road. When you are out of your studio element, you begin to notice things while you're driving, riding a train, or whatever. Take your songs with you, as well as a notepad. And while you're at it, take the voice recorder that I mentioned in earlier chapters. (Some portable MP3 players actually have voice recorder adapters!) While you are in a peaceful environment, it's easy to get little spurts of inspiration and new ideas about material.

I think you're beginning to understand the importance of a wave editor to the composer. As mentioned before in Chapter 4, if you're a Mac user, Peak is your main choice. If you use a PC, Sound Forge or Wavelab serve you well.

Soft Synths

Synthesizers go with video game music like peanut butter goes with jelly. The two just work together. Any sci-fi or action title will most likely have a synthesizer in it. Even kids' titles will have synthesizers to emulate the bouncy little pieces of music that kids love to hear.

For many years, composers have relied on synthesizers to create atmosphere and emotion in their scores for movies, TV shows, and video games. There's just something cool about hearing haunting string melodies accompanied by some soaring resonant sweep in that Vangelis sort of way.

Many great composers still employ a couple of hardware synthesizers in their arsenal of music gear. In some cases, great composers use several hardware synthesizers. It all comes down to preference. But make no mistake, the software synthesizer has infiltrated its way into the world of video game music, and you'd do well to know about them.

And why wouldn't you want to use a soft synth? They will fit on any laptop that has the processing power to run them, which means you can take them with you! They are also cheaper than most hardware synthesizers, and they even have more capabilities with a more intuitive interface than most hardware synthesizers.

But do they sound as good? This is a question that many an audiophile will debate regarding the thickness or thinness of the sound. Soft synths, in some cases, may not sound as good as hardware synthesizers. In my opinion, though, usually it's the soft synth that's trying to emulate a classic piece of hardware that is the object of scrutiny. Yeah, it's definitely hard to emulate the characteristics, the depth, and the frequencies that come from some of the classic synthesizers.

But what about soft synths (such as Absynth) that aren't trying to emulate any one synth in particular? These soft synths—out to break new ground with unheard of forms of synthesis, using technology that was never even possible with a hardware synthesizer—are truly turning some heads. They can mix several forms of synthesis, from granular to FM synthesis with three different kinds of filters or more, into one sound.

And how will it sound? It will sound unique. And that's how I try to look at soft synths. I don't really care about how close the Arturia Minimoog V sounds to the original or how close it emulates it. I care about getting really thick, really great sounds quickly when I'm in the middle of a project, and I don't have time to screw around with a hardware synthesizer.

Soft synths are great for getting good stuff quickly. They are perfect for adding a little spice to that musical composition you've been agonizing over. They are the perfect companion to that beautiful string section you've just placed in your music. Soft synths are a composer's weapon. Are they his main weapon? No, absolutely not. But they are a means to an end. They are a vehicle for matching up your music with that one special sound that sets your performance over the edge.

In this section, we'll focus on some soft synths that have come up in several interviews that I've conducted with video game and TV composers alike. We'll go over what's cool about these synths, and why you might want to take a gander at them.

Absynth for PC and Mac

In one key press, Absynth can do what it would take several instances of another synth to pull off. For example, you can have a high synth lead doing a melody, an ambient bed of music playing in the background, and a bass line going in syncopation with another synth. And it will all be in 5.1! The patches you can make with this synth make it a pleasure to work with for both composition and sound design.

Several forms of synthesis and sampling are available to Absynth, shown in Figure 11.8. Granted, Absynth is not a sampler, but it can play back sound files, and you can do some very exciting things with them. One of the things that I find enjoyable about Absynth is its ability to create new waveforms and envelopes simply by drawing. It's an incredibly visual synth, and nowhere is this more evident than in its interface.

Absynth's graphical user interface (GUI) is like no other synth out there. It's literally like you're working with an instrument from another planet. All of the menus are rounded and curved in a greenish-blue hue. It's almost as if you're working with a synthesizer designed by Captain Nemo.

Figure 11.8

Absynth is an all-around great choice for video game composers. Even sound designers can benefit from its numerous uses.

And its sound is definitely from another planet. Basically, the sound is reminiscent of the look—very subtle, very ambient, almost haunting.

The program banks that ship with the program lend to film, TV, and game composition in many, many ways. Many of the patches can simply be used as ambience, where other patches in Absynth's line-up can be used as ambient pads or even other-worldly percussion.

In its latest incarnation, Absynth is equipped with 5.1 surround patches, but it also gives you the ability to create patches in 5.1, as well. You've heard me say it before, and I'll say it again: Everything in entertainment is steering towards 5.1. This is a great feature to have in a synth, especially for game composition. With platforms like the Xbox 360, the ability to have *your* music played back in 5.1 has never been more real. The composer who can accommodate this will definitely reap the benefits. To be sure, most music scores for games are played back only as stereo files, even when they are in a surround environment. But who knows? It could happen.

Absynth's ability to manipulate audio as a granular synthesizer is another bonus to composers, as well as sound designers. Granular synthesis is remarkable for its ability to take any audio file and twist it and shape it in ways that can be beautiful, as well as disturbing. One thing's for sure: It's great for making all new instrument sounds out of whatever the original recording was.

Like most Native Instrument plug-ins and instruments, Absynth can be used as either a plug-in or a standalone synthesizer. So no matter what multi-track package you're using, your Absynth will work with it.

It's literally one of those synthesizers that you can spend forever and a day with. The more you work with it, the more you discover. The more you discover, the more you want to try experimenting. This synthesizer comes highly recommended by sound designers and composers alike.

Reason for PC and Mac

Of course, you know Reason as a standalone program. But Reason can also exist as a rack of synthesizers that you can use like plug-ins with other host programs through a protocol known as ReWire. This is excellent, because Reason has two really handy synthesizers that can be used for many, many things. ReWire allows you to slave Reason to another host program, like Logic. When you start Logic, and then start Reason, you'll notice all of Reason's outputs are illuminated. Now Reason's clock is synced with Logic's, and all of Reason's outputs are going into Logic. But that's not even half of what's cool about Reason. With Reason wired to Logic, you also have the ability to select instruments in Reason as if they were instruments in Logic. This is awesome because you can use Logic's more advanced sequencing capabilities to sequence Reason's instruments.

The Subtractor in Reason, shown in Figure 11.9, is a subtractive synthesizer that is similar in many ways to the Nord Lead. You can get quick, punchy little bass sounds out of it, as well as pretty thick leads, if you know how to play with the phase and LFOs.

Figure 11.9

The Subtractor in Reason can be a handy, basic subtractive synthesizer that fulfills many different sounds.

The Malström in Reason is a granular synthesizer that has its own sound, to be sure. The Malström has a large wavetable to draw on that offers everything from choirs to raw synthesizer waveforms. As Malström is a granular synthesizer, you can manipulate these wave files in very interesting ways. Really, with a simple flick of the knob, a sound can go from a bell to a car crash. Granular synthesis is just cool like that.

You're probably asking yourself how these two synthesizers stack up to a synthesizer like Absynth. Well, these two synthesizers are in no way as advanced as Absynth. But the word "stack" definitely fits in with this next Reason device. The Combinator, pictured in Figure 11.10, is essentially another rack that is contained inside the already-existing Reason rack, which can be manipulated and used as one instrument or effect box.

Figure 11.10

The Combinator allows you to make elaborate synthesizer patches out of the smaller, simpler synthesizers already available in Reason.

With the Combinator, you can stack multiple versions of the Subtractor synthesizer with the Malström if you desire, or you can stack a Subtractor with an NN-XT sampler with effects. Or really you can stack any instrument or device in Reason with as many different instances as you want in one device. Basically, you can make one patch based on several synthesizers, samplers, and effects boxes built into one device.

Now, really, this section is for composers, and composers need sounds on the fly to get the music going quickly and sounding good. Well, you'll be happy to know that Reason's Factory Sound Bank has many, many different kinds of sounds broken down into categories like pads, basses, guitars, and so on. The Reason browser actually has a search window at the top where you can type in the sound you are looking for, and it will find you all the pads that go along with your search. It's just like using an Internet search engine—cool huh?

Reason also ships with the Orkester sound bank. This bank is filled with patches and samples of instruments used to build orchestras. Everything from oboes to cellos has all been lovingly recorded. In Chapter 12 you get into sample libraries and such, but it's important to note that you can get a pretty good sound library included in Reason.

The RV-7000 reverb is another device of note in Reason. It's an extremely programmable reverb that is great for adding a haunting quality to your sounds. I particularly like to use this reverb with strings. It adds a full sound to things that makes my heart flutter. The RV-7000 has a programmable EQ, as well, for adding a little something to your patches or taking away a little something that's not quite working.

Another thing that I mentioned earlier is how loops can really help a composer get a piece of material together quickly. Reason has a device called Dr.Rex that allows you to play recorded loops along with your existing song, or you can use Dr.Rex as a percussion device.

Speaking as a person who uses "the Dr." quite a bit, there are tons of handy loops available in Reason. I tend to use Dr.Rex as a percussion device or to manipulate existing loops in strange and distorted ways. At times though, I've needed guitar strumming in the background of a song, and Reason has many different types of instrument loops, as well as drum loops, to accommodate many different situations.

Redrum, Reason's drum machine, is equally handy. There are several different drum kits found in the Reason Factory Sound Banks based on different genres and styles. Redrum is an extremely programmable device that you can either manipulate in real time or with its step-time sequencer. It also has multiple outputs that allow you to route each drum sound to different effects and routings. This is great when you need to tighten up the kick with a compressor and add some reverb to the snare.

As you can see, Reason offers a lot to the composer in many ways. While it's an extremely robust package, it's also an extremely affordable one that tends to be the Swiss Army Knife in my arsenal as a sound designer and composer. I can also attest that it's an extremely stable program. There are so many things that you can't rely on in this life, so it's nice to have programs like Reason that always hold true!

Beyond being an all around, great program, Reason has an extremely cool community that is known for being very helpful.

Atmosphere for PC and Mac

Wavetable synthesizers have been around for a while; and when they are put together with the kind of love that went into Atmosphere, they are wonderful to hear.

Atmosphere is built off of a 3.7GB core library. The sounds that reside within that library come from legendary synthesizers that have been lovingly recorded and cataloged. Some of these synthesizers include the Yamaha CS-80, the Virus, and the Roland Super Jupiter. The list is so long that it would astound you.

Atmosphere, pictured in Figure 11.11, was originally intended as a synthesizer that would behave more as a pad synthesizer, but it evolved over time. Apparently, they noticed that it was capable of a lot more. From dense pads to vocoded choirs to ambient strings, Atmosphere is very capable of setting a mood.

Eric Persing was the sound designer behind Atmosphere. You may know his name from all of his work that went into many of the classic Roland synthesizers. Some of these synths are the legendary JV-1080, the JP-8000, the D-50, and the Jupiter 6. These synthesizers were amazingly prominent and influenced the sounds of many great composers over the last 20 years. It goes

Figure 11.11

Atmosphere supplies some beautiful sounds in a down-to-earth interface—a perfect companion for the composer.

without saying that you will find something for almost any track you're working on with this synth. Another great Atmosphere feature is that its patches are meticulously cataloged so that you can quickly find the type of sound you need when you need it.

Atmosphere isn't usually the composer's main synth, but it's always being used. And in a sense, this means that the software is living up to its namesake. Even if it's not the main synth, it's at least providing "Atmosphere."

Blue for PC and Mac

Rob Papen, responsible for designing sound sets for the Virus as well as many other synths, started his own line of soft synths a while back. Blue is one synth of his that is consistently the subject of conversations I've had with composers lately.

Blue is a fine example of a soft synth doing its own thing, rather than trying to emulate an older synthesizer. It's got a large amount of modulation options, a sequencer, and a very powerful arpeggiator (see Figure 11.12). The interface is intelligently laid out, and it's a very pretty synth to look at in general. The colors, blue and silver, resemble the Virus Indigo. I wonder if it's coincidence?

This synthesizer is capable of several forms of synthesis, and that seems to be the key that makes it so robust. It features FM synthesis, phase distortion, waveshaping, and subtractive synthesis. This gives you a lot to work with to help you come up with your sounds. Also, having the ability to merge these forms of synthesis will definitely create some powerful sounds, indeed.

Blue's preset banks carry a wide array of thick synth basses and cutting leads. This synth would work well in any action game or sci-fi title. The pad presets that ship with this synth are nothing short of epic. They have a regal quality about them that can come off as either somber, beautiful, or uplifting, depending on how you play them.

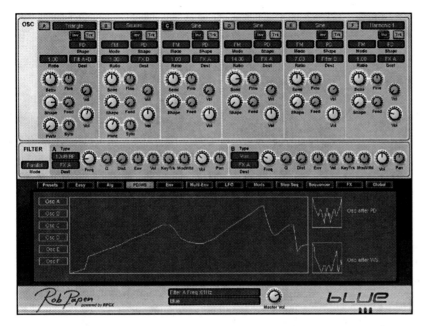

Figure 11.12

It's always good to have a workhorse synthesizer like Blue. The sounds are thick, and it has a regality that adds to a composition.

The interface is intelligently thought out, and it has an Easy edit mode that's great for the composer who needs something quick and doesn't want to jack around with menus all night, or day.

If you're a composer who likes to make his own sounds, you've got plenty of power with Blue. This synth has up to six oscillators, two filter banks, a step sequencer, and an arpeggiator. I find arpeggiators to be wonderful sources of inspiration when you have that great idea, but you need a little something to drive it. Blue is priced competitively, and you'll have a hard time finding a synth that is as capable and robust.

Minimoog V for PC and Mac

In a relatively short amount of time, Arturia has made a name for itself by recreating classic synthesizers in the software environment. The synthesizers not only come very close to replicating the sound, but they also have really cool interfaces that resemble the hardware interfaces of the synth that they seek to replicate.

One synth that has been invaluable to me at moments when I just couldn't find a sound that would fit is the Minimoog V. The Minimoog, shown in Figure 11.13, has the classic knob layout of the original Minimoog synthesizer. It also can be installed with three different wood finishes to suit your taste. (No, it doesn't affect the sound at all.) It even has a button that gives you access to the added features and embellishments that the company has added to the classic synth. Some of these features include an arpeggiator, a chorus, and a digital delay.

Figure 11.13
The classic Minimoog was used for years in many productions and compositions. The software version seems to be continuing the tradition.

One area that will benefit the composer is how thoughtfully Arturia has categorized the sounds by the sound designers (and there are some very reputable ones, such as Jean-Michael Jarre, for example).

The MinimoogV is capable of very thick leads, basses, and even polyphonic synths. It's got some pretty beautiful pads, too. India is one pad that I've found myself playing around with for the sheer enjoyment of it. It's warm and regal, with a nice attack.

Pretty much any time I'm having trouble finding a bass to go with whatever composition I'm working on, I turn to the Minimoog to answer my bass needs. Recently, I was trying to do a retro composition, and none of the basses in my usual arsenal were sitting quite right. With just a few minutes of tweaking the Minimoog, I had a success that helped make the composition as a whole.

While it may not sound exactly like the original synthesizer, in terms of dynamic quality and the frequency range, the Minimoog still covers all the basses. You almost have to be careful with it because it can take up your whole mix if you let it.

I don't necessarily think this is a synth that you can't live without, but I do think it's great for special situations where nothing else seems to work. It's not an incredibly expensive soft synth, so I recommend at least taking a moment to check out the demo and see if it might work in your palette.

Well, I've covered multi-track programs, wave editors, and soft synths for the composer. In the next chapter, we're going to get into one tool that is of the utmost importance to the modern day composer—the soft sampler. And in doing so, we'll go over some of the sample libraries that other composers in the industry are using right now!

12 } Samplers

If you have never worked with a sampler, let me give you a brief description of how one works. A sampler takes one or more recorded sounds and then spreads them out over a keyboard. The sampler allows you to play the recorded sound by pressing a key on a keyboard. Each key will play the recording at either the recording's original speed or pitch or a different speed or pitch. This description, however, is only the basic function of a sampler, the function most commonly associated with a sampler.

When I was still in elementary school, Casio released the SK-1 keyboard pictured in Figure 12.1. At an affordable price, it was one of the first keyboards to let you sample external sounds and then do some light manipulation. A friend of mine had one, and we'd record any number of sounds to entertain ourselves. We'd play "Mary Had A Little Lamb" with whatever crude sounds we could think of.

When I got older, I got a real sampler—a Roland S-550. At the time, it was one of the hottest samplers on the market. You could hook it up to a computer screen and actually see the waveform, while performing very surgical edits compared to what other samplers were capable of. It even had a mouse that you could use with it (see Figure 12.2). I used to stay up for hours sampling different sounds around the house and then manipulating them in different ways. It was always a goal of mine to see if I could take one kind of sound and then use it for something entirely different.

I also got acquainted with layering samples on top of one another. I thought this was one of the coolest features! I'd record my voice singing "ahhh," like a choir boy. Then I'd record a female friend of mine doing the same thing. I used to make layered choir samples and use them in songs of mine.

The other thing I loved to do was make velocity-sensitive patches. With these patches, I'd make one sample of a small chink of metal, which I tagged as the low-velocity sample. The next sample would be a very hard chink of metal. This I tagged as the high-velocity sample. I'd assign both of

Figure 12.1

The Casio SK-1 was one of the earliest, affordable samplers on the market. I remember it fondly.

Figure 12.2

The Roland S-550 was one of the first samplers to allow wave manipulation with a mouse and monitor. It was way ahead of its time.

these samples to the same key. When I'd hit the key softly, the small chink of metal would play. When I'd strike the key in a harder manner, the hard chink of metal would play.

When I think back to the old days of tooling around with my sampler in school, I learned a lot about sample editing, patch creation, and sound design. The great thing about all I learned, though, is that sound design really hasn't changed much since samplers became, more or less, all software.

Software samplers have all the same functions as my old sampler and much, much more. There are several layers of velocity sensitivity, real-time manipulation features like sound morphing, and real-time time-stretching and pitch-shifting.

On top of all the editing features, graphically working with a sampling program has never been easier. You can see all of what the waveform is doing. You can see where the loop begins and ends and look at the sample in different views. You can perform on-the-spot edits. You can bring your sample into your wave editor and perform some very surgical edits. The sky is pretty much the limit with the amount of audio manipulation available today.

But does a composer have time for all of these functions? Not really. Composers need sounds that are already great and ready to go. They also need sounds that are as close as possible to the real thing. That's where samplers come in really handy. There are orchestras that have been painstakingly sampled and edited. The patches that contain each sample are well thought out and meticulously laid out. We will look at a few of these sample libraries later in this chapter.

Sampling programs, or samplers, accommodate all of this. They make having the orchestra right at your finger tips a reality. To an even greater extent, it means you have entire choirs right at your finger tips. Take East West's Symphonic Choirs, for example. This package is a complete set of samples and patches recorded from a full choir. Every vowel sound that is commonly used by the choir is recorded, and every voice within the choir has been recorded. It even comes with a program that will cause the choir to sing certain words.

The sampler is one of the great tools of the modern day composer. And this is the chapter to tell you about it. You're going to explore several different samplers and how they can be useful to you. We'll also take a look at different sample packages that have come recommended by other composers in the field.

Sample Formats

Over the years, there have been several different sample libraries made for several different software and hardware samplers alike. Unfortunately, the sample libraries were usually made in a format that would only work with one kind of sampler. Thankfully, with the rise of the software sampler, many sampling programs can read multiple formats. This not only includes the old samplers (like my old Roland) but also the new samplers.

But why would you want to read old libraries of the samplers of long ago? Well, the quality that went into some of these libraries is quite extensive, and there are some very beautiful patches to be heard. Not to mention, you can get these older libraries at a much smaller price than what they used to sell for back in the day. But the new libraries are all in different formats as well, and that's why it's important to pick up a soft sampler that can support as many different formats as possible. You just never know when you'll stumble upon an old gem that might be in a different format than what you currently use.

Now, don't think that you're stuck if your sampler doesn't support the format of a library that you just can't live without. There are programs like CDxtract that can convert a sample library into another format with the touch of a button. But even as great as CDxtract is, you may still have some functions that aren't carried over from sampler to sampler.

Take a look at some of the big sample formats that are around today:

❋ **Akai:** At one point, Akai was the big player on the block that made the most sought-after samplers on the market. As a result, there was a large library of samples for the Akai series of samplers. Don't be misled! You may have a sampler that supports some Akai libraries but not all. For example, Kontakt 2 supports the S-1000/3000 series and the S-5000/6000 series. Take a look at an S5000 in Figure 12.3.

Figure 12.3

The Akai samplers were at the top of the heap for a long time. They still have a huge library of wonderful sounds that you can take advantage of with your soft sampler.

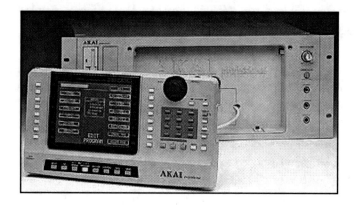

❋ **E-mu:** Another big player from back in the day was E-mu. Here is another sample format that will have several different variants. There were several different samplers, from the E6400 series to the ESI series.

❋ **Roland:** The Roland sample formats are still as widely used as the last two mentioned. There were only two big series to think about with Roland—the S-7X and S-5X. Roland captured some beautiful samples and made some wonderful presets and patches out of their hard work.

❋ **SoundFont/SoundFont2:** The SoundFont format was developed by E-mu and its owner, Creative labs. It is a simple-to-use bank management and authoring tool with Sound Blaster and E-mu cards that play back sound like a synthesizer. Essentially, a SoundFont is a patch that will work with sound cards, samplers, and synths that support SoundFonts. There have been some nice SoundFonts created by companies and individuals—there are a lot of SoundFont enthusiasts out there!

❋ **GigaStudio:** GigaStudio is at this moment a very popular format, especially for professional composers. There are gigantic libraries on top of libraries available in all the Giga formats (.gig and .gsi). These formats are usually limited to users of GigaStudio, but Kontakt 2 has the ability to play these Giga formats as well.

Soft Samplers

As stated in previous chapters, the soft sampler has filled the niche at being a main tool of the modern-day composer. The editing features are superb, and every soft sampler has something to offer. Whether it's an intuitive interface or a vast amount of libraries, there is something for everyone.

There are some, like Logic Pro's EXS24, that are native only to a certain host program. But you may ask, "Why would you want to be limited to a sampler that only works in a host program?" Usually a plug-in or instrument native to a program will integrate seamlessly with the interface of the program and the functions contained therein. Some soft samplers even allow you to drag audio parts within a song you are working on into the sampler so that you can manipulate it or play it musically.

But then there are standalone software samplers and some that can run either as plug-ins or as a standalone program that can be manipulated via MIDI by another sequencer. This is a very common scenario among many modern composers. Some of the software samplers and their extensive sample libraries use a lot of resources. It's very common to hear of one composer having one PC as a host sequencer and five other computers merely acting as samplers.

Is this kind of scenario required? No, not at all, but it works out well for some. They've got the cash for it, and they have the need. But if you think about it, it's not really that difficult to pull off. PCs are getting cheaper and cheaper; a lot of people even have old machines just lying around that they aren't using anymore. Some of these discarded machines may make good little plug-in hosts for samplers. Of course, you should check the specifications out before you jump to any conclusions, however.

Which soft sampler is right for you? You're going to examine a few of the more popular ones in this chapter. These soft samplers are the chosen applications of several of the composers that I've interviewed while writing this book. So take a look at why these are recommended.

Kontakt for PC and Mac

I've heard a lot about samplers from various composers—a *lot*. And when samplers are mentioned, Kontakt has always been one of the first. This makes sense; Kontakt is undeniably powerful and offers a sleek interface with a robust feature set that runs transparently in the background.

Kontakt offers a modular architecture that allows you to modify the signal flow that your samples go through. It has a handy browser that lets you see an overview of your samples, modules, and so on. This is great for finding sounds and modules that you need quickly and letting you add them in as needed. A picture of the all of the modules within Kontakt is shown in Figure 12.4.

Kontakt can work as a standalone sampling instrument or as a plug-in that can be launched in programs like Nuendo or Logic. This is awesome because, as I was saying in the soft sampler overview, you could feasibly have a dedicated Kontakt machine that acted as a sound module while you ran another machine as a sequencer. As a plug-in, it will run VSTi, Audio Units, RTAS, or DXi.

Figure 12.4
*Kontakt is made up of a
modular architecture that
you can use to edit and
manipulate your samples.*

Kontakt is a multi-timbral instrument that allows you to take several different instruments available in Kontakt that are made up of your samples and play them individually. You can, for example, have one instrument in Kontakt act as a drum module, while another instrument in Kontakt is playing guitar samples. You can combine these instruments into what Kontakt calls **multis**. When you have several instruments working together in a multi, you are able to assign each instrument to its own MIDI channel. This gives you individual control over each instrument, and it's also a system common to most computer music users. Multis also contain output and aux settings for routing your sounds to the appropriate sound sources within your host audio program or your audio interface.

Kontakt also has a sophisticated browser that logs all of the Kontakt-compatible files available on your computer or on your network, if you have your computer set up on one. This is paired with the browser I mentioned earlier that allows quick drag-and-drop functionality. This allows you to drag and drop instruments and multis into Kontakt's virtual rack.

There are also multiple playback engines for use in Kontakt, five of them in all. There is the standard Sampler mode, which alters pitch like a standard sampler by resampling files to stretch across a keyboard. There's also the Tone Machine feature, which alters pitch without altering the duration. I could see this being a great tool for voice samples, guitar stabs, and so on.

There's also the Time Machine feature, which can do a variety of pitch, duration, and other alterations. Additionally, there's Time Machine II, a version of the Time Machine, optimized for quality pitch transposition and tempo-stretching. And finally, there is the Beat Machine, which is a method of slicing digital audio to allow for high-quality time-stretching.

When you are editing instruments, you can work on a much more detailed level. Individual samples that make up an instrument can be mapped in different ways using the map editor to cover a keyboard and group them together for further editing. For example, you might want to group some tom samples together in a drum kit and process them as a group. There is also a looping editor that works with individual samples, allowing repeating portions of the sample to create sustained or rhythmic effects.

Kontakt also has extensive signal processing options and a large roster of effects. You can drag effects as inserts for samples and groups, as master effects for instruments, as sends or aux effects, and as master effects for outputs. These effects include filters, modulations, and time effects. There's also a convolution reverb for extremely realistic reverbs. Convolution reverbs are incredibly hot with many composers and sound designers at the moment. They are great for creating atmospheres as well as replicating halls and environments. As you can see, Kontakt is a comprehensive package that offers a mighty palette of tools. Beyond what I've already discussed, it also includes a 14GB library of sample material, which includes guitars, orchestras, pianos, and more.

The convolution reverb even includes impulses. Impulses are samples used to replicate the environment of certain spaces, like subway tunnels and churches. It's pretty exciting, if you think about it. You can bring up a full orchestra and then apply a reverb using the impulse of the kind of auditorium that an orchestra would actually play in.

There are also several libraries of samples available for Kontakt, and it reads multiple formats like Akai, GigaStudio, SoundFont2, EXS, .wav, and .aiff. If you have any additional questions about the functionality of Kontakt and its current versions, you can visit www.native-instruments.com.

GigaStudio for PC

GigaStudio, shown in Figure 12.5, is known as the hottest soft sampler on the market, and for good reason. It was one of the first soft samplers available, period. It's got an extensive list of libraries available for it, and it's used by many, many major composers for film, TV, and video games, which include greats like Hans Zimmer and Trevor Rabin. Some versions of GigaStudio may be overkill for your way of working. Thankfully, it comes in three different versions:

✳ **Orchestra** features unlimited voices, or whatever your host system can handle, and can accept up to eight ports at a time. It's fully ReWire 2-compatible, so you can use it with programs like Reason, Cubase SX, and Logic. To add to its versatility, you can also host VST plug-ins out of GigaStudio Orchestra. It also has up to 24-bit/96kHz support. The included sample libraries are the Full and Light Edition of MegaPiano II and an additional 17 GB of samples that include the custom Vienna Giga Symphony.

Figure 12.5

Like Kontakt, you'll notice GigaStudio has several modules, or interfaces, resembling hardware devices to help you edit your patches.

- ❋ **Ensemble** is limited to 160 voices, but lets face it, that's quite a bit. It will definitely get you by. It only has four MIDI ports, but it does include the Full and LE versions of MegaPiano II. It also has an additional 11 GB of samples. Like the Orchestra version, it is also ReWire 2-compliant and can host VST plug-ins.

- ❋ **GigaStudio** Solo is geared more for the type of chap who only needs a little bit of Giga support but loves it nonetheless. It still has a whopping 96 voices and two MIDI ports, so it's far from useless. It only comes with the Light Edition of MegaPiano II, but it still comes with 3 GB of sample data. It's also ReWire 2-compliant and can host VST plug-ins.

One thing you'll notice is that GigaStudio is for Windows only. However, this shouldn't dissuade Mac users. Plenty of Mac musicians use a PC to host GigaStudio and have it controlled by a Mac running sequencing software. With the constantly falling prices of PCs, you can put together a screaming system for less than the price of many synth modules. If you look at price versus performance, a GigaStudio computer workstation will give you much more realistic sound than most synth modules, not to mention more multi-timbral parts, higher polyphony, and better effects.

Another way for Mac users to take advantage of GigaStudio is through the recently released Boot Camp from Apple. This allows the new Intel Macs to dual boot Mac OS X and Windows XP. As a standalone application, it can take advantage of Kernel-level processing power. This means that it gets to dig underneath the Windows layer and get down to the root of your computer's CPU for more processing power. Reportedly, this results in more polyphony and lower latency than plug-in–based software samplers.

One newer component of GigaStudio is GigaPulse, shown in Figure 12.6. This is a convolution reverb that can be used within GigaStudio. The Pro version of GigaPulse is available only in the GigaStudio Orchestra version, but there is a light version available for Ensemble and Solo. Additionally, it also does mic-modeling and instrument-resonance simulations. Can you think of a better way to give your performances that pro sound?

If you are dead set on working in only your host DAW and know that you won't be working with another PC, there is GVI. GVI is the VSTi/RTAS plug-in version of GigaStudio 3. You get regular access to all of the libraries, the power of the program, and the same interface. Things to know about GVI are that its fully multi-timbral, supports multiple instances, and has up to 16 MIDI channels. At the time of this writing, GVI support for Mac OS X is promised for the future.

As you can see, GigaStudio is very flexible and gives you a slew of different choices in configurations. As it's one of the hottest-selling software samplers to date, it would be a good idea to keep it in mind for your future pursuits as a composer. If you would like to know more about GigaStudio, there is a wealth of information at www.tascam.com. You can even download a demo of GVI!

Figure 12.6

GigaPulse is a convolution reverb that ships in different forms, depending on the version of GigaStudio you pick up.

Additional Samplers

While Kontakt and GigaStudio tend to be the most talked about samplers by video game composers, there are several others available that are well designed and will do a great job in supporting your needs. The rest of the samplers I'll be talking about act as plug-ins inside of host audio programs, like Nuendo, Digital Performer, and Logic Pro. These samplers are well regarded, can support extensive sample libraries, and also have great libraries created for their sole use.

Logic Pro EXS24 for Mac

Logic Pro is a very popular program among composers today. It's owned by Apple, and it's been engineered to work flawlessly within the Mac OS.

The EXS24 sampler, pictured in Figure 12.7 works inside of Logic Pro. It's maintained by Apple for Logic, so you can expect the same great quality that you're used to receiving from all of the Apple product line. Additionally, because it runs native to Logic Pro, when working with the EXS24, it's like working with an extension of Logic Pro rather than switching to another app.

So what file formats does the EXS24 support? For starters, it supports the Akai format, which is almost a given with any soft sampler out there. There are vast numbers of sample volumes available in the Akai format. The GigaSampler library is also supported. If you're not a fan of using GigaStudio, but you like certain volumes available in the GigaSampler format, this is great. If you're an old SampleCell user, or you have come across some old SampleCell volumes that you think might be cool, you'll be pleased to know that the EXS24 supports the SampleCell 2 format.

Figure 12.7
The EXS24 is a powerful sampler that comes in Logic Pro and supports a wide variety of sample libraries.

The REX format is also supported, which is great if you're into sampled loops. The REX format is a type of loop file that slices every beat in a loop down to individual "slices" but still keeps all of the loop tempo, MIDI information, and audio bundled together in one audio file. When you load up a REX file, you can either play the loop as an audio file or have the loop laid out across the keyboard like a drum kit—instant drums!

The SoundFont 2 file format is supported as well. As mentioned previously, there are vast numbers of SoundFont 2 patches available online and in stores. You may not use it now, but it might come in handy.

The EXS24 is also capable of creating complex routes for your audio through its extensive modulation matrix. This provides you with several possibilities for manipulating your audio. You can make your strings pulse to the beat like a synthesizer, or you can give your synth pad a percussive quality. Modulation matrixes can breathe new life into plain sound patches. Additionally, you can give your sounds greater movement in the stereo field by tying their panning to an LFO within the EXS24. There are endless things you can do with this feature!

The EXS24 also provides you with a multi-mode filter. It comes with adjustable slopes, variable filter overdrive amount, and a fatness circuit that ensures excellent low-frequency response, even at high resonance settings.

These are just a few of the great features within the EXS24. It is also one of the most famously CPU-friendly samplers on the Mac. This is certainly a wonderful sampler that can provide a wealth of abilities to you as a composer if you're working in Logic Pro.

HALion for PC and Mac

You will find few samplers that can match the features available in HALion, pictured in Figure 12.8. Of all the plug-in–based soft samplers, it's one of the first, and Steinberg has been building on it for several years.

Figure 12.8

HALion is a versatile sampler that has a cool interface and supports a wide variety of formats.

HALion supports all the standard plug-in formats, such as VST, DXi, AU, and ReWire. It can also work as a standalone for live scenarios and similar applications.

One of the things that made me drool from the start was that HALion uses filters designed by Waldorf. The synthesizers that Waldorf has produced have a very warm and full sound, due in no small part to the awesome filters that are present within. Now in HALion, you can apply these same filters to your sample patches.

HALion also offers an advanced audio engine that works in up to 5.1 surround and supports audio files recorded in up to 384 kHz. Granted, there aren't a whole lot of files recorded in 384 kHz, but it's nice to know that HALion is a sampler that can grow with the pushes of technology.

You'll be pleased to note that HALion is a fully multi-timbral instrument that accepts up to 16 MIDI channels and can be opened multiple times as a VST plug-in.

One of the things HALion is widely noted for is its user interface. Everything is drag and drop and intelligently laid out. There's even a little control ball in the corner of the interface that lets you quickly navigate to other windows.

For editing multi-samples, HALion has an extremely intelligent editor that allows you to see where each layer of the samples are and when and how they occur while being played in a patch. It's an incredibly easy way to work. I can tell you that when setting up velocity-sensitive patches in hardware samplers of old, this was a very tedious task that HALion has made easy.

HALion also reads an enormous amount of sample types: Akai, E-mu, Kontakt, Kurzweil, Roland, Giga, EXS24, SF2, LM4, LM4 MkII, REX, ZGR (ZeroX BeatCreator), .wav, .aiff, and SD II (Mac only). HALion pretty much covers it all for you. Another really cool feature is that HALion can access Nero CD images without needing them burned as CDs. This means that you can have multiple disc images on one drive that HALion can access at a moment's notice!

HALion also ships with over 160 sampled instruments. These include synthesizers, strings, guitars, drums, and pianos. The sound library is clearly organized and arranged in instrument categories, making it easy to pull the right instrument for the right occasion.

For performance boosting, HALion employs RAMSave technology. This technology limits the amount of sample data stored in your internal memory, based on what you're actually using in your composition. It actually scans MIDI notes and deletes all samples that are not assigned to any used notes. This lightens the RAM's load and ensures faster loading times.

In addition to the features listed previously, HALion has a very nice effects section, an elaborate modulation matrix, and Q controls that allow you quick access to specified parameters, each rotating on every specific patch. This is handy for tweaking the sweet spots of certain patches and getting a good sound in a short amount of time. For more information on HALion visit www.steinberg.net.

MachFive for PC and Mac

MOTU (Mark of the Unicorn) also offers a very, very powerful sampler—the MachFive. This soft sampler can work as a plug-in with any of these plug-in types: VSTi, RTAS, DXi, MAS, Audio Units, and HTDM.

MachFive's interface has been designed to look like hardware, but don't let that scare you. The layout is well thought out and is quite intuitive. I might add that it's really cool to look at sporting black, red, and blue hues. It has one of the more sleek interfaces of the sampler line-up.

Like many of the soft samplers we've covered, MachFive supports many sample formats: Akai, SampleCell, EXS24, and GigaSampler, as well as legacy formats like Kurzweil, E-mu, and Roland. This compatibility is made possible by UVI-Xtract, an import utility included with MachFive that allows you to import programs and samples from all the formats listed here.

MachFive, pictured in Figure 12.9, is 16-part multi-timbral and each part has multiple choices of audio outputs, including volume, pan, and so on. Additionally, MachFive supports up to 5.1 audio files in real time and has multi-channel effects to support this format.

It boasts a powerful synthesis engine that offers eight filter algorithms that include crucial parameters like Filter Resonance, Cutoff Frequency, and Overdrive. These parameters may be automated by MIDI. It even has modulation options available at every stage of the synth section. Additionally, this engine is capable of unlimited polyphony and ultra-low latency. Support for up to 24-bit/192 kHz audio is available within MachFive as well.

Figure 12.9

MachFive is a powerful sampler that has a great look and a great feature set.

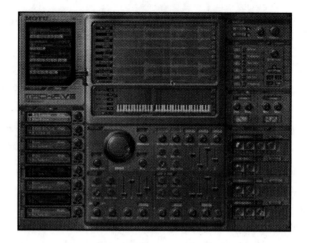

Like the other samplers in this class, MachFive offers drag-and-drop capabilities. It allows you to drop in samples from your desktop and host application to the MachFive keyboard. You can also audition samples while importing them, listening to each note as you stretch a key map over a range of keys.

Each multi-timbral part can have up to four insert effects plus four preset effects. Additionally, you can add four global aux effects and four master effects, all operating simultaneously. Basically, you can have up to 136 total FX and 85 separate FX chains per instance of MachFive with instant recall.

Many different kinds of effects are included. Reverbs, tempo-synced delays, tremolo, chorus, filters, and BitCrushers are just some of the effects that you'll find with this sampler.

MachFive is definitely a formidable sampler that competes with the best of them. Its flexibility makes it ideal for the game composer, and its large effects array will work well for you when creating broad musical atmospheres. For more information, visit www.motu.com.

Sample Libraries

Now that you've gone over the soft samplers available to the composer, I'll talk about the sample libraries that you'll want to accompany your soft sampler.

There are tons of packages out there, and none of them are cheap. Occasionally, you can find some deals on legacy sample libraries that were available for the hardware samplers of old, but for the new cutting-edge sample libraries, you're probably going to have to spend some money.

Why are sample libraries so expensive? Where orchestral libraries are concerned, a lot of time and money is spent on hiring the studio and musicians, producing the material, organizing the files...you get the picture. These libraries have been lovingly put together by some of the best names in the business, and, when you hear them, you'll get an idea why they are so good. You'll also get an idea of why they cost so much.

Do not forget that these libraries are made up of thousands and thousands of sample files. They spend months creating these libraries, recording minute details like fret slides and reed clicks. The end result is a full-fledged replication of whatever you've purchased, right there at your finger tips.

But how do you know which libraries are worth the money? In this section, we'll go over some of the picks of several composers working in the industry. We'll examine why they're cool, and why you might want them in your compositions.

Vienna Symphonic Library

The Vienna Symphonic Library stems from a frustration that many of us feel when composing—we want a real orchestra, but we can't afford it. This is the same thing that Herb Tucmandl felt when he was inspired to put this project together. He was working as an orchestral film composer, but there were no budgets available for full orchestras. He quickly turned to samplers and the limited sample libraries that were available at the time, but these libraries didn't live up to the challenge.

In the end, Tucmandl decided to create his own sample library based on his own abilities with the cello. On top of being a film composer, Tucmandl was also a substituting cellist for the Vienna Philharmonic Orchestra and knew what things were supposed to sound like. He booked some time at a studio and recorded several thousand samples of his cello. He made a demo of his idea and convinced some investors and experts that he had a great idea.

Herb went on to find other musicians to record their instruments, as well—from string artists like Christian Eisenberger and Anett Homoki to renowned harpists like Ruth Rojahn. There is nothing but talent going into these recordings, and there's definitely talent in recreating the instruments coming back through your sampler. Since then, Vienna Symphonic Library has been built up from the instruments of several orchestral musicians. Not only is there cello, but there are all the other instruments making up a real symphonic orchestra.

There are several ways to purchase the Vienna Symphonic Library. One new convenient way doesn't even require a soft sampler. You can purchase Vienna Instruments, which is made up of some of these vast collections. There are several different instruments available: solo strings, orchestral strings, woodwinds, percussion, and so on. These instruments support VST and AU and also can operate as a standalone.

You can purchase these instrument volumes separately or purchase the Symphonic Cube, which is made up of all the above and more. These virtual instruments help organize a vast array of samples over one MIDI channel, allowing you to mimic the nuances and emotions of the instruments with ease.

If you would rather use your soft sampler to control these samplers, you can go with the Orchestral Cube. This package includes strings, brass and woodwinds, and percussion. It comes in the GigaStudio 2.5 format, as well as the Emagic EXS MKII format. All of the volumes can be purchased separately as well, if you don't have the funds or the need for the whole Cube. Vienna Symphonic Library also offers the Horizon series. These are individual volumes that focus on specific instruments or instrument groups. These volumes work with the Giga formats, EXS24, Kontakt, and HALion.

For an all-inclusive library from the Horizon series, you can purchase the Opus 1 and Opus 2 products that contain strings, brass, woodwinds, and percussion. Or you can purchase more specialized volumes that come in the Opus series like solo strings, Vienna harps, and woodwind ensembles.

One suggestion is that when using this library, you'll need to use a lot of reverb. It's much more dry than the Symphonic Choirs by East West (see the section, "Symphonic Choirs," later in this chapter). This is because the Vienna Symphonic Library is recorded in a dry environment, while some of the other libraries are actually recorded live in a concert hall. With the convolution reverbs that are available these days, you can pretty much put the Vienna library in any hall you want to, however.

The Vienna Symphonic Library is a beautiful recreation of an amazingly talented orchestra. If your compositions are in need of an orchestral kick, you won't find a better one anywhere else. For more information, check out www.vsl.co.at.

SAM Orchestral Brass

If you're looking to supplement your brass arsenal, Sam Orchestral Brass may be just what you're looking for.

This library was recorded in an actual concert hall, covering the French horn, trombone, and trumpet section. There are also solo instruments and essentials, like the tuba and cimbasso. A wide variety of articulations and modern playing techniques and effects have been recorded for all the brass in this library. Sustains, multiple marcato lengths, multiple staccatos, staccatissimos, mutes, stopped notes, crescendos, diminuendos, and glissandos are all available to flesh out your compositions.

A number of short phrases are available for the solo horn, trumpet, trombone, and tuba, as well as for the trumpet section. These phrases include 8th-note triplets, 8th-note and 16th figures, and repeated staccatos in 16ths. The full brass set covers three orchestral brass sections and seven orchestral solo brass instruments, which comes to an impressive total of 150 sampled articulations.

In movies, there are lots of orchestrations taking place throughout the score. Since video games are becoming more and more cinematic, it makes sense that the music would start to emulate the scores heard in movies. With that in mind, having some good orchestral brass at your disposal isn't a bad thing. For more information on SAM Orchestral Brass, check out www.projectsam.com.

Symphonic Orchestra, Gold Edition

As I mentioned with the Vienna Symphonic Library, virtual instruments are becoming a new trend in the soft sampler community. Basically, when you buy a sample library, a soft instrument is included that already has all the articulations, velocity maps, and nuances mapped to the keys in a logical way.

Symphonic Orchestra, Gold Edition ships with Kompakt, a light version of Kontakt, that is basically a sample instrument that supports VST and DXi2 for the PC. For the Mac, it supports VST, Audio Units, and RTAS. You can do basic edits to each patch, such as edit the release and attack, as well as other basic adjustments. The software also does a few things for you that may alleviate the need for some of these edits, though. The included software analyzes the amplitude of the waveform when the key is released, activating the release trail and adjusting the dynamics so the two samples blend seamlessly.

But what if you want to use the library with your existing soft sampler? If you are a Kontakt user, you can import the sampler patches into the full version of Kontakt for added flexibility. Or you can use programs like CDxtract to convert the included libraries to the format that you are using.

The person responsible for the engineering of the Symphonic Orchestra library is Prof. Keith O. Johnson, who recorded this colossal library in a $125 million concert hall. His idea was to recreate the orchestra in its native environment, where an orchestra is known to sound best.

So what does the library include? Eighteen violins, 10 cellos, 10 violas, nine basses, a solo violin, solo cello, harp, three flutes, three oboes, a piccolo flute, six horns, four trumpets, four bass/tenor bones, a solo tuba, and an entire percussion section. And that's not all!

The Symphonic Orchestra, Gold Edition comes highly recommended, and you get a lot out of it for one initial price. For more information, check out www.soundsonline.com.

Symphonic Choirs

When composing for video games, getting that epic sound is really important. If you're composing for a sci-fi title, or an adventure title, or for any title whose music should transport the player, you want them to feel like they are a part of the adventure and existing in one of their favorite movies.

One color that I might recommend for your palette would be human choirs. Choirs add a true human element to any orchestral composition. Well, the choir is the one element that can only sound human—that's its job, right? It's singing. And what's more beautiful than hundreds of male and female voices there to back up your orchestra?

It's become a pastime of mine to listen to scores in video games and to try to figure out if it's a real orchestra or a sampled orchestra. You'd be surprised how hard it is to tell. Some of the time, composers will have just enough of a budget to book part of an orchestra. For example, they might book a brass section and that's it. They'll have the brass section play along with the sequenced composition. Later, the composer will mix in the real orchestral elements with the sampled orchestral elements, thus creating an amalgamation that sounds very authentic...because in reality it is. When you add in sampled choirs, it takes the already authentic-sounding composition and knocks it right over the edge. I mean, hey, it's got to be real. There's singing in it, right?

East West has created a truly remarkable product with the Symphonic Choirs package for adding choirs to your composition. The Symphonic Choirs package is startling in its depth. It contains five choirs altogether: a boy's choir, alto (female), soprano (female), basses (male), tenors (male), and solo singers. It was recorded at the same concert hall, and with the same team of engineers and producers, as the Symphonic Orchestra mentioned previously. This is great if you own both packages. It sounds like the choir and orchestra are in the same hall because they are! The choirs were even recorded with three simultaneous stereo mic setups (close, stage, and hall), so you can mix any combination of mics to control tone and ambience.

For added authenticity, all the singers were recorded in position and chromatically sampled with multiple dynamics (non-vibrato, light vibrato, and heavy vibrato). Really, it's almost like having the singers right there for you to direct. Having this kind of control can really lend to the emotion and depth of your compositions.

I mentioned previously that many of these packages are starting to be sold as virtual instruments. Symphonic Choirs is one of these. It comes with Kompakt, like Symphonic Orchestra, but the choirs cannot be imported into Kontakt, like the orchestra. As with Symphonic Orchestra, Symphonic Choirs supports VST, DXi, ASIO, and Direct Sound for PC and VST. For Mac it supports VST, Audio Units, Core Audio, Core MIDI, and RTAS.

You can't import these samples into other soft samplers because this package is more like a very large soft synth that uses a large sample library. However, this package can do one thing that is exceptional, and it relies on proprietary software to work. All of the choirs also recorded extensive singing vowels that can be formed together to build words. This is made possible through the Word Builder software that comes with Symphonic Choirs. You can make your choir sing more than just simple "ahhs" and "ohhs." They can sing the words that you tell them to, the way you want it! Granted, the Word Builder more or less only supports Latin, but I hear that if you play around with it enough, you can mimic certain words in English.

This package comes highly recommended for its 24-bit recording quality, its realism, and its flexibility. And let's face it, having five choirs at your command is a powerful feeling. And when you hear this package, you'll know what I'm talking about. East West has posted demos on its Web site (www.soundsonline.com), where you can hear how awesome this package really is. Its Web site also has additional information.

❋ Perusing the Libraries

As you can see, there is an increasing trend in some of the hot new sample libraries to be used as virtual instruments, rather than sample packs, so to speak. Before investing in a soft synth, you may want to take a look at some of the libraries available to see if they come as all-in-one instruments, rather than buying a sampler and then spending more money on the samples.

For instance, some of these sample libraries can cost far more than the actual sampler itself. Some go up into tens of thousands of dollars! The libraries covered in this chapter come highly recommended by working game composers. They are also newer and on the cutting edge. The sounds from these libraries are current and will serve you well in your endeavors.

13 } Editing Prerecorded Music

After reading the title of this chapter you are probably asking yourself, "Why would I have to edit prerecorded, licensed music within a video game?" You're probably thinking that you're only going to compose original music and that's that. I understand your train of thought; most composers I know have, at one point or another, thought the same thing. But all too often it does not work out this way.

I'm sure that you, like me, have some old movies lying around that you are a big fan of. These movies were ground-breaking and have inspired a huge following. Some of these movies are so big that they are still inspiring people on a daily basis, and, as a result, several video games have been made so that the huge fan base can still relive these wonderful flicks.

You would probably think that, when these new video games are being made, people would want fresh music that nods to the classic film scores of these monumental films, or maybe even new renditions of the classic scores. This does happen sometimes, but it usually affects the game adversely. Why? Fans tend to like what is most familiar when reliving their childhood fantasies. The quirkiness of the old scores and the antiquated quality of the recordings are still consciously and subconsciously dear to their hearts, and, as a result, it makes the fans feel more immersed when they are playing the game.

It isn't that strange if you think about it. You have those old songs that you love, and you prefer to hear the original recording artist. It's exactly the same thing when it comes to old movie scores.

Another trend has become popular with some of the mainstream games, like *Grand Theft Auto: San Andreas*. Game companies are starting to license mainstream hits for their video games. Does it matter to whatever lead or exec that the song may not be right for whatever cut scene that has been selected or that it's entirely too long? Nope, it's your job to fix it!

So does this go on a lot in the video game industry? It depends on what company you are working for and what style of games the company creates. But either way, it's important that you know how to edit existing music when and if the time ever comes up.

I know, I know—you pride yourself on only writing original music, but humor me with this chapter. You might even find that this is actually a challenging craft that can be very enjoyable. In fact, it's a skill that may earn you some easy cash now and then.

So what do you need when editing existing music? Usually just a multi-track editing program and a decent version of the music that you intend to edit. Additionally, it's helpful to have a good understanding of how to use automation to blend different parts seamlessly together.

This chapter will give you some prime examples of how to tackle this endeavor. And it can actually be pretty fun and rewarding. But it can also give you some self-inflicted bald spots, depending on the track!

Cutting Audio

What's really cool is how easy you have it when it comes to cutting music to either extend it or decrease its length. With computer editing capabilities, you can actually see where the music drops out and comes back in. As shown in Figure 13.1, notice where the audio's **amplitude**, or volume, gets bigger and smaller.

Figure 13.1
It's really helpful to be able to see where the audio rises and falls throughout its play time.

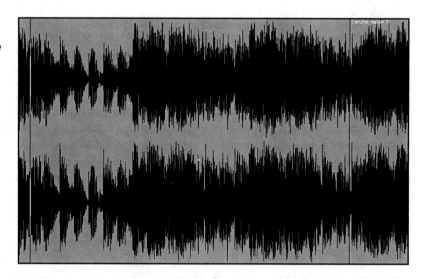

While the most important thing when editing music is what you hear, seeing what's going on helps as well. In the following exercise, I'll be using Nuendo to edit all of my audio. But this exercise is possible in all other multi-track programs, so don't be discouraged if you don't have Nuendo.

For example, say that I've been asked to make an existing piece of music shorter and also edit out all of the slow parts to keep it more fast-paced and intense. When the track starts, it's very intense and action-oriented, but then it slows down for a while. But you're doing an action game, so there's no time to slow down!

As shown in Figure 13.2, I go ahead and use the Scissors tool in Nuendo to separate the two pieces of audio. Notice that I cut where the level of the track is at its lowest volume. I do this because I would like the cleanest possible exit, regardless of what I plan on doing with the audio later. Most likely, I'll end up making the fade more drastic, but if I end up crossfading it, then I'll want that decay to be as natural as possible when fading in the next part of the music.

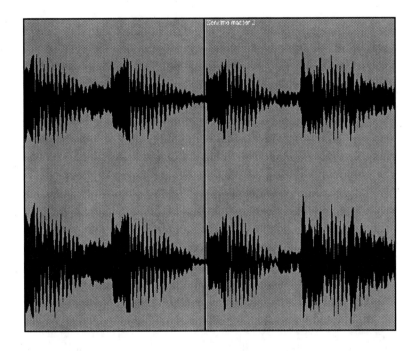

Figure 13.2
I find it best to cut where there is the least amount of volume within the track. This gives you the freedom to fade, crossfade, or end in any situation.

❋ **What You Hear versus What You See**

I'm going to say it again because it's important—what you hear is way more important than what you see in this kind of work. Seeing is also helpful, but if it doesn't sound right, then you need to keep trimming until it does.

If you find yourself questioning whether it sounds right or not, this is usually a good time to rest your ears for a few minutes, and then come back later and take a listen.

It's really convenient that you have such a great place to cut in this audio file. But what about when you are working with a piece of music that doesn't have a such a great point where you can cut? For example, say that the producer of the project likes a certain piece of licensed music.

As a matter of fact, he really likes one part of the music and he'd like it to continue a second time, regardless of how the song actually goes. When you listen to the music, you realize this piece just goes on and on—the part that he likes doesn't have any stops at all where you can create a good cut. What do you do?

Listen and look! Even an apparent steady stream of music will have small areas where it will drop out. It may be between a drum or between a guitar lick, but there will be a drop there. Also make sure that when you are cutting into a steady stream of music, you cut at a zero crossing, as shown in Figure 13.3.

Figure 13.3

Make sure that you cut at the zero crossing of an audio file if you are cutting during the middle of a sound. If you don't heed this warning, you may get a pop!

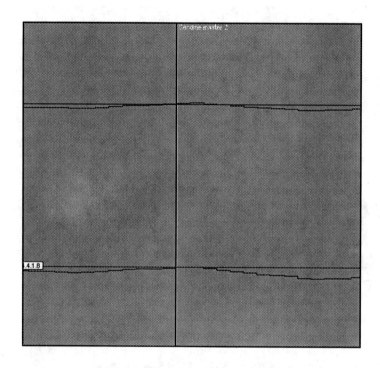

The Zero Crossing

There is a line that is displayed in between the alternating currents of audio in audio editors. The line is known as the **zero crossing** and is the single point at which there is no voltage present. The zero crossing is important for systems that send digital data over AC circuits. If there is a shift or break within the discrete gain settings generated by an audio file, artifacts like pops will occur.

The way that you ensure you're cutting at a zero crossing is to zoom in as close as you possibly can. Once you're all the way in, move to a point where the line of audio is touching the zero line.

Cut at the point where it intersects, and you've done it! Granted, this is only part of it; you also need to make sure you cut at a point where it sounds good, too! Once you get used to looking for both the zero crossing and an adequate spot within the music file to cut, the procedure will become second nature. Cutting audio is just a skill that one gains through continual practice.

So far we've only focused on the exit of the beginning of music. Now we'll move to the first part of the music that the producer likes. Start looking for a clean spot for entrance. In Figure 13.4 you will notice an audio file that just looks like a steady stream of sound...from a distance.

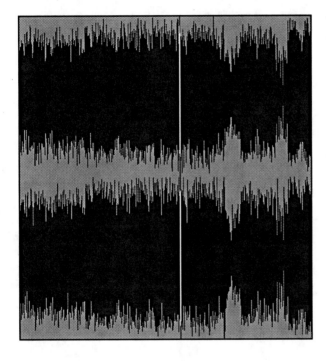

Figure 13.4
From a distance, this just looks like a wall of sound. Where could you cut this piece of music?

As you start to zoom in on the audio file, you'll notice that it's not as steady as it originally appeared. You can see jagged edges, like what's pictured in Figure 13.5. This particular audio track is a piece of electronic dance music with vocals. The jagged edges are the kick drum hits within the song.

You could actually cut in between the kick drum repetitions at the zero crossing and maybe, just maybe, make a seamless repetition of the audio file. You start listening to the area of the song over and over again. Once you feel like you've gotten comfortable with the start of the area that you want to cut, you make an incision with the Scissor tool, as shown in Figure 13.6.

Figure 13.5

When you zoom in closer on an audio file, you will begin to see more areas where cuts can occur. Granted, you still need to listen!

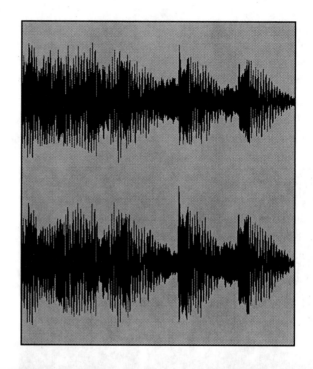

Figure 13.6

Here you carefully make an incision. Even if you aren't careful, however, it doesn't matter. You're using non-destructive editing!

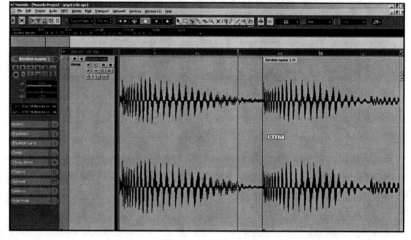

After you've cut the entrance point, start looking for the exit point (the place where the audio stops and repeats). You listen to the end of the part that the producer wants over and over again until you find a spot. With the Scissor tool, make another incision.

> ❋ **The Beauty That Is Undo**
>
> Keep in mind when editing audio digitally within programs like Nuendo and Pro Tools, you can make as many mistakes as you want when cutting. If you mess up, just go up to the Edit menu and select Undo. It's that easy!
>
> It's called **non-destructive editing**, and it basically means that anything you do to the audio file does not affect the actual audio file at all unless you render your work. And even then you are actually creating another audio file entirely. So have fun!

Notice what's been done to the audio file: There are cuts at the beginning and at the end of the segment that the producer wants, as shown in Figure 13.7.

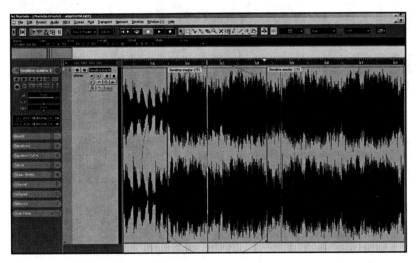

Figure 13.7

You've cut out the beginning and the end of the segment that you want to repeat.

Now comes the moment of truth! Using the Cursor tool, select the segment that you've cut. Once it's selected, it will be gray. Now you're ready to copy it back to back with the original part!

First things first, though. You need to make some room. In Figure 13.8, you'll notice that I've slid the beginning of the part after our repetition over a little bit to make some room. This is easily done just by selecting the segment of audio and dragging it to a later measure.

Now that there's room, I go up to the edit menu and press Copy, and then I position the song right where I want to insert the new segment copy. The song position was right after the other segment, as shown in Figure 13.9. It should be perfectly back to back with the other copy, but either way you need to take a listen.

After playing it back, I figure out that I should probably edit a little more. It's pretty close, but it's still a little off.

Figure 13.8

You can move the audio file segments around as needed within your editing program in order to make room for new segments.

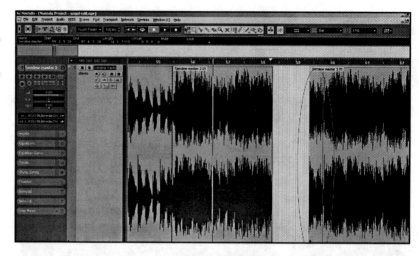

Figure 13.9

You can make copies of segments or entire audio files with the Copy function.

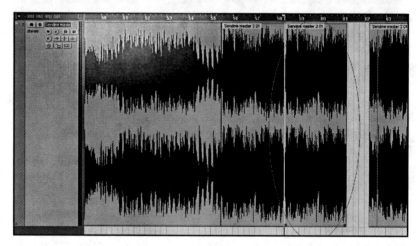

What's really cool about non-destructive editing is that you can always drag out portions of the audio that are from the original file but that were cut out when you made the copy. In fact, you can elongate the file to be a complete copy of the original file. This is done by dragging the right-hand corner of the audio file whichever way you want it to go. You'll find that you aren't dragging the audio file itself, you're just extending it, as shown in Figure 13.10. You actually don't want to extend it out that long, so I go up to the Edit menu and press Undo. Now it's back to normal!

The reason I mention the ability to resize audio is this: After I made the copy and placed it after the part that I wanted to repeat, I realized it wasn't an exact fit. So I needed to elongate the file a little to make it match up a little more, just a smidgeon here and a smidgeon there, until it started

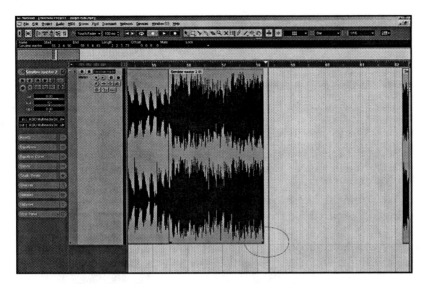

Figure 13.10
By dragging the lower corners of the audio files out, you're actually extending the segment to reveal other portions of the original recording.

to sound right. So take a listen again. It's pretty close this time. I move it over just a smidgeon again, and then take one more listen. We've got it!

Basically, editing music is a lot of trial and error. The more repetitious it is, the easier it is to make repeats in an audio file or to introduce new elements into it. Pop music tends to be pretty easy because it's got a beat that lets you know if you're in time or not. If it's pop music with vocals, though, it can be a little trickier because you have to work around the vocals.

Orchestral music can be much harder in some circumstances and really easy in others. It just depends on the composer. For example, some composers can be so random in their compositions that it's really hard to match certain segments up. Then again, you can use their randomness to your advantage sometimes!

Sometimes a composition will be so random that you can feasibly drop audio in at any point and still get away with it. As long as it seems like it's in beat, the listener may never notice. Tribal beats and jazz fusion are great examples of this. Sometimes, though, there may be one instrument that has a long decay in what would otherwise be a perfect cut. What do you do at that point? Crossfade!

Crossfading

There are times when even the most brilliant cut-and-paste job is not enough. Sometimes you have to rely on trickier methods.

What if you could actually have one part of an audio file fade out as the other was fading in? Wouldn't that allow for the release and decay of an instrument while another part comes in? This is entirely possible, and it's called crossfading. **Crossfading** is having one piece of music fade out while the other piece of music fades in. It's basically a very controlled and pleasant segue. There are two ways to do this in all multi-track editors:

* You can use the Crossfade function within your multi-track editor.

* You can create another track and automate the volume so that one track fades in, while the other fades out.

Start off by taking a look at the Crossfade function in Nuendo.

Crossfading: The Function

In Figure 13.11, you'll notice that there are two audio files. I'm going to drag the audio files so they overlap, like what you see in Figure 13.12.

Figure 13.11
Compare this with Figure 13.12.

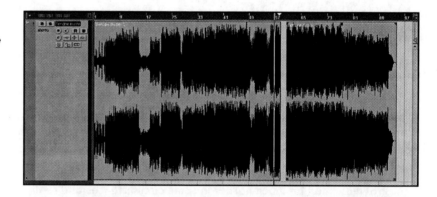

Figure 13.12
You can see where I dragged one file to overlap the other.

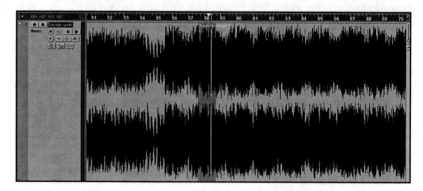

Once you've dragged one file on top of the other, go ahead and select both files. Then you can go up to the Audio menu and select Crossfade, as shown in Figure 13.13.

Figure 13.13
After overlapping the files,
go up to the Audio menu
and select Crossfade.

After the crossfade has been selected, a blue X appears over the junction where the two files overlap. This is the crossfade! See Figure 13.14 to get an idea of what I'm talking about.

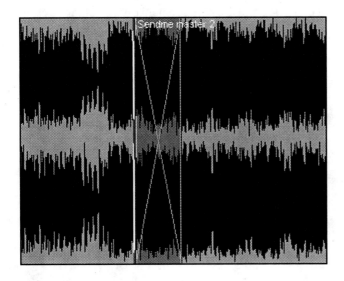

Figure 13.14
Once you've added the
crossfade, a blue X will
appear where your files
overlap.

Once the crossfade is in place, you can make it larger or smaller by dragging it farther up or down the timeline. You can even stretch it so that the crossfade happens gradually over a period of time. Figure 13.15 shows how I've increased the crossfade to extend the amount of time over which it occurs.

Figure 13.15
After the crossfade is in place, you can edit it to make it happen more gradually or very rapidly.

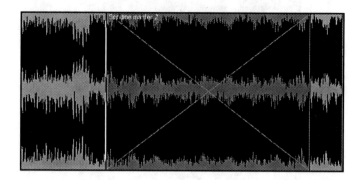

Now that you understand the Crossfade function, take a look at how to crossfade without using this tool.

Crossfading: Manual

You're probably wondering why I would even bother explaining a different way of crossfading. The reason is simple: When you apply a crossfade over a single track between two different audio segments, it can be difficult to tell where the fade actually occurs. To counter this problem, a lot of people will place one segment on one track and the next segment onto another track, like what you see in Figure 13.16.

Figure 13.16
Sometimes it's easier to place one segment on one track and another segment on another track, and then blend them manually. This gives you a little more control over the crossfade.

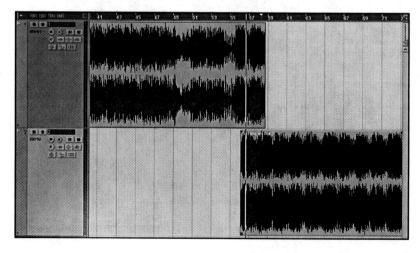

Obviously, in Figure 13.16, the tracks are overlapping. If you were to play these two tracks back to back, it would sound like a total mess once you heard the overlap section. That's why you still have to fade each audio track in and out, or crossfade them.

In Figure 13.17, you'll notice that I selected and dragged the upper-right corner of the beginning audio segment backward to initiate a fade out.

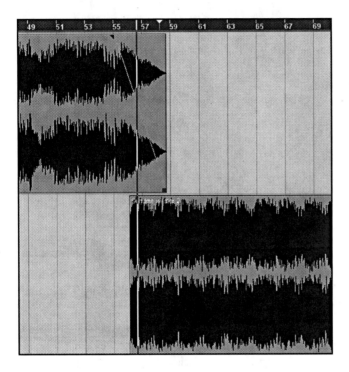

Figure 13.17

If you select and drag the upper corners of the audio files horizontally, a fade in or out will occur, depending on where you are in the audio file.

That takes care of the first segment—I've created a fade-out that will occur every time that point of the music occurs. Now I need to fade in the second segment. That is done the same way, but at the beginning of the audio file instead of the end. I select and drag the upper-left corner, and instantly a fade-in occurs, like the one shown in Figure 13.18.

There you go! This is an easy, manual crossfade where you can see the action exactly as you hear it. It's a little easier to edit this way because you can just keep dragging the second audio track around until it finally matches up.

Figure 13.18
To fade in, select the file and then drag the upper-left corner to the right.

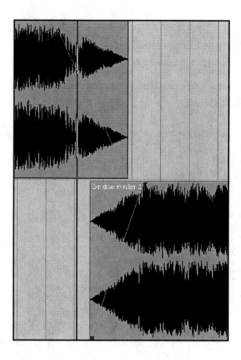

Automation

If you need more elaborate volume controls during a crossfade—for example, if you want to raise the volume for part of the beginning of a segment and lower it a bit before it really kicks in—you can rely on another feature that is standard in all multi-track programs.

Automation lets you send multiple cues to a certain parameter of your multi-track program. For example, if you want your audio segment to pan in several different ways or fade in and out over several points within its playtime, you can totally do that.

By opening the automation track lanes, as shown in Figure 13.19, you can enter an area where you can control your audio as much as you want. You do this by clicking the plus and minus signs that I've circled for you in Figure 13.19.

The first is the Volume track lane that is used for—you guessed it—volume automation. Notice a black line in the upper middle of the Volume lane waveform. This shadow of the audio file is really handy when you have to zoom in close on your automation points. Using this, you can see the peaks of the file and where you should concentrate your automation points.

The black line that you see is the current volume of the audio file. Right now, I am unable to move this line because automation is not yet enabled on this track. By pressing the R button (that stands for Read), as shown in Figure 13.20, the line turns blue and I'm able to start automating.

Figure 13.19
Click the little plus and minus signs to open and close more track lanes for automation in Nuendo. Many other multi-track editors work the same way.

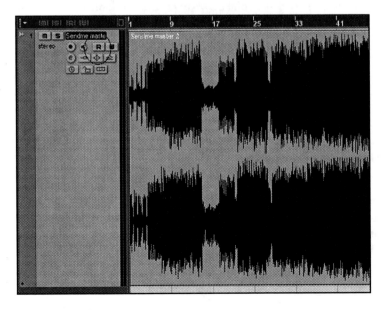

Figure 13.20
Push the R or Read button to enable automation within the track lanes.

Now that I've enabled automation, I can go ahead and start doing creative and necessary things with the volume for the first and second audio clips. As soon as I click on the blue line, an automation point is made, like the one you see in Figure 13.21. From here, I can drag the blue line up or down and drag the automation point to whatever area of the audio clip that I want.

Figure 13.21

Clicking the blue automation line automatically creates an automation point.

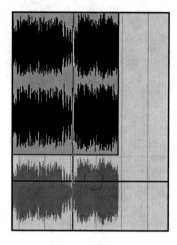

If I decide that I want to delete the automation point later, all I have to do is select it and then press the Delete key.

I decide to move the automation point almost to the edge of the audio file. Once it's in place, I make another automation point, and then drag this point down to create a volume slope, as shown in Figure 13.22.

Now I decide to move down to the next segment. I enable automation on this track, and then proceed to make a fade-in. In this track however, I'm going to allow a small part of the segment to fade in and out rapidly to introduce a small part of the clip before it comes in completely. See Figure 13.23 to see what I'm talking about.

So there you have it—automation in a nutshell. But don't think that's all there is to it. You can automate many different parameters, such as panning, mutes, effects—you name it! Check out Figure 13.24 to see some of these other parameters.

But do you think you would ever really use all of these different components of a multi-track program? Actually, you'd be surprised how much you will end up using. When you are rushed to get a music edit together for a one-minute cut scene, and you're supposed to make one five-minute song sound like it fits in there naturally, you'll find yourself making quick creative cuts in the audio, time-compression, and whatever else you can think of to make it work.

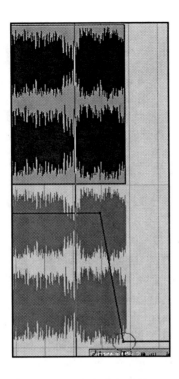

Figure 13.22
Clicking in a different part of the automation lane will create another automation point. This shows how I've made the volume fade out using automation.

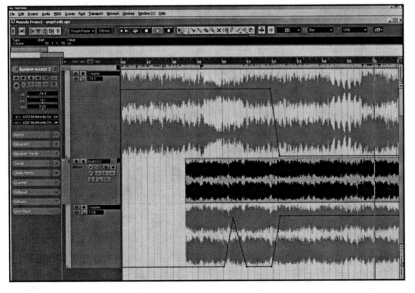

Figure 13.23
With this next clip, I've made a more elaborate use of automation. Here it fades in rapidly, fades out, and then comes in quickly again.

❊ ❊ ❊

Figure 13.24

There are many different parameters that you can automate. Your program may not have automation parameters set up in exactly the same way, but, trust me, they will be there.

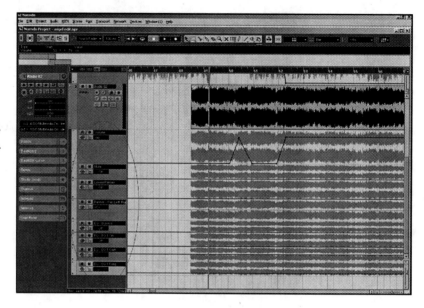

Automating Effects

One trick that ends up saving all sorts of edits is using reverb to blend two different segments together. How could this possibly be helpful? Say you've got some epic orchestral piece that doesn't quite end the way you need it to in order to go into the next segment of audio, and this next segment is crucial in order to tie up the ending. If you just let it cut out, as is, it's not going to sound right. But, if you can fade in a little reverb with a long decay, right as the ending occurs and then fade it out rapidly, you can easily transition into the next piece. Give it a shot!

The first thing I do is click the Project menu and select FX Channel under Add Track (see Figure 13.25).

Figure 13.25

An FX channel is basically the same thing as setting up an auxiliary channel on a mixing board.

212
❋ ❋ ❋

Setting up an FX channel is like setting up an FX loop on an analog mixing board. I use FX channels so that I'm not adding a plug-in to every track. This way, I can use one reverb to affect many different channels. After I select FX Channel from the Add Track menu, the Add FX Channel Track dialog box appears (see Figure 13.26), asking what kind of plug-in to use for this channel. I select Reverb A, one of the reverbs that ships with Nuendo.

Figure 13.26
Once you tell Nuendo that you want an FX track, it will ask you what kind of plug-in you want to use.

After setting up the FX channel, I open up the Sends section of track 1 and select FX1-Reverb A as my first send (see Figure 13.27).

Figure 13.27
After you've set up your FX channel, you need to enable it on the tracks where you intend to use it.

Once the FX channel is set up properly, all I need to do is automate it. I could go through a lot of different automation lanes until I find the right parameter, but I'm going to avoid the endless searches and automate it by hand. It won't be perfect, but I can fix it later.

The first thing I do is click the W (for Write) on the channel I want to add automation to, as shown in Figure 13.28. I'll actually record my automation with the mouse movement this time.

Figure 13.28

The W button lets you to record parameter adjustments on the fly!

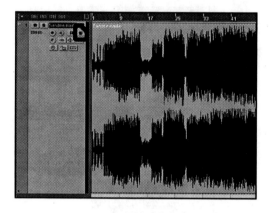

Once I've enabled the Write setting of the track, I can now record my automation. I'll rewind a little bit so I can have my automation occur in the right spot, and then I press Record. While recording, I adjust the level of the FX send on channel 1, as shown in Figure 13.29.

Figure 13.29

I adjust the amount of reverb being mixed into this channel while recording.

Once I've recorded the automation in the right spot, I decide to inspect my work. With the track selected, I go up to the Project menu again and select Show Used Automation under the Track Folding submenu, as shown in Figure 13.30. Instantly, the Sends:1-Send Level track lane appears, as shown in Figure 13.31.

From here all I need to do is apply just enough reverb to make it sound natural as it transitions into the next part. It doesn't need to be a lot; a little burst will do. Now that the automation track lane for the reverb send is open, I can edit it as needed until I get the appropriate result and my edit sounds either natural or, even better, completely undetectable.

Figure 13.30
Nuendo automatically shows all the parameters that you automated.

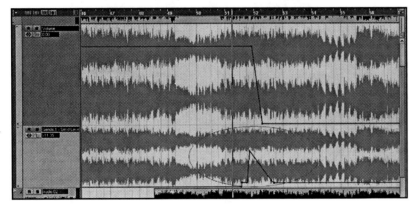

Figure 13.31
The Sends:1-Send Level track lane appears.

215
❋ ❋ ❋

14 } Creating Music for Cut Scenes

The lights begin to dim and the chatter of the audience dies down. Suddenly, the curtains begin to slowly lift up. A movie title fades in from black and a scene fades in. It looks cool, but where's the music? That's what this chapter is all about: scoring the cut scenes that occur in every video game title, the small little movies where major plot points occur. They're just as dramatic as what you hear in the movies, and they are just as dynamic. What separates the two?

The main difference is that a movie has to be scored from start to finish. A movie just isn't interactive; you don't decide what will happen—someone else does. Games work a little differently because you are playing the hero and the big musical cues occur when you progress. In every level of a video game, you usually have the regular music, the action music and so on. A triggered cut scene, however, is where a game and a movie become a similar type of production.

Cut scenes, as explained in earlier chapters, are pre-rendered (or sometimes rendered within the game's own engine) performances where the character loses control for a moment and gets to watch his character go on to fulfill its greater destiny. This is where you hear the hero talk and say the big lines like, "You're gonna pay for that!" and "You've got a lot of explaining to do!" Cut scenes are where characters face off and discuss, over a warm cup of cocoa, how they got their feelings hurt. (Yeah, right!) It's where you get to see subtle facial expressions. Cut scenes are where major plot points occur. During two characters' battle, a cave-in separates them and the cut scene ends, leaving you to figure out how to get them out of the mess.

All of these dramatic sequences are completely boring if they don't have music. Action sounds help a bit, but without the music to create atmosphere and suspense, what's the point?

Go through a dramatic scene without music:

Cut scene opening:

Our hero climbs up a large mountain. As he slowly reaches the top, he notices he's not alone. Directly in front of him is his nemesis, waiting patiently, as if he's been there for some time. There is complete silence, besides the wind blowing and the shuffling of gravel and rock as the hero climbs.

(Hero): I hope I didn't keep you waiting too long.

Still silence.

(Nemesis): I've always got plenty of time for you. Too bad your time is almost over.

More silence.

(Hero): If that's what you're thinking, then I hate to disappoint you. You're going to be waiting a little longer than you thought.

The hero slowly unsheathes his sword. You hear only the sword slowly sliding out of the scabbard. He points the sword toward his nemesis.

(Nemesis): We'll see about that!

There's a quick swish of metal and a clashing of swords. Like lightning, the nemesis has unsheathed his sword and is immediately on our hero.

End scene

Now try this with music:

Cut scene opening:

A low orchestra drones, playing slowly.

Our hero climbs up a large mountain. As he slowly reaches the top, he notices he's not alone. Directly in front of him is his nemesis, waiting patiently, as if he's been there for some time. Flutes trill as rocks fall with our hero's every movement; then he finally reaches the summit.

(Hero): I hope I didn't keep you waiting too long.

A Spanish guitar sounds a small couple of notes, denoting a challenge is in the air.

(Nemesis): I've always got plenty of time for you. Too bad your time is almost over.

The guitar sounds again, denoting that the challenge has been answered.

(Hero): If that's what you're thinking, then I hate to disappoint you. You're going to be waiting a little longer than you thought.

The strings play faster; French horns explode. The guitar is strumming. The hero slowly unsheathes his sword. You hear only the sword slowly sliding out of the scabbard. He points the sword toward his nemesis.

(Nemesis): We'll see about that!

Timpani drums begin to sound and you can tell that the challenge has begun. There's a quick swish of metal and a clashing of swords. A cymbal crashes as the swords clash. Like lightning, the nemesis has unsheathed his sword and is immediately on our hero.

End scene

Of course, you couldn't actually hear any of that. But you could imagine what it sounded like, right? You could hear the rock scrapes, the raspy voices, the French horns, the Spanish guitar? Isn't it much better, even in text, with music? I'd like to think so.

This chapter covers scoring cut scenes or small movies. You learn simple tricks of the trade that keep things simple and help your cut scenes work with what's onscreen.

Start with Action

In many situations, you start off slowly and work your way up. That's how a lot of people work with music in general: While strumming away on a guitar, you decide "Hey, this would make a good verse section for a song!" So you keep strumming after that's established and then start playing into another part that's bigger and fuller. The song sort of takes off here. You say to yourself, "This has to be the chorus!" And from there the song just sort of writes itself.

Scoring a cut scene works in a similar fashion. Most composers start with the action sequence within a scene and then figure out how the music will build into that fast, exciting music. The action sequence is the climax, where everything has exploded and there is the most activity. As a result, the music is the "most active" here as well. Once you have the big part composed, you can slowly build up by bringing in one or two tracks at a time until it finally explodes.

For example, the scene laid out at the beginning of the chapter begins with dialogue. After the dialogue has gone on for a bit, the fighting begins. The fighting scene would be a proper place to begin working on music. Again, the fighting sequence has the most activity. It's really easy to bring in the big drums, the strings, and the cymbal crashes, and have them jive. Once you've determined all the instruments in the big fight scene, you can add one instrument at a time at the scene's start until the fight commences.

According to Style
What type of music you compose largely depends on the style established at the beginning of the title.

For the sake of demonstration purposes, say this cut scene is to be orchestral with some contemporary elements like synthesizers added for spice. Overall, the game developers want the music to be epic and similar to a modern film score. With this in mind you decide to bring in some orchestral percussion first. Drums are always a good way to begin a fight scene because they almost instantly say, "Action."

1. Bring the cut scene into the host sequencer. I use Nuendo in this chapter. Once you have the movie in, line it up at the beginning of the sequence, at 0, as seen in Figure 14.1.

Figure 14.1

I've imported the movie file to Nuendo. I line it up at the beginning of the sequence. Now it's ready to go!

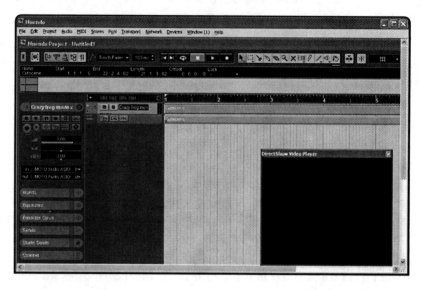

✳ B.Y.O. DAW

If you don't have Nuendo, don't worry about it. Simply use a host application like Pro Tools, Logic Pro, Cubase SX, or whatever digital host application you have. Just make sure that you can import video! For instructions on how to import video into your digital audio program, consult with your software documentation.

The video that you use can be anything, for practice purposes. Just kill the audio attached to the video so that you can add your own.

2. Watch the video again and look for significant points. The kind of points I'm referring to are where the character notices a clue or physically accomplishes a certain task.
3. Take notes and leave some markers, as I have done in Figure 14.2.

Figure 14.2

I've added some markers to help me keep track of what's going on.

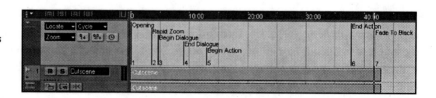

> ❄ **Markers**
>
> **Markers** are visual cues that act as reminders of what goes on in a certain section; that way you can quickly go from one section to another. Adding markers when composing a cut scene is especially helpful because there are so many things to be aware of within a scene. It's always great when the music seems to react to things that the characters are doing, and markers help you remember actions. Also, you can easily use markers to tell yourself when the music should be louder, softer, or harder. They are great for helping with your dynamics. You can use them to tell you where the music should have completely faded before you've composed any of it!

4. Set markers for these things:

   ❄ Beginning of the track

   ❄ Significant scene changes

   ❄ Bold actions

   ❄ Conversations

   ❄ Beginning of the cut scene

   ❄ Ending of the cut scene

   You can usually title certain markers with "dialogue begins," "dialogue ends," "begin action," "end action," and the like.

5. Begin composing.

In this example, you've established the scene's action, so you add some percussion. You load up the East West Symphonic Orchestra Gold timpani set to get things cracking. You add some heavy hits and try to make a little rhythm while at the same time match the action. You also load up some cymbal crashes as well. How about some cello to fill in the low end? You start making a low melody that works along with the beat of the timpani drums that you've already added. This ends up being the fight's overall theme. At this point you decide to bring up some brass as well. There's nothing like a little brass to bring some action to the forefront. A little trumpet will do a nice job of enriching the experience. You decide to do a few stabs here and there.

At this point your composition is slowly but surely filling out, but just for one part of the scene, as shown in Figure 14.3.

The Dialogue

Right before the action sets in on the scene, there is a lot of dialogue. It would be easy to add some low strings in the background here to set the mood. The main part is filled with strings, and the low strings would blend in perfectly.

Figure 14.3

The composition is fleshing out quite well, but only in one area of the scene. What will you use to build up to this point?

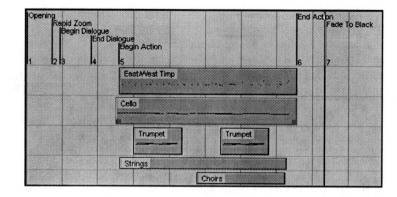

Now there's something that you should know about video game cut scenes: Because music is the first thing added to a scene, you generally have no other sounds (including voice) to work with. It can be especially annoying not to have voice, because it's always fun to have the music react to something the character has said (like in the soap operas).

For example:

(Hero): Why do you continue to persecute me?

He stands with one leg propped up on a large rock, his hair blowing in the wind. His fist is clenched toward his nemesis. The background music is slow and mysterious.

(Nemesis): You don't even remember me, do you? Don't you remember that small boy you picked on in summer camp?

An oboe pipes in, almost questioning listeners.

(Nemesis): That was me. You embarrassed me. Now I'll hunt you to the ends of the world!

The music begins to build and get more urgent. When the character's background is revealed, the music rises for a moment.

When you don't have voice to work with, as will most likely be the case, have the script in front of you. The characters will at least be working in the same order as the script, so you can follow along. If the characters have lips, the voice will already be in. Artists need to have the voice in and working to properly lip sync the character animations. You definitely don't want too much interaction between the music and the actors, or it will just get annoying. Try to focus on major points. In Figure 14.4, some music appears during the section marked Begin Dialogue, but not much. I've kept it minimal on purpose so I don't distract from what's going on.

Ultimately, how your music interacts with what is happening onscreen is up to you. This is merely a suggestion. A lot of the time music dies down to a minimum with just a couple of notes playing; that may be how you want to work it for your scene.

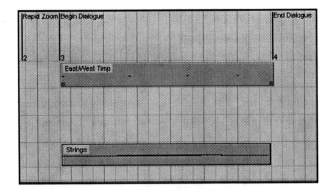

Figure 14.4
During my cut scene's dialogue, I've kept the music to a minimum so I don't distract from what the characters are doing.

Of course, when the final cut scene is being mixed, the sound designer can and will pull the music back in volume when the dialogue is going on. However, having huge, active music during a passive conversation is a distraction, even if it's at a lower volume and fills up the mix.

You might want music to remain consistent, despite conversation, when

- ❈ Characters are gearing up for an intense battle
- ❈ Characters are in the beginning of a big battle
- ❈ A major victory has taken place
- ❈ A major tragedy has taken place

In the end, your best judgment and instincts will help you know when to hold back and when to let loose. And, as always, if you're in doubt, take a break and come back with fresh ears.

The Intro

The way that you begin the intro largely depends on what's going on when it begins. If there is a large opening shot of a windy meadow, then you might want to create something that is light and fades in with the video. If your opening scene is a massive deployment of spaceships, then you might want big music that explodes with the intro.

One important rule to observe is this: Make sure the music begins before the video fades from black. There should never be utter silence at the beginning unless the script calls for it. The music should be heard even before anything is seen. Not by much, mind you, but the music begins first. It goes back to the old silent movies. They used to have a live organist, and even sometimes a live orchestra, performing while the movie played. Before the curtain had even been raised, the music would have already started to get people all pumped up and ready for what they were about to see.

A couple ways to get some intro ideas is to check out other cuts scenes in other video games, or go online. A Web site like www.gamespot.com offers trailers for upcoming video games.

In my cut scene, I've started in a very simple fashion with sustained strings and some small hits of percussion here and there. Things will gradually build up, as you can see in Figure 14.5, until things explode at the fight, toward the middle of the scene.

Figure 14.5
I'm keeping things simple at the beginning and slowly building up. This augments the rising tension already in the scene.

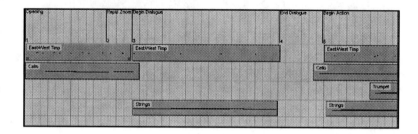

All in all, make sure that your beginning goes with what's going on in the video. If you're in doubt, do one intro, save the file, go back and try another intro, and then save that file. You can check out both beginnings when you've had some time to rest your brain and see which one works best.

The Ending

Ending your cut scene is similar to the beginning. What's the flow of the end of the cut scene like? Is it faster than the beginning? This can occur, you know. It's been a popular trend of many current film editors to lull the audience in to a sense of security by having the opening of a scene be very slow and normal. Just when the audience thinks that everything is dull and boring, suddenly things go very quickly to create level of dynamics within the scene.

Music can and should perform the same way. If a scene opens up with a normal family eating dinner, then the music should have a modest, family-oriented piece of music. If a tank busts through the dining-room wall and soldiers come running through the house taking hostages and lobbing grenades in the kitchen sink, the music should become more intense.

❄ **Keep Your Eye On the Cut**

Keep an eye on how often the scene cuts from one shot to another. I love it when I get to watch a high-intensity scene that has the music in time with the shots. This isn't easy to achieve. (It's actually easier if the scene is edited to the music and not in reverse). Is this mandatory? Not by a long shot. I just like to encourage it when possible. Even if only a couple of shots are in time with the beat of the music, it creates a feeling of fluidity.

The main thing to accomplish (after scoring your fight scene and then creating a scene entrance) is working your way out of the fight scene. If you're paying attention, the scene can tell you how that occurs.

Visit our familiar hero and his nemesis:

The fight has been raging back and forth. Swords clash with loud metallic jolts, blows are parried, blows are dodged. With expert skill, the nemesis kicks the hero dead in the chest, causing him to land on his back. Before the hero can raise his weapon, his nemesis slides his blade underneath the throat of the hero.

(Nemesis): Finally, I've got you where I want you! Take your hand off your weapon!

(Hero): This isn't over, villain!

(Nemesis): Ah, but it is! Guards!

From out of nowhere, two hulking guards in crude armor appear, holding chains. Using their brute strength, they grapple, bind, and drag the hero out of the picture.

The nemesis is left alone. The camera closes on him laughing maniacally.

The fight rages at the beginning, but ends abruptly due to the hero's lack of skill. When the hero lands on his back, you have a wonderful spot for percussion to hit big and then stop. At this point, eerie strings can create a dark mood as the nemesis informs the hero of his defeat. When the guards come to pick up the hero, it's the perfect time to introduce a slow, tribal rhythm to announce the arrival of a military faction. Once the hero has been pulled out of the scene, the drums can die down and you can create some dissonance within the strings to make the villain seem creepier and crazier. As the scene fades out, the strings can die down too, which is what you see in Figure 14.6.

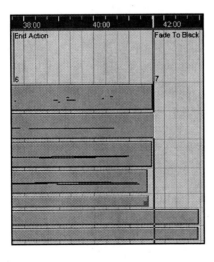

Figure 14.6
At the ending of the scene, the music looks almost as if it's going to pick up again before it suddenly dies out.

Is this the way the scene has to end musically? Not at all. The only rule you have to observe is this: Music has to be the last thing heard in a cut scene. To end before causes players to think there was a timing or audio problem. With that in mind, enjoy finishing up your cut scene!

15 } Breaking into the Game Industry

The veil of mystery surrounding the game industry is thin but dark. A lot of people have a huge interest in making music and sounds for games. From artists to engineers to programmers, game companies offer a chance for many people with many different talents. Game company analysts even report the buying habits of different demographics!

My History in the Game Industry

I got my start in the game industry in March of 1998. I started off working as a tester, but ended up working in compatibility within a few months with a company that will remain nameless for legal reasons.

My first year was a very strange and disorienting time. So many young people like myself were passionate about creating games. It was difficult playing games, having an opinion about it, and having that opinion count—mainly because, to a hard-core gamer, the idea of changing a game based on your suggestion is like changing reality. I ended up working in compatibility for several years. **Compatibility** functions to test the various forms of computer hardware with a game, ensuring that it functions properly for the end user. For example, I tested each video card that a game could technically support. I also tested each sound card, CD-ROM drive, and so on. During my time in compatibility, I became the lead audio tester for compatibility and quality assurance. I had a knack for understanding positional sound, and I knew how to communicate bugs to the sound department.

For a few years, my daily ritual was playing games with a 5.1 surround speaker set and listening to make sure sound was properly implemented in each level. In addition, I was leading a test team in compatibility testing of each available sound card. I spent many late nights working with my teammates. I finally got my chance to really test my skills in audio production when a position opened up in my company's voice department. Normally video game companies don't have voice departments; this company was an exception. After a few interviews with people in the department, I was hired as a voice editor assistant. Not only did I get to edit, process, and database all the voices that went into the games, but I also got to engineer voice sessions. As the years went by, the voice department eventually merged with the regular sound department. After this union, I tried my hand at sound design ... finally! I quickly found out how rewarding and difficult the job could be. I had to learn to think of everything, and I got to use the sharpened ears that I'd acquired working in compatibility.

Not everyone goes the path that I went getting into game audio. I was very zealous to work for a specific company doing sound design. All in all, I think I became a stronger sound designer because I saw every angle of game development.

Going to School

Will you need to start through the lower ranks of a company to move into sound design? If you don't have a degree in audio production of some sort, you might have to start off small. I'm not degreed. I spent several years in audio and video production during the army and while producing music for two record labels. This experience didn't matter to the person hiring in the sound department. He just cared about the degree. Not having a degree meant a much rockier road. But I should also mention that having a degree does not necessarily guarantee that you can get a job in game audio. Thousands of starving sound engineers who work in music stores across the country can vouch for me on this one. Having a degree that supports the possibility of working in game audio is not a bad idea at all. As I mentioned before, employers do look at degrees. Granted, experience counts, too. If you've already had a few audio gigs in gaming, that will get you in a few doors already, especially if it's with a reputable company. Take it from me though, it's a difficult road without a degree.

What are some good schools?

* The **Berklee School of Music** based out of Boston, Massachusetts has definitely brought some successful colleagues of mine into the limelight of game audio. Granted, it's first and foremost a musician's college. They do, however, have a very comprehensive music production and engineering course that has brought some great players to the table. Equally, this is a great place for composers as well. Berklee offers film scoring as a major! For further info check out www.berklee.edu.

* The **Expression College for Digital Arts** based in Emeryville, California offers a sound arts major that is uniquely engineered for a career path in the video game industry. Not only does this school offer extensive hands-on experience with digital audio software, it also offers courses in analog technology, acoustical design, and so on. The school offers intern programs for work with actual game companies, so it's seriously worth checking out at www.expression.edu.

Loads of other colleges out there offer great courses that are compatible with game audio. These two happen to be the alma maters for successful designers. I definitely recommend checking out your local colleges as well, but always remember: The degree itself will not guarantee you anything. It's what you do with it that counts!

Networking

The ability to network has most helped pave the road for me (and for everyone else I know who's had any level of success in this business). When I say **network**, I don't mean the flashy smile, false persona, "I'll call you, you call me" garbage. I mean going out to the trade shows and conferences and being genuine to the people you meet at these shows.

Try these things as well:

✳ **Get to know the people during a seminar.** Talk to the people at the booths and enjoy the company. They might not be in the department you want to work in, but they have one thing going for them that you don't: They're working in the game industry. They know people in other departments, they know how their company works, and they know if any positions are open.

✳ **Attempt some company trade-offs.** For example, if you work at a music store, sell a new contact on doing some trades for some CDs for some games. You may not even be interested in the games, but this is a good way to build up a good contact. Even after I was working in the game industry, I still worked my ability to trade. I'd trade games for car repair, musical gear, games from other companies, and discounts on computers. If you're savvy, you can save yourself a lot of money and make some valuable friends!

✳ **Know where your contacts live.** If you are going to be in their area, drop a line to schedule a lunch date. The goal is to build up a good rapport. Every time I go on trips, I try to remember if there's someone in that region that I know. When I come up with a list, I drop each person a line. In reality, this is just building up friendships, but it's also a good way to see what's going on in these different regions. You occasionally find out about jobs, opportunities, etc. It also places you in a great position because you are there as a buddy, not as someone sniffing around.

✳ **Start a contact list.** Most e-mail programs have the ability to keep a rolodex of names, e-mail addresses, and phone numbers. This list is just as valuable to the freelance sound designer as the sound database. Keep track of the people on this list periodically. Just send out a personalized e-mail every now and then ask how things are going.

✳ **Check with friends.** Maybe they know someone working in the industry. If so, ask if you can meet that person or get his e-mail address. Like any big business, nepotism is rampant. Companies tend to hire based on the recommendations of people who work for them. If you can get a recommendation from someone on the inside, you have a much better chance of success.

✳ **Have business cards on you at all times.** I've met people in similar industries in the strangest places and having a business card makes it very likely that you'll be remembered. Your business cards should have your e-mail address, phone number, position title that you're accustomed to working under, and your Web site URL. Make sure that it's a sharp business card. If you need to spend a little extra money, do it! Flashy cards make it easier for you to be remembered.

✳ **Make a CD and keep it on you.** Some people keep mini CD-ROMs with their demo reel and their Web site. Having small discs available makes it easy for people to check out your work and your Web site.

The Internet

When it comes to the sound designer or the composer, it can be very, very difficult to even figure out who to talk to about a job. Thankfully, the Internet has made things a lot easier in terms of finding information about a company and what jobs are open.

Job Hunting

Every game company has a Web site, and every game company Web site has job listings. Granted, sending in a resume for a listing is often considered impersonal, but it's an effective way to spread the word about yourself. Creativity may be your goal, but while you're looking, you have to play the game.

Offer a cover letter with your resume. If you don't know how to write a cover letter, look online for examples and borrow a cover-letter writing book from the library. Many people forget this important step when sending in their resumes; as a result, they are seen as just another number that falls into a stack of others. Writing a cover letter lets the HR person get a little more of a glimpse into your personality and experience.

For the actual resume, I suggest looking online for effective examples. When it comes to resumes for the sound designer or composer, your technical expertise should be available for viewing. Your expertise includes what kinds of software and hardware with which you have experience. Additionally, add some special skills that set you apart, but do so on a small part of the page. The most important part is your experience. Make sure and include your Web site! This gives the person hiring a good view at who you are and what you can do with your creativity.

One Web site I'd like to leave with you is www.gamasutra.com. This Web site breaks down each listing by date, and it's purely for the video-game industry. You can even post your resume for the many companies to view.

Your Web Site

Web sites are very important, pretty much for any line of work. If you are skilled with Web design, make your page as polished as possible. Make sure that you have good, professional-quality photos if you have any available. Photos are not essential in this business, but it doesn't hurt. A picture says a thousand words, right?

If you are new to Web design, talk to friends who are good at Web design. Ask to see if you can work out a trade or reduced pay for their design of your site. Like business cards, this is not an area where you want to cut corners.

A Web site should consist of the following:

❋ **Bio:** This brief biography of your history should pertain to the business. It should also contain your college major, a brief illustration of the projects that you've worked on, and other career-related accomplishments. Make it short.

❋ **Credits:** Include games you've worked on, audio productions you've worked on, and so on.

❋ **Press:** Just put in the positive clips.

❋ **Music or sound examples:** Have some MP3s available. You can set them up to stream only. Make them easy to download but pleasing to the ear. You should use only your best work!

❋ **Equipment list (Optional):** A gear list tells what software and hardware you use.

Above all, your Web site should be a reflection of you! Make it fun, pleasing to the eye, and something that you're proud of. Several great books and online sites can walk you through making a Web site. However, if you know a pro, that's the way to go.

Sound designers: Bay Area Sound has a wonderful example of a very successful, very professional Web site at www.basound.com. This small company has done some huge business over the years. After you've taken a look at some of their credits, I'm sure you'll be impressed. Not only does this site provide a comprehensive look at all of its services, but it even has a demo reel online for you to check out.

Composers: You should check out www.griskey.com and www.petermc.com. These Web sites are for two highly successful game-industry composers. They offer a top-notch, concise design that informs you of what they are up to and what they have done. They even offer samples of their work.

Trade Shows

Each year hundreds of companies get together and set up in massive convention centers. The lights and booths are amazing to behold. The companies must spend loads of money setting up. The great thing is walking around and actually talking to people who work for these companies.

Figure 15.1

This is the main page of Bay Area Sound's Web page. Notice the neat, to-the-point layout.

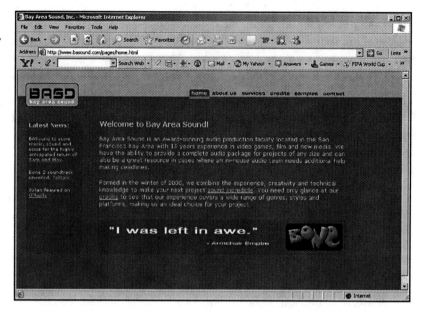

Make sure you don't come off as pushy, however. Be calm, yet enthusiastic. The game industry is full of very quiet people who are used to working solitarily in an office for several hours a day. They do not react well to loud, obnoxious people. Just be calm and confident; go easy on the sales pitches. Definitely sell yourself—just don't oversell.

Do Your Homework

GDC is a great way to get an on-the-spot interview, and you want to be prepared. Books can help you with interviews and how to behave during them. The Internet is full of articles like this. Take some time and read through these things if you aren't sure of your abilities.

Additionally, I'd recommend being careful of how you dress during trade shows. The game industry is compromised of people that dress extremely casually. You should be dressed the same. You should dress in clothes that are both casual and fashionable. No business suits—that's a great way to blow it right there. Most people in the game industry frown on business suits. It reminds them of working in a corporate job that they might have had once.

As you are walking around and meeting new people, you might notice that some of the people might seem aloof or awkward. Don't take this personally; people skills are not necessarily something the game industry is known for. You can definitely expect warm personalities coming from the HR department and the marketing department, but don't expect it out of some of the other areas. Most of these guys tend to work at computers nearly all day. They are used to getting most of their interaction out of e-mail and such. When a live human being comes along, it can be a little jarring, especially one that isn't in the business. My main point in telling you this is for you not to feel defeated if you feel like you've been brushed off. This is just how it is with some of these guys. The most important thing is you continuing to meet new people in the business and sell yourself in a positive light to the right people.

GDC

Game Developers Conference, or GDC (see Figure 15.2), is geared more toward hardware and game development than new games. Occasionally you get a glimpse at some new stuff, but it's usually from a hardware manufacturer's booth whose new technology is playing the game.

But there is this: Game developers set up booths there as well. These booths are not as big as they would be at a convention like E3 and are usually staffed by someone from the human resources department. If you haven't picked up on why you should be excited, let me say it outright: If human resources is manning a booth, it can only mean one thing: They are there looking for people to hire! This should make you absolutely excited! You'll have the ability to actually show up, hand in a resume, and talk to someone.

Figure 15.2
GDC is a prime opportunity for getting your name to different game companies.

Photo courtesy of the Game Developers Conference.

So would I recommend taking some extra resumes to GDC? Absolutely. You should take a stack. Additionally, you should be smiling, talking, and handing out your personal business cards. Above all, talk to the HR people. Be warm and energetic. Ask them what positions they are trying to fill currently. If they don't have any positions open for sound, ask them if there is from sound who you could talk to. Just mention that you'd like to know how things work in the department and see if there might be anything open in the future.

Nine out of ten times, someone from the sound department *will* be around. They may not be standing at the booth, but they will be coming by at certain points. Generally, you should ask if you could speak to the sound department supervisor. That's the main person you want to impress. Even if nothing is available, you can hand over a business card and resume and ask the supervisor to hold onto both in case something does open. You can also talk about yourself and ask if she knows any other companies looking to hire.

Even though the video game industry is doing bigger business than ever, it's not a very big industry (in regards to how many people work in it). Most people that have been working in the game industry for any number of years will have met several people at other companies, and if they are smart, they've kept up communication with them. Supervisors have been in the game industry for years; they know plenty of people at other companies, including other supervisors. Sometimes they know if another company needs someone. You may even get lucky and talk with the other person hiring or get an introduction from one supervisor to another. You can read more about the conference at www.gdconf.com.

E3

Electronic Entertainment Expo, or E3, is not geared for recruiting. This show, which you can read more about at www.e3insider.com/portal, is all about letting companies show off new titles. Additionally, because E3 is so crowded, it can make networking a little tricky. It is worth checking out, however. Through E3 you can get a good idea what each company is doing and what kinds of people work there. You also have a chance of meeting some of the employees, which means some networking possibilities; it's just a little more difficult here than at GDC.

16 } Reviewing What You've Learned

You've covered a lot of ground in this book. You've gone over getting into the business, getting your project rolling, and getting to know the team. You should have a clear idea of what happens in the gaming industry—how it works and how a sound designer or composer fits into the whole equation. I hope at this point you're dying to get your career started in this fast-paced, quirky, and artistic field.

Any motivational speaker will tell you that goals are of the utmost importance when trying to achieve anything. There's something about writing goals down on paper that makes things more official. It puts your mind in gear, rather than just talking about it. As competitive as the game industry is, having a firm set of goals will definitely help you to persevere in what might seem like a difficult endeavor. Like many books that focus on achieving a certain level of success or landing a specific career, I encourage you to make a list of goals for yourself if this is the career you want to work toward. Decide what your long-term, ultimate goal is. From there you can break the steps into short-term goals.

This chapter walks you through reaching this goal. Start off with getting yourself ready and then move into the doing-the-job part of it.

Step One: Demo Reel, Web Site, Business Cards

The first thing you want to do is begin preparing a demo reel. The demo reel is a showcase of many different sounds, ambiences, effects, or music that you've made.

Demo Reel

A demo reel should be flashy. It needs to be your best work, period. Take special consideration with the CD as well. Writing "demo by Rodney" with a permanent marker on the CD will not garner much interest. If you have access to a CD printer, print your name, Web site URL, e-mail address, and phone number, and make the graphics flashy. You want the CD to catch someone's eye and say, "Listen to me!" Go with loud colors if you need to—anything to get some attention.

You can put your demo reel on your Web site. Some sound designers offer links to each sound. A good example of a great demo package is up at www.basound.com under Samples. There is a section for sound and for music.

How you do your demo depends on what's on it.

Figure 16.1

Your demo reel should include your name, e-mail, phone number, and Web site. Also, feel free to throw in a small logo or graphic.

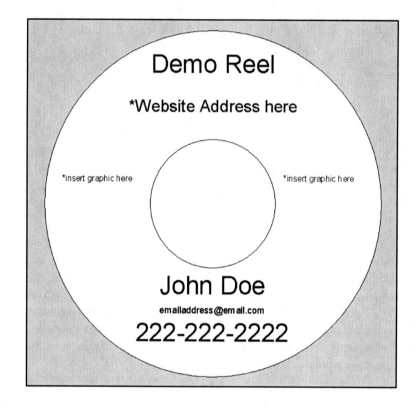

Sound Designer

As a sound designer, you usually create a one- to two-minute mix of many sounds that you've created, in a sequence. Include ambiences that set the mood and create the background; mix this scene with your own sounds over the top. You're creating an audio experience, essentially. For example, you'll have a war-time ambience with bomb explosions low in the background. Over this, mix some footsteps and breathing. Then add some vehicle sounds and mix in music that you've composed yourself. You can borrow from a soundtrack, but list in the credits where you got the music.

Composer

As a composer, you can go about creating a demo reel a few ways. The easiest and most straightforward is to include two or three compositions. In the CD liner, include what they were for.

Composers have commonly begun including video with their work as well, since DVD burners have become cheaper. Some use a video clip from a game or movie. A movie with sound effects but no music is ideal. If the movie has music and sound effects, kill them in your multi-track program and simply score the video yourself. You will, of course, explain in your liner notes that you used this footage for demonstration only and that you did not create it. The cool thing about using a movie is that it's something your audience can see and hear. Granted, you didn't do anything visually, but your audience can see how you are capable of not only composing, but scoring.

Web Site

It doesn't matter if you are a sound designer or composer: You should have a Web site to put on your business cards and direct people to through e-mail.

It's important that your Web site

* Look really good. The more interactive and interesting, the more interest you'll gain.
* Be easily navigated. Things should be clearly labeled.
* Offer your e-mail address in an easily visible place on the page.
* Host a well-written biography about yourself and what you've done.
* Make you look like a demi-god among men. This is a shrine to you and, above all, a visual and audible reason people should hire you!

Not everyone, me included, is gifted with the ability to create good-looking Web sites that catch the eye. You may need to enlist the help of a friend. You may even want to have someone write your biography and come up with an introduction for your Web site. If you have the cash, consider hiring a Web designer.

It's also possible to use places like www.myspace.com to host your individual Web page. If you make a MySpace music page, you can actually host your music up there if you are a composer. As www.myspace.com has become a great networking tool for musicians, sound designers, and bands alike, you may consider having a Web site in addition to a MySpace page. It's free publicity, right?

Business Cards

As mentioned earlier, get yourself some business cards. They should state your name, e-mail address, Web site URL, and telephone number. It should also state whether you are a sound designer or composer. If you are both, include both!

Figure 16.2

This is a screen shot of Bay Area Sound's demo section. They go out of their way to let you hear many different examples of their work.

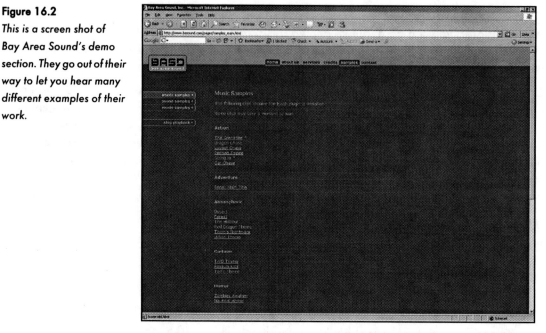

Again, try to get the business card as flashy as possible: You want it to look good and stand out. The most important thing is to get people's attention with it. Don't be stingy with business cards, by the way. Any time you meet someone who emits even the slightest smell of the game industry, hand out one of your cards. Any time that someone you meet has a brother or sister or a distant cousin who works at a game company, hand out your card. The only time you should hesitate giving out your business card is when someone appears to be overly shady and possibly a threat to your safety.

Remember to post your resume up at www.gamasutra.com. There companies can review your work and see if you might be a fit for their current project. Also check out www.craigslist.com, which covers many cities within the U.S. It's not uncommon for companies to post help-wanted ads for contract and intern positions. Intern positions don't always pay top dollar, but they get your foot in the door.

Step Two: Game Conventions

As mentioned in a few of the chapters, game conventions are excellent places to get some great contacts and potentially land some sound-design gigs.

Do you have your business cards and demo reel? Is your Web site together? Good, because the conferences are the best places to make use of them. Again, Game Developers Conference (GDC) is the best place to start. It always has companies there for the express purpose of hiring talented people like you. Most of the time, human resources departments man the booths. However, department leads usually stop by to meet new prospects, especially if they are in need of people.

Head over to these booths and do some of that smooth talking that you are so good at! There's nothing better than making a new friend. Get those business cards; follow up with e-mails. Express how good it was to meet. Ask when he or she might be in your neck of the woods. Maybe you have something to offer them? Be yourself!

E3 is worth attending but is more a show-and-tell thing that is open to most of the public. Tons of people from the gaming industry are here, but not usually to recruit. Still, it's always good to meet as many people as you can and build up a list of contacts. You may meet someone who later lets you know of a position or who needs a score or sound design.

Step Three: A Gig

After you have the contract or position making sounds or composing, it's time to start the preparations. Now you get to go over the design doc and check out the game. This is also the part where you are introduced to the people on your team, start going to meetings, and become part of creating a game—it's really exciting. During meetings you start learning what the milestone dates are and when your share of the work needs to be done. You learn what's planned for the sound engine and how it affects you. Needless to say, this is the time that you start taking notes!

If you are a sound designer, you'll start making placeholder sounds now as well. This is an excellent way to learn how the engine is going to use your sounds and in doing so, make the team happy by giving them something to hear. As you do your placeholders, go through your database to see what you've got and put together a database for the game. You're also determining what sounds need to be field recorded. Doing this, start tracking what sounds you have in your library and what you need to record. From the document, line up locations, set dates, and get your gear ready.

If you're a composer, you're in the middle of composing your score. You're prioritizing by the needs of the team and the milestones. You're supplying music for upcoming demos, advertisements, and so on.

Step Four: Stockpile Tools of the Trade

You know these edits are a given: minute, final recordings, final mixes, new sound FX. You also have to create loop files for ambiences. This is where two-track editors come into play. Programs that fall into this category are Wavelab, Sound Forge, Peak.

There's also the multi-track editor. This program mixes several audio sources for composing music, creating ambiences, adding sound to cut scenes, and scoring cut scenes. Programs that fall into this category are Nuendo, Cubase SX, Pro Tools, Logic Audio, Digital Performer, and SONAR.

Figure 16.3

Nuendo is a multi-track program covered earlier in this book.

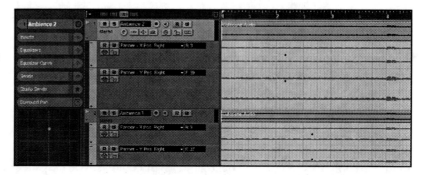

I talked about FX libraries and how it's perfectly acceptable to use them for inspiration and building blocks to create your own sounds. After all, there simply isn't enough time in the day to record all the sounds that you will need for a game. Not everyone has access to F-16 jet fighters and M-1 Abrams tanks!

I talked about FX plug-ins, which allow you to add FX like reverbs, delays, choruses, EQs, filters, distortion, and tons of others that add depth, dimension, and noise. Plug-ins are available in different formats like VST, Audio Units, Direct X, RTAS, and TDM. Instruments fall into the plug-in category. Different software synthesizers and samplers supply sounds and music for sound design and composition. These synthesizers sometimes emulate classic synths of old (like the Pro-53 from Native Instruments) or a totally unique synthesizer (like Absynth, also from Native Instruments).

Then there's the software sampler. It allows you to take recorded material and play it back over several keys. I talked of ways to quickly merge sounds with samplers and make all new sounds with samplers. You also read about sample libraries that have thousands of sound FX, like the Sound Ideas General 6000. Finally, you read about sound volumes that cover every possible recording of every orchestral instrument known to man. These things play back on software samplers (like the East West Symphonic Orchestra, Gold Edition or the Symphonic Choir), which are essentially software instruments unto themselves. These volumes have phenomenal sounds that can convincingly emulate all of your orchestral needs.

Game's Complete

Once the game has been completed, several things generally happen: Marketing begins its massive campaign to let the world know about the game. You'll start seeing it advertised in every store (well, every store depending on your project's budget). You'll also see reviews pop up on Web sites like www.gamespot.com. Reviews are important to follow. Why? Beyond criticizing every inch of the game play, the reviewer also remarks on the sound and music.

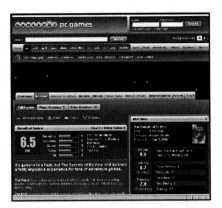

Figure 16.4
Gamespot is one of several sites that reviews games for their playability, graphics, sound, and music.

It's important that you do these things:

- ✳ **Track anything that mentions your work.** For one thing, you can learn from what they have to say. Another thing, you should add any favorable review to your Web site.

- ✳ **Merge your work.** Put what you did on this title with your resume, Web site, and demo reel. It's important to keep these things as up to date as possible.

- ✳ **Archive in a concise, organized manner.** It's a good policy to copy your database over to a DVD along with the entire library of sound. You'll probably also want to begin merging the data in with your regular database as well.

- ✳ **Attend wrap parties.** These parties are great ways to find out what projects are coming up next, to meet other people at other companies, and to let people know how much a part of the team you were.

Freelance Contractor

What if you were working as a contract sound designer? Pretty much all the above still applies—you just want to be a little more aggressive in your outgoing communications with the company you've been working for. For example, do not constantly drop hints that you don't have anything to do after your contract is up. However, *do* go out of your way to get the job done and be a constant source for solutions. Getting good at subtle ways to point this out is an extremely good idea as well. Record these accomplishments in a notebook with dates. That way, if the proper opportunity comes about with the big boss, you can let him or her know what work you've done.

And while you're working on the game, keep an eye out for new work! As a contractor, you're ultimately looking out for yourself. Make as many friends as you can around your team—after all, it's through friends that a lot of work is obtained. People are constantly bouncing from company to company in the game business. Often, when moving to the next company, they get a better position. This makes it easier for these people to recommend others. As a contractor, keeping up to date on who is where and how they are doing can really help your career. Web sites like www.linkedin.com actually help you in this pursuit. This particular site maintains a database of your contacts while letting others know what and where you are as well.

Figure 16.5

Web sites like www.linkedin.com are excellent ways to keep tabs on everyone.

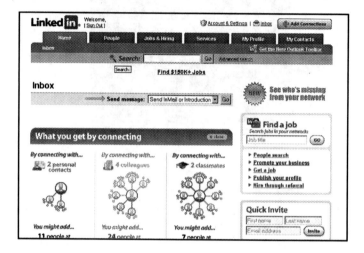

Going Full Time

Full-time positions for sound or music within video-game companies are becoming scarce. Most companies continually hire freelancers or outside businesses to handle sound. Many sound designers prefer to remain freelance for assorted reasons: working their own hours, working from home, or working for better pay. This isn't always for everyone, however. Steady, reliable income and health benefits are two reasons you might pursue a full-time job.

By staying active within the game-development community, making a good name through your work, and continually making good industry friends, you could find yourself in a full-time position. Sometimes simply dropping someone a line may turn on a lightbulb over that person's head: "Wait, we have a position open for a full-time sound designer; you should send me your resume!"

Why would someone sound that eager? That's an easy answer. Most companies offer incentives for recruiting. One lovely incentive is known as a **hiring bonus**. When someone refers you to a job within their company and you are hired, companies often kick back a small bonus to the person who made the referral. As hard as it is to find jobs within the game-development world, it can be just as hard to find people to fill the positions.

So hand out that business card, collect some of your own, and keep them on file. Use tools like www.myspace.com, www.gamasutra.com, and www.linkedin.com to promote yourself and to keep up with your friends and colleagues. Keep updating your demo reel with new work, techniques, and things that you come up with through experimentation. You never know what opportunity may be right around the corner!

Appendix A

Online Resources

Here is a compilation of the all URLs I mention in this book. Some companies are hard to classify, as they offer more than one kind of product. In that case, I've listed the company in each category that it fits into.

Hardware and Software

Audio-Technica
www.audio-technica.com

BaseHead
www.baseheadinc.com

Cakewalk
www.cakewalk.com

Edirol
www.edirol.com

KVR Audio
www.kvr-vst.com

M-AUDIO
www.m-audio.com

Mark of the Unicorn
www.motu.com

Native Instruments
www.native-instruments.com

Peff
www.peff.com

PROJECTSAM
www.projectsam.com

Propellerhead Software
www.propellerheads.se

Quick Keys
www.quickkeys.com

ReasonStation
www.reasonstation.net

rgc:audio
www.rgcaudio.com

Soundminer
www.soundminer.com

Steinberg
www.steinberg.net

TASCAM
www.tascam.com

Microphones

Audio-Technica
www.audio-technica.com

M-AUDIO
www.m-audio.com

Rode Microphones
www.rode.com.au

Sennheiser
www.sennheiserusa.com

Shure
www.shure.com

Sound Devices
www.sounddevices.com

EastWest
www.soundsonline.com

Vienna Symphonic Library
www.vsl.co.at

Conventions
Electronic Entertainment Expo
www.e3expo.com

Game Developers Conference
www.gdconf.com

Sound Effects
The Hollywood Edge
www.hollywoodedge.com

Sound Ideas for sound effects
www.sound-ideas.com

Soundrangers
www.soundrangers.com

Vienna Symphonic Library
www.vsl.co.at

Miscellaneous
Creating Music and Sound for Games' companion Web site
www.courseptr.com

Appendix B}

Tools of the Trade

What you need to get yourself going as a sound designer or composer definitely can be subjective. Different people use different programs, operating systems, and organization methods. It's okay to vary in what you use, and one person's opinion isn't necessarily "right." People just tend to recommend what's worked best for them. There are certainly tools in my arsenal that lead to questions from others, but when they see how I use whatever program it is, it all makes sense to them.

This book has recommended tools that are universal within the sound designer and composer fields. There really isn't one program that's recommended over another; that just isn't what this book's about. This book simply recommends the basic programs and hardware that you'll need, tells you about several of the programs available, and then leaves it up to you to decide what will work best for you.

One thing you should understand is that all of the programs available for editing and creating sounds and composition tend to have hundreds of options, but most of the time only a few of the options ever get used. To me, this is unfortunate. Computer software isn't cheap by any means and to have useful functions within a program going unused, I feel, is a real tragedy. With this in mind, I'd like to encourage you to really take some time and get to know all the tools that you pick up.

But you may be saying, "Some of these programs have owner's manuals that are the size of dictionaries!" Yes, it's true. Many of the programs that are available for audio editing and manipulation need very elaborate manuals to completely cover all of the functionality available within the program. To go completely through one of these manuals can be a long and boring process, I know.

The good news is, there are usually tutorials or quick-start books that tend to come with each program! These books are usually written by someone who words their tutorials in simple terms, and they usually force you to do each exercise with the shortcuts for each function.

How does this benefit you? Simple! By learning shortcuts and going through tutorials, you get to learn each function in a work environment and at your own pace. In my opinion, this is one of the best ways to learn.

Simple key commands (like the ones used on computers) are extremely easy to forget unless you perform them over and over again. Tutorials make you repeat these commands, and they also show you what each command does. For example, the tutorial might say, "Highlight the beginning portion of the audio file and then press control-c. Now place your cursor at the end of the audio file and press control-v. The audio file beginning appears at the end. Now highlight the beginning of the audio file again and press control-c...." Are you following me? Repetition is the best way to learn!

Another thing about tutorials is that each one of them also covers functions that may not be obvious to someone just stumbling into using the program. For example, Nuendo (like many multi-track recording or sequencing programs) has markers available to help you keep track of where you are within any project. These markers can be labeled and placed wherever you like. However, as a brand-new user, you may completely miss this feature when you first enter the program! By going through the Getting Started manual that ships with Nuendo, you can learn about this feature and more by just following along with the exercises created by the people who actually made the program!

It all comes down to this: With computers these days, your skill largely depends on your knowledge of each program that you use. There is definitely a lot to be said for creativity, and it's still the most important factor in determining how good your sounds or composition will turn out, but it's your knowledge of each program that helps you realize that creativity.

Within this appendix you will find quick breakdowns of the types of programs you will need accompanied by a small list of available programs that fall within these categories. I encourage you to research each program before you buy!

Tools for Sound Designers

The main tool for sound designers is the two-track editing program, or wave editor: a program with multi-function editing tools used to perform precise, microscopic sound edits. This is outlined in the following sections, in addition to multi-track programs, plug-ins, samplers, synthesizers, sound databases, and field recorders—all weapons in the sound designer's arsenal!

Wave Editors

As often mentioned throughout the course of this book, wave editors are two-track editing programs that allow you to perform very intricate edits on sound files, and then process them as needed. A sound designer will use a wave editor to mold specific sounds through tools like EQ, fading, effects, and gain settings.

- ❀ Wavelab
- ❀ Peak
- ❀ Sound Forge
- ❀ DSP Quatro
- ❀ SADiE
- ❀ Wave Creator
- ❀ Wave Editor

Multi-Track Editors

Multi-track programs serve several different purposes for the sound designer. With one of these programs you can mix many sounds together into one sound. You are also able to sync up audio to video so that you can mix and edit audio tracks. These programs allow automation that enables you to control panning, gain, and effects throughout a sequence. They also allow you to mix in surround.

- ❀ Nuendo
- ❀ Cubase SX
- ❀ SONAR
- ❀ Pro Tools
- ❀ Digital Performer
- ❀ Logic Pro

Plug-Ins

Plug-ins are smaller applications that run within your multi-track editors and wave editors. Plug-ins are generally used for effects. These effects include compression, reverbs, distortion, filtering, delays, and choruses. There are many plug-in types that only work with specific programs. For example, VST plug-ins only work with programs that support them. Make sure to research this when you are trying to determine whether you can run a specific plug-in.

Following are some packages that include several plug-ins or effects:

- Waves Platinum Native Bundle
- Reaktor
- T.C. Powercore
- WaveArts Power Suite
- PSP Audioware Everything Bundle
- Nomad Factory Blue Tubes bundle
- Arboretum Hyperprism Bundle

Additional Plug-In Information

A great place to find new information on plug-ins in many different forms is the Web site www.kvr-vst.com. While the name implies VST only, there are actually several Audio Units plug-ins listed here as well. There's even a database to help you find the exact plug-in you're looking for!

Synthesizers

While there are many wonderful hardware synthesizers available, this book only covers the software synthesizers. Synthesizers are devices that allow you create many strange and quirky sounds from the ground up. Synthesizers are available as plug-ins, as well, and come in several different forms, like VST and Audio Units.

Following are some of the different software synthesizers available:

- Reason
- Reaktor
- Minimoog V
- Pro-53
- Absynth

Samplers

Samplers can be used in many ways to manipulate sounds that you already have at your disposal, as well as sounds that you may have picked up from libraries. The ability to do quick mixes and tweaks with samplers make them an intuitive way to get your job done in a fun and timely fashion.

The following list outlines several software samplers available:

- Kontakt
- Reason
- HALion

- ※ MachFive
- ※ GigaStudio
- ※ EXS24

Field Recorders

Field recorders are your way of capturing the outside world and its many sounds. This a great time for field recording because the smaller and more compact digital devices available these days get impressive recordings while you are on the go.

If you already own a digital camcorder, this can be used in place of a digital field recorder. It's also great because you can get a visual reference of what you are recording, as well.

Following are examples of different field recorders:

- ※ MicroTrack 24/96
- ※ Edirol R-4
- ※ Sound Devices 702

Sound Databases

Sound design is as much about data administration as it is artistry, so it would behoove you to get to know Filemaker Pro (it's the main program used by most game companies for creating sound databases) and build your own personal database.

The following are examples of database programs:

- ※ Filemaker Pro
- ※ BaseHead
- ※ NetMix
- ※ Soundminer

Sound Libraries

Sometimes you will need sounds that are not available for you to record, and you may need the sound quite badly. For example, how many of us have jets that are available to record at a moment's notice?

This is why sound libraries are great. You can use these sounds as source material to create your own new sounds. How? Blend them with other sounds, use your FX plug-ins on them, pitch them up, or time-stretch them. Digital sound manipulation allows you many ways to create new sounds from existing material.

Following is a list of existing sound libraries that are available for purchase:

- Sound Ideas General 6000, Basic Set
- Hollywood Edge Historical Series
- Universal Sound Effects Library

Tools for Composers

Many of the tools suggested for sound designers are also suggested for composers. However, the programs are the only main similarity, besides the fact that both jobs create audio. Composers use these tools very differently. A sound designer will spend most of his time in a wave editor and in the databases. A composer will spend most of his time in a multi-track program using its MIDI-sequencing functions.

Once again, let's go over what tools composers use most and why.

Multi-Track Editors/Sequencing Programs

Composers use multi-track recording and sequencing programs to do the bulk of their work, essentially. These programs allow them to score scenes in video games like they would in a movie. In fact, most of these programs are used for movies, too. You can record audio in these programs, as well as MIDI, and that's just what you need when you are working with soft synthesizers and soft samplers.

Here's a short list of the programs that can be used to fulfill this purpose:

- Nuendo
- Pro Tools
- Cubase SX
- Logic Pro
- SONAR

Wave Editors

The composer's use of a wave editor is quite minimal. However, it is still a necessity. Multi-track editors are able to export mixes as stereo audio files, but they still need to be edited slightly after the export has taken place. What sort of edit? Too much space may have been rendered at the beginning and end of the audio file. Wave editors are ideal for correcting this problem. You also might want to do some light mastering or level-balancing to ensure that the audio file is at the appropriate volume. Wave editors are great for quick edits that my be really cumbersome within a multi-track program.

Here's a look at some of the wave editors that are available:

- ❄ Wavelab
- ❄ Peak
- ❄ Sound Forge
- ❄ DSP Quatro
- ❄ SADiE
- ❄ Wave Creator
- ❄ Wave Editor

Samplers

Samplers are one of the main instruments used by most modern composers these days in both games and film. Why? There are tons of great sound libraries that have extremely detailed audio replications of orchestras, choirs, and most any instrument that you can think of. Samplers allow you to replicate many different instruments that you either don't know how to play, may not have access to, or that have been recorded in concert halls that none of us has access to.

Following are some of the samplers available to the modern composer:

- ❄ Kontakt
- ❄ Reason
- ❄ HALion
- ❄ MachFive
- ❄ GigaStudio
- ❄ EXS24

Sample Libraries/Sampled Instruments

As mentioned previously in the "Samplers" section, there are tons of great sample libraries out there that let you emulate almost any instrument you can think of. And if you're clever, most people won't even know that it isn't the real thing! Some of these sample libraries are filled with thousands of sample patches that work on certain soft samplers. Other sample libraries, like Symphonic Choirs from East West, include a special version of a software sampler that has been optimized for recreating choirs in the most authentic way possible. In a way, this library is a highly authentic instrument in its own right and actually reproduces full choirs!

Here are some of the libraries/instruments available:

* East West Symphonic Orchestra, Gold Edition
* East West Symphonic Choirs
* The Vienna Symphonic Library
* SAM Orchestral Brass

Appendix C

Potential Employers

In this section, you will find a list of game developers that either regularly employ sound people or are growing so rapidly that it's feasible they might hire in-house sound people in the future.

Take your time and check out the sites. Be sure and note any preferences that they may have on receiving demo reels and how to submit a resume to them!

Game Developers

Activision
www.activision.com
3100 Ocean Park Boulevard
Santa Monica, CA 90405
United States

Bandai Electronics
www.bandaigames.com
5551 Katella Ave.
Cypress, CA 90630
United States

Bethesda Softworks
www.bethsoft.com
1370 Piccard Drive
Rockville, MD 20850-4304
United States

Big Fish Games
www.bigfishgames.com
100 Fourth Ave N
Suite 630
Seattle, WA 98109
United States

BioWare Corporation
www.bioware.com
#302, 10508-82 Avenue
Edmonton, Alberta T6E6H2
Canada

Blizzard Entertainment
www.blizzard.com
P.O. Box 18979
Irvine, CA 92623
United States

Bungie Studios
www.bungie.net
1 Microsoft Way
Redmond, WA 98052
United States

Capcom Entertainment, Inc.
www.capcom.com
475 Oakmead Parkway
Sunnyvale, CA 94085
United States

The Collective
1900 Quail St
Newport Beach, CA 92660
United States

Deep Fried Entertainment, Inc.
www.deepfriedentertainment.com
#400 - 1062 Homer St.
Vancouver, BC V6B 2W9
Canada

Disney Interactive
www.disney.com/disneyinteractive/
Burbank, CA 91201
United States

DreamWorks Interactive
Los Angeles, CA 90049
United States

EA Sports
www.easports.com
933 Salisbury Road
San Mateo, CA 94404
United States

Eidos Interactive
www.eidosinteractive.com
San Francisco, CA 94107
United States

Electronic Arts
www.ea.com
209 Redwood Shores Blvd.
Redwood City, CA 94065
United States

Elixir Studios, Ltd.
www.elixir-studios.co.uk
Millennium Business Centre
London NW2 6DW
United Kingdom

Factor 5
www.factor5.com
101 Lucas Valley Road
Ste. 301
San Rafael, CA 94903
United States

Gas Powered Games
www.gaspowered.com
Seattle, WA
United States

Id Software
www.idsoftware.com
10662 Los Vaqueros Circle
Mesquite, TX
United States

Infinity Ward
www.infinityward.com
15281 Ventura Blvd.
Suite 270
Encino, CA 91436
United States

Irrational Games
www.irrationalgames.com
125 B Street
2nd Floor
Boston, MA 02127
United States

Konami
www.konami.com

MetaGear
www.metagear.com
2824 SE Bella Vista Rd.
Vancouver, WA 98683
United States

Microsoft Corporation
www.msdn.microsoft.com/directx
1 Microsoft Way
Redmond, WA 98052-6399
United States

Midnight Studios, Inc.
www.midnight-studios.net
PO Box 2507
Georgetown, TX 78627
United States

Midway Games, Inc.
www.midway.com
2704 West Roscoe Street
Chicago, IL 60618
United States

Monolith Productions
www.lith.com
10516 NE 37th Circle
Kirkland, WA 98033
United States

Namco
www.namco.com
2055 Junction Avenue
San Jose, CA 95131
United States

Neversoft Entertainment
www.neversoft.com
6041 Variel Ave
Woodland Hills, CA 91367
United States

Nintendo of America, Inc.
www.nintendo.com
4820 150th Avenue NE
Redmond, WA 98052
United States

Pandemic Studio
1920 Main Street
Santa Monica, CA 90405
United States

Planet Moon Studios
www.planetmoon.com
323 Pine Street
Sausalito, CA
United States

PSEUDO Interactive, Inc.
www.pseudointeractive.com
80 Bloor St., West
Suite 400
Toronto, Ontario M5S 2V1
Canada

Radical Entertainment, Ltd.
www.radical.ca
369 Terminal Avenue
Vancouver, BC V6A 4C4
Canada

Raven Software
www.ravensoft.com
3 Point Place
Madison, WI 53719
United States

Red Storm Entertainment
www.redstorm.com
2000 Aerial Center
Suite 110
Morrisville, NC 27560
United States

Relic Entertainment, Inc.
www.relic.com
#1500 - 550 Burrard Street
Vancouver, BC V6C 2C1
Canada

Rockstar San Diego
www.rockstarsd.com
5966 La Place Court
Carlsbad, CA 92008
United States

Rockstar Vancouver
www.rockstarvancouver.com
800-858 Beatty Street
Vancouver, BC V6B 1C1
Canada

Secret Level
www.secretlevel.com
123 Townsend Street
3rd Floor
San Francisco, CA 94107
United States

Section 8 Studios
www.s8studios.com
Suite 201
Carlsbad, CA 92008
United States

Sega of America, Inc.
www.sega.com
650 Townsend Street
San Francisco, CA 94103
United States

Shiny Entertainment, Inc.
2901 W. Coast Highway
Ste. 370
Newport Beach, CA 92663
United States

SoftEgg Enterprises
www.softegg.com
4758 Forman Ave #10
Toluca Lake, CA 91602
United States

Sony Computer Entertainment America, Inc. (SCEA)
www.scea.com
919 East Hillsdale Blvd.
2nd Floor
Foster City, CA 94404-4201
United States

Square Enix North America
6060 Center Drive
Suite 100
Los Angeles, CA 90045
United States

Sucker Punch Productions
www.suckerpunch.com
500 108th Ave. NE #390
Bellevue, WA 98004
United States

Taito
www.taito.com
Japan

Take-Two Interactive Software, Inc.
www.take2games.com
622 Broadway
New York, NY 10012
United States

Tecmo, Inc.
PO Box 5553
21213-B Hawthorne Blvd.
Suite 205
Torrance, CA 90503
United States

THQ, Inc.
www.thq.com
27001 Agoura Road
Calabasas Hills, CA 91301
United States

Turbine Entertainment Software
P.O. Box 747
60 Glacier Drive
Suite #4000
Westwood, MA 02090
United States

Ubisoft Entertainment
www.ubisoft.com
625 Third St.
3rd Floor
San Francisco, CA 94107
United States

Valve Corporation
www.valvesoftware.com
520 Kirkland Way #201
Kirkland, WA 98033
United States

Appendix D }

Glossary

Here are a list of terms that have been used throughout the book. Please feel free to take a look if something in the book confuses you, or if you simply forgot and don't feel like going back to the chapter where it was originally described.

Alpha. Alpha is the first phase in the production cycle. In order for the game to be eligible for Alpha status, it must have the majority of the art in place, the story line, and prototype sounds.

Ambience. Within a game, this is generally a looped recording of a collage of audio that sounds like the environment that is being displayed. Basically, it's the environmental audio that makes up a level.

Art Team. The art team is made up of several artists and technical artists that are responsible for supplying environments, models, textures, and FX for the game.

Assistant Producer. Assistant producers are usually responsible for assisting with the management of a project. They'll make sure the team is fed, they'll keep an eye on the bug count of a project, and any other tasks that they can do to pick up the slack for the producer.

Audition. The composer will usually have to audition for a composing gig with any game company these days. The audition process consists of the team handing over reference and design material to a composer, then having the composer come up with a piece of work specific for that game. New material is requested for almost every audition.

Beat-Synchronous Instructions. This feature allows the composer, with the help of a programmer or level designer, to introduce instructions within a music track. These instructions tell the game's audio engine to transition at a musically sensible location, like a measure.

Beta. Beta is the second phase within the production cycle. When the Beta milestone is reached, all of the art and game play elements, as well as the bulk of the music and sound, are within the game.

Bug. A bug is a term used to describe problems, crashes, or glitches that occur within a video game...or any other program for that matter. One of the big goals when shipping a game, despite making a great game all around, is making sure that it ships with as few bugs as possible.

Chorus. Chorus is an effect used to make a sound "thicker" or "bigger." The effect is achieved by actually creating a repetition of a sound almost instantly after it's played, essentially doubling the sound on top of itself.

Composer. A composer is responsible for composing all of the music for a game. Additionally, he may be called upon to edit music that he did not create so that it fits properly within the game.

Compressor. A compressor is a tool or effect that is used to keep a sound within a certain volume range. In many cases, when an actor is speaking, her volume range will be very dynamic, which causes the volume of her voice to decrease and increase as she speaks. A compressor will make sure that the volume stays within a certain range. Compression can also be used to boost the perceived volume of a sound by squashing the peaks and dips in an audio file, and then through the gain setting, increasing the overall volume.

Concept Art. At the beginning of every game project, there are only a few people working on the game. One of these people is the lead artist who is responsible for creating artwork that reflects what the game, its locations, and all of its characters will look like. The initial art created in this early stage is referred to as the concept art.

Cut Scene. A cut scene is a scripted or prerendered movie within the game where the player has no control and a part of the story is being told. They are basically in-game movies.

DAW. A DAW (or digital audio workstation) is a term used to describe a computer that is running audio software like Nuendo, Pro Tools, or Logic Pro and several other audio programs needed to fulfill the production needs of sound designers and composers alike.

Delay. A delay (or echo) is an effect used to create a single or several repetitions of a sound after it has been played. A delay can be used to recreate the effect of a voice or sound being played through a vast cavern or off the top of a mountain. Just think, "Hello, hello, hello..."

Design Document. The design document is created before any work is started on a game and is, in reality, the outline of what the game intends to be. It includes the story of the game, the basic game-play mechanics, concept art, reference material from movies, and sometimes reference sounds. Design documents are used in the beginning to get approval from the executives to create the game. Once the design document has been approved, it is copied and distributed as needed within the team.

Field Recorder. A field recorder is a portable recording device that is used to obtain quality sound recordings in an outdoor or indoor environment. They are generally rugged and are predominantly digital these days.

Field Recording. Field recording is the act of leaving your studio to go out and capture sounds in outdoor environments (like the woods or an airport) or in some cases indoor environments (like factories or metal shops). Field recording takes place when you do not already have an adequate sound within your library.

Foley. Foley is the art form of creating sounds like footsteps, breathing, door openings, and other sounds that we usually take for granted in daily life. Foley is required during cut scenes to make them more immersive. Usually, Foley recording takes place at elaborate recording studios with stages and surfaces like tile and grass and gravel. You can, however, do some really great Foley work if you are creative with things lying around your own house.

Foley Pit. A specialized stage at a recording studio that has several different surfaces available for simulating real life as well as foreign environments.

Gold. The Gold phase means that the game is complete and nearly ready to ship. Usually, there are only minor bugs left over, and the media that the game is shipping on is being tested.

Level. Games are usually divided into several sections. When one section is beaten, you move on to the next section. These sections are called levels. Every level within a game will have its own music and sounds that will be specific to the level, along with its characters and art. In many cases, a level is part of the overall story, as well.

Level Designers. Level designers are responsible for building, scripting, and devising levels within a game. There will usually be two or three levels per designer. Most of the time, the game story line will be divided into levels, and the level designer is responsible for making the overall puzzle that is each level. In some cases, level designers are responsible for wiring in sounds that are created for the game.

Loop. A loop is an audio file tagged to start over once the file is finished. Essentially, it's an audio file that will play over and over again, seamlessly, until it's programmed to quit.

Marketing Department. The marketing department is responsible for creating hype for a video game. It does this by coordinating Web content, print ads, TV commercials, and special events.

Multi-Track Editor. A multi-track editor is a program that can play several tracks of audio at once, as well as mix and automate them. The program is primarily used for creating music, mixing audio within a scene, and for mixing many sounds together to form one. Most modern multi-track programs are capable to mixing audio back in surround and are able to support several effects plug-ins. Programs that fall into these categories are Nuendo, Pro Tools, Logic Pro, Cubase SX, and SONAR.

Plug-In. A plug-in is either an effect or software instrument program that runs within a multi-track program or a wave editor.

Producer. The producer runs and oversees the game project. This person is generally who everyone on a game team ultimately reports to with their progress.

Production Cycle. The production cycle is made up of several phases, or milestones, that are needed to complete a project. These phases are Alpha, Beta, QA, and Gold. In order to complete each phase of production, certain parts of the game must be in place and working.

Programmer. A programmer is one of the people creating the game through computer code and scripting. He is responsible for keeping the game running as well as, in some cases, creating the engine that actually makes the game run.

Prototype. Prototypes are temporary sounds placed in the game during the Alpha phase so that the team can ascertain how well the sound engine is working and get an early idea of how the game will play with sound when the true sounds are finally in.

QA Milestone. The QA milestone consists of having everything within the game, period. At this point there are only light tweaks that are happening to the sound, and these are only on a severe "as needed" basis. Testers and their bugs predominantly rule this phase.

Quality Assurance Department. Quality assurance (QA) is made up of testers who go through the game and search for crashes, art bugs, game bugs, text bugs, and sound bugs. Occasionally, a tester will be assigned to keep track of all sound bugs and to specifically hunt sound bugs within a game. (See also **Tester** and **Bug**.)

Reverb. Reverb is an effect used to emulate cavernous, large, or live rooms. For example, a reverb can be applied to a voice recorded in a studio to make it sound as if it's in a giant cave with a large ceiling.

Sampler. A sampler is an instrument that uses real audio. Samplers are used to replicate real instruments or audio events, and they do an excellent job because they are actually using raw audio of the subject. The audio is spread over a key range and can be played faster or slower, depending on how high or low the key is that has been pressed.

Shockmount. A shockmount is used to keep vibrations that occur when the microphone is physically handled from being picked up in the recording.

Slate. A slate is usually a verbal indicator recorded at the beginning of a field-recording session, indicating what the subject of your recording is and any other relevant information.

Sound Database. A sound database is used to keep track of all of the sounds within either your personal sound library or the sound library that has been created for a specific game.

Sound Designer. A sound designer is the person on a game team who is responsible for getting all of the sound effects and ambiences into the game. Additionally, they are responsible for assuring the overall quality of the mix.

Sound Engine. The sound engine is the software component of the game that manages when, where, and how all of the sounds are cued and played back within a game. Each sound engine is proprietary to each game engine and each sound engine, depending on the game engine, will have different capabilities.

Synthesizer. A synthesizer is an instrument that combines electronic tones and plays them back as musical notes. Synthesizers can be used to emulate specific instruments or can also be used to create completely alien textures.

Tester. A tester is one of the people who makes up the quality assurance department. Testers find and document bugs (or technical issues) within a game, making sure that when the game finally ships, the customer will not experience any problems within the game.

Wave Editor. A wave editor is a computer sound program that is primarily used by sound designers to perform intricate edits and processing on sounds and by composers for mastering music.

Windscreen. A windscreen is a device used to cover a microphone in a field-recording environment so that natural elements, like wind, don't interfere with the recording.

 Index

INDEX ♩

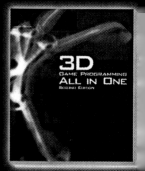

ADVANCED
VISUAL EFFECTS
WITH DIRECT3D

BASIC DRAWING
FOR GAMES

BEGINNING
GAME ART IN
3DS MAX 8

BEGINNING

GAME
GRAPHICS

SHADERS
FOR GAME PROGRAMMERS
AND ARTISTS

CHARACTER DEVELOPMENT
AND STORYTELLING

FOR GAMES

GAME ART
FOR TEENS
SECOND EDITION

THE DARK SIDE OF
GAME TEXTURING